NAZIS ON THE POTOMAC

NAZIS ON THE POTOMAC

The Top-Secret Intelligence Operation
that Helped Win World War II

ROBERT K. SUTTON

CASEMATE

Philadelphia & Oxford

AN AUSA BOOK
Association of the United States Army
2425 Wilson Boulevard, Arlington, Virginia, 22201, USA

Published in the United States of America and Great Britain in 2021 by
CASEMATE PUBLISHERS
1950 Lawrence Road, Havertown, PA 19083, USA
and
The Old Music Hall, 106–108 Cowley Road, Oxford OX4 1JE, UK

Hardcover Edition: ISBN 978-1-61200-987-2
Digital Edition: ISBN 978-1-61200-988-9

A CIP record for this book is available from the British Library

Printed and bound in the United States of America by Integrated Books International

Typeset in India by Lapiz Digital Services, Chennai.

For a complete list of Casemate titles, please contact:

CASEMATE PUBLISHERS (US)
Telephone (610) 853-9131
Fax (610) 853-9146
Email: casemate@casematepublishers.com
www.casematepublishers.com

CASEMATE PUBLISHERS (UK)
Telephone (01865) 241249
Email: casemate-uk@casematepublishers.co.uk
www.casematepublishers.co.uk

*Dedicated to the memory of the families and loved ones of the men
featured in this story who perished in the Holocaust.*

Contents

Contents

Preface

Imagine that between 1943 and 1946—in the midst of World War II—there were 3,451 German soldiers and sailors, including 15 Nazi generals living on the banks of the Potomac River, only 12 miles from the Pentagon and 14 miles from the U.S. Capitol. Thank goodness these men were all prisoners. Now, imagine that these German prisoners were interrogated by former German or Austrian Jews, who had escaped from their homelands with the rise of Adolph Hitler. As far-fetched as this scenario seems, the story is true and one of the most fascinating untold stories from World War II. The narrative that unfolds here took place at Fort Hunt Park. It was a well-guarded secret; the American soldiers stationed there were sworn to secrecy, and, in time, the story might have vanished from the annals of history.

In 2006, however, National Park Service staff learned the identity of one of the men who was stationed at Fort Hunt during World War II. His name was Fred Michel, and he and his wife were living in Louisville, Kentucky, at the time. Brandon Bies, the historian at George Washington Memorial Parkway (which manages Fort Hunt), contacted Mr. Michel and tried to arrange a time to conduct an oral history interview. The session was on, then off, then on again, and Brandon ascertained that Fred was reluctant to talk about his experiences at Fort Hunt. He understood why. As Brandon and park staff were beginning to piece together the story of the fort during the war, they understood that soldiers' lips and the documents related to the program had both been sealed. But now, 60 years later, the documents were declassified, and the soldiers were allowed to share their experiences.

Brandon traveled to Louisville in May 2006, and in his briefcase, he carried copies of interrogations Fred Michel had conducted with German prisoners during the war, with his name on them. His hunch was correct. Fred was uncomfortable discussing his work at Fort Hunt because he had been sworn to secrecy and was expected to carry his knowledge to the grave. When Brandon showed him the transcripts of his interrogations, he began to open up and talk about his experiences. At the end of his two-day oral history interview, Fred not only discussed what he had done at the fort; he provided the names of several of his former colleagues, which opened up the opportunities for multiple oral history interviews.

Between 2006 and 2010, National Park Service historians from the George Washington Memorial Parkway, in partnership with the Friends of Fort Hunt Park, located, interviewed, and transcribed oral history interviews of 65 World War II veterans. Most had either interrogated prisoners or translated and analyzed enemy documents. Others had worked in the escape and evasion section—helping American airmen escape capture or providing resources to prisoners of war (POW) held in German prison camps. Several former German prisoners were interviewed, as well as German scientists who came to the United States after the war. Collectively, their stories are remarkable, giving us a window into the American intelligence operation during the war. This book tells their stories.

Unfortunately, most of the interviewees are now gone. It would have been wonderful to have asked them to elaborate on some of their stories. One man escaped from a prison camp in Poland and made it back to the United States. How did he manage that? Many left Germany or Austria as children and emigrated to the United States. Some provided hair-raising details; others offered very little. For the latter group, finding out more would have been a bonus. Still, others led interesting lives after the war, of which we know very little. Missing these details is minor compared to what we have learned from this oral history project. Together, their memories of their time at Fort Hunt were so vivid after some 60 years of having to remain silent, it quickly became clear that, for many, this time was a pivotal period in their lives and the details remained fresh.

While most of these men have passed away, Peter Weiss, George Weidinger, Arno Mayer, Guy Stern, and Paul Fairbrook are still very much alive, well, and as sharp as ever. Although well into their 90s, they have been very gracious and helpful, filling in many of the blanks for this story. Three of the four elaborated on their intelligence training prior to their assignments to Fort Hunt. Peter Weiss shared more details about his early life in Europe before his family emigrated to the United States. Conversely, I knew a great deal about George Weidinger's early life in Austria but not much about his experiences after he left the army. He was gracious to fill in those details. Arno Mayer elaborated on his new life after his family settled in New York City. He shared much more about the time he spent with Wernher von Braun when the German rocket scientist came to the United States. Arno and Peter were both picked up by Mamie Eisenhower on separate occasions, while hitchhiking, and they wanted to make sure that I understood that both stories were not made up. Paul Fairbrook made sure I understood the nuances of how the Military Intelligence Research Service (MIRS)—in which he was an integral part—worked. He sent me dozens of documents produced by his office, which filled in the holes I had encountered as I focused on this program. He also helped me understand how the German Military Documents Section (GMDS) program functioned after the war. Guy Stern elaborated on how his early life, growing up in Germany, was a great benefit to him, as he interrogated German POWs during the war. He also helped me understand the value of his training at Camp Ritchie, as it prepared him for his intelligence-gathering assignments in Europe.

This story could not be told without the rich resources Peter, George, Arno, Guy, Paul, and the 60 other men provided in their interviews. I owe them a debt I will never be able to repay. However, without the vision, persistence, and tenacity of several National Park Service employees, tirelessly tracking down and interviewing these men, this story could not have been told. Ranger Dana Dierks passed along the name of Fred Michel, the first interviewee to her supervisor, Vincent Santucci, who in turn sent park historian Brandon Bies to interview Mr. Michel and his wife. From that start Brandon and Vincent conducted most of the interviews, along with David Lassman, Sam Swersky, Eric Oberg, Matthew Virta, and others. Transcribing the interviews was a critical part of the project. The Friends of Fort Hunt Park, in particular Robert Rosenthal, president, Eric Johnson, vice president, Dorothy Cantor, and others devoted hours and financial assistance for this critical function.

George Washington Memorial Parkway Superintendent, David Vela provided the support and budget necessary to complete the program. Kimberly Robinson, park curator, catalogued the photographs and artifacts associated with the project, and made the interview transcripts accessible on the internet. Her assistance was absolutely critical in this endeavor. Even though the park archives were closed during the Covid-19 pandemic, she posted interviews on the internet and sent images for this book. Thank you again Kimberly.

Many of the men stationed at Fort Hunt received their intelligence training at Camp Ritchie in Maryland. Fortunately for me, Beverley Eddy was nearing completion of a comprehensive history of that facility when my study was underway. She answered numerous questions, and my chapter that focuses on Camp Ritchie is much better as a result. Late in the war, and after Germany surrendered, a number of generals passed through Fort Hunt. Their stories, and their significance, was an area in which I felt I needed some assistance. Fortunately, Derek Mallett, who had written the definitive work on German generals in the United States was happy to share his expertise with me and answer numerous questions.

Finally, Dan Gross has an interest and skill that I wish I possessed. He loves to collect information and put it into databases. Not only that, but he can retrieve his data instantly. During the course of pulling this study together @ RobertSutton, I cannot even begin to count the number of times I called or emailed Dan with questions—some general others specific and esoteric—and I honestly do not remember a time when he did not have an answer. With nearly all of the repositories, such as the National Archives, closed during the course of writing this study, due to the pandemic, I honestly do not know what I would have done without Dan's help.

I enlisted the assistance of colleagues, friends, and family to review style and content. Brandon Bies and Vincent Santucci helped to fill in details that were not included in certain interviews and corrected several misstatements. Paul Fairbrook read the entire draft and made valuable corrections and suggestions on the Camp Ritchie and MIRS chapters. Eric Johnson and Robert Rosenthal read the draft manuscript and offered valuable suggestions. David Martin and Christopher Tourtellot helped clarify statements and correct inadvertent errors. My son, Lee Sutton made valuable recommendations. Jared Weatherford formatted and arranged the images in the appropriate size and resolution. Finally, I am exceedingly fortunate that my wife, Harriet Davidson, is, quite possibly, the finest editor anywhere. She corrected grammar and style throughout and made numerous organizational recommendations that made the entire document flow much more smoothly. I simply cannot imagine writing anything without her amazing editorial skills.

Writing a manuscript is one thing, getting it into print is often a daunting task. Fortunately, I had worked with Joseph Craig, who is the Director for the Association of the United States Army Book Program, on an earlier book project, and he was enormously helpful with helping me put together a proposal to submit to Ruth Sheppard at Casemate Publications. Ruth has been an absolute joy to work with. She provided encouragement when needed; pushing—but not much—when necessary; and the resources to make this a success. I also have to thank the rest of the team at Casemate: Felicity Goldsack, Declan Ingram, Megan Yates, Mette Bundgaard, Daniel Yesilonis, and David Farnsworth.

A note about quotes: The quotes that follow come mostly from the National Park Service oral history transcripts, from interrogation transcripts, or directly from the men with whom I interviewed. In nearly every instance, I copied the quote verbatim, but in some rare cases, I edited the quote to make its message clearer. At some places in the text, quotes are in *italics*. These are not direct quotes but rather amalgamations of multiple quotes from multiple sources. So, for example, from the interrogation transcripts, opening questions and answers were similar, and by creating generic quotes, I believe I have captured the verbiage common to most.

Send These, the Homeless, Tempest-Tossed to Me

With silent lips she cries:
"Give me your tired, your poor,
Your huddled masses yearning to breathe free"

EMMA LAZARUS[1]

In 1654, six families totaling 23 people disembarked from the *Ste. Catherine* ship in Dutch New Amsterdam (later New York City). They were Sephardic Jews who had fled the former Dutch West India Company outpost of Recife, Brazil, fearing they would become victims of the Portuguese Inquisition. They were the first known group of Jews to permanently settle in what would later become the United States. Several years later, other Sephardic families settled in nearby Newport, Rhode Island, and eventually built the Touro Synagogue, the first synagogue in the American colonies.

Through the late 1600s and early 1700s, a trickle of Jewish immigrants came to the colonies. Then, in July 1733, 43 Jews arrived in Savannah, Georgia, after sailing on the ship *William and Sarah*. They were invited by the colony's founder, James Edward Oglethorpe, a liberal member of the British Parliament, who opened his Georgia colony to mostly destitute English subjects. As their names—Francis Salvador, Alvaro Lopes Suasso, and Antonio da Costa—suggested, they were refugees from the Portuguese Inquisition, like many of the earlier Jewish settlers in the northern colonies. One new arrival, Samuel Nunes Ribeiro, immediately used his expertise as a physician to successfully treat many colonists who were suffering from yellow fever. Another new resident, Abraham de Lyon, was an expert in viticulture (producing wine), which made him an important contributor to the fledgling wine industry in the Georgia colony. During the 1700s, more Jews came to the colonies. Most, like the group who came to Georgia, were Sephardic, and like them, a large majority settled in the South. with the largest concentrations in Savannah and in Charleston, South Carolina. They were merchants, professionals, farmers, and plantation owners. By the 1830s, there were as many as 6,000 Jews in the United States, mostly in the South.[2]

After the 1830s, Sephardic Jews continued to arrive, but their population was soon eclipsed by increasing numbers of German and Ashkenazi Jewish emigrants from Eastern Europe and Russia as well. They settled in all corners of the United States and its territories, so that by the 1860s, the estimated Jewish population had expanded to nearly 200,000.[3]

Among this new group of migrants, Luis Gold and his children came to the New Mexico Territory in the 1850s, where he and his sons established The Old Curiosity Shop and Free Museum in Santa Fe. He and one of his sons joined other Jews in the first known Yom Kippur High Holy Days service in Santa Fe in 1860. In 1857, another Jew, Aaron Meier, ventured to Portland in the Oregon Territory and established a small mercantile store. By 1870, his business had expanded to the point where he took on two brothers—Emil and Sigmund Frank—as partners. The company continued to expand until it became the largest department store chain in Oregon, known as Meier and Frank. The Meiers and Franks were pillars in the Oregon community and active in politics; in 1930, Aaron's grandson, Julius Meier, was elected Governor of Oregon. But Julius Meier was not the first Jew elected as governor of a state. Moses Alexander, in neighboring Idaho, was elected governor in 1914.[4]

Between 1860 and 1890, the Jewish population of the United States doubled to about 450,000. Over the next 30 years, from 1890 to 1920, a surge of immigration brought the population to nearly 3,500,000. As with earlier migrations, Jews were facing oppression in their homelands of Eastern Europe and the Russian Empire. However, this wave of migrants settled in cities, in contrast with earlier Jewish immigrants who had settled in both urban and rural parts of America. By the 1930s, half of all American Jews lived in and near New York City, mostly in Brooklyn, the Bronx, and the Lower East Side of Manhattan.[5]

No matter when or where Jewish people settled, from the American Revolutionary War to the present day, they have participated in nearly every U.S. military engagement. They even fought against each other in the American Civil War. When the United States entered World War II, nearly 550,000 Jewish men entered military service. American Jews, unlike many of their fellow soldiers, knew that if they were in the European war theater, they likely would face great danger, even death, if they were captured by the Germans.

Several Jewish soldiers reported experiencing antisemitism.[6] One recalled that he and his bunkmate had become close friends, but when he said he was heading home for the Jewish holidays, his bunkmate refused to say another word to him for the remainder of their time together.

Of course, not all American soldiers were antisemitic. Most, in fact, welcomed them as partners in the war effort, and some risked their own lives to protect their Jewish comrades. During the Battle of the Bulge, from December 1944 through January 1945, nearly 15,000 American soldiers were taken as prisoners and sent to POW camps. A group of 1,275 enlisted men and non-commissioned officers were taken to Stalag IX-A near Ziegenhain, Germany. The senior U.S. soldier of the group, Master Sergeant Roderick A. "Roddie" Edmonds, was ordered by the camp commandant to turn over all of the Jewish soldiers in the camp the next morning. Edmonds passed the word around for all 1,275 men to turn out instead. The German commandant was furious with Edmunds. He pulled out his Lugar pistol, pointed it at Edmonds's head and demanded that if he did not turn over the Jews, he would shoot him. Edmonds calmly said: "We are all Jews here," and if the commandant wanted to shoot anyone, he would need to shoot every single U.S. POW in the camp. He added that the war was nearly over, Germany would lose, and if the commandant shot anyone, he would be considered a war criminal and be punished accordingly. The commandant backed down, and Edmonds singlehandedly saved the lives of some 200 Jewish POWs.[7]

Of the Jewish men stationed at Fort Hunt—admittedly a small sample size—none said they experienced antisemitism during their military service. Many Jewish soldiers, both at Fort Hunt and elsewhere, were terribly upset when the military decided to deploy them for their language abilities, rather than their fighting skills. Several later said that all they wanted was for the army to give them guns to go to Germany and kill Nazis.

Several Jews who served in the U.S. armed forces during World War II would become prominent Americans after the war. Writers Leon Uris, Joseph Heller, and Noman Mailer served and picked up some of their ideas for later work from their service. J. D. Salinger was assigned to counterintelligence, accompanying the 12th Infantry Regiment and the 4th Infantry Division of the army. He landed at Utah Beach on D-day and served in the Battle of the Bulge and the Battle of Hürtgen Forest. He was also present when the U.S. Army liberated Kaufering IV concentration camp, which deeply affected him; Salinger spent several weeks after the war in a military hospital for what we now know as post-traumatic stress disorder (PTSD). Melvin Kaminsky, later known as Mel Brooks, was drafted and served in Europe, defusing land mines left by the Germans. For Brooks, the military diet was a new experience compared to his childhood in Brooklyn. He was raised in a Kosher household, meaning that his family he did not mix meat with dairy products. He noticed that the other men in his unit were eating cheeseburgers. He finally decided to try one and decided that he liked this new "delicacy." Carl Reiner was trained as a radio operator, but shortly before he was deployed, he was reassigned to the Special Services entertainment unit; for two years, he traveled around the Pacific theater, performing for troops in Hawaii, Guam, Saipan, and Iwo Jima.[8]

These men, and a large majority of Jewish American soldiers and sailors, were second- or third-generation Americans. However, in this story, I will focus on more recent immigrants to the United States at the outset of World War II, who were forced out of Germany, or Austria, or other areas of Nazi reach and influence. While some had relatively straightforward departures from Europe, others went through harrowing, but ultimately successful, experiences to emigrate to the United States. Still others came to the United States as part of a program that allowed European parents to send their children to live with relatives or foster families to escape Nazi Germany. Many of these parents who sent their children away believed that Hitler and Nazis were aberrations, convinced that the German people would come to their senses and vote these men out of office.

As new United States residents, the young men and boys who had escaped from the Nazis were anxious to do whatever they could to end Hitler's reign of terror. Because of their language skills, many were recruited into or volunteered for top-secret military intelligence operations, and as such were sworn to secrecy and understood they would likely carry their wartime experiences to their graves. Unfortunately for historians, many did just that. Some had fun with the secrecy. One soldier told his wife, who was badgering him for what he was doing, that his job was to make brassieres for the Women's Army Corps (WAC). Fun aside, these men took their oath of secrecy seriously. Most were unaware that in the late 1990s, the government declassified this part of the American war effort. Documents were now available in the National Archives and the soldiers involved in the program were now allowed to share their experiences.[9]

Slowly at first, Americans started learning about these secret programs. The first exposure came when a former soldier, Lloyd Shoemaker, published his memoir, *The Escape Factory*, in 1990. The U.S. military was not yet ready to reveal anything about these secret programs and went to great lengths to purchase as many copies as it could to suppress the story. Shoemaker's book revealed the site of a classified operation based at Fort Hunt, Virginia, 12 miles from the Pentagon. He focused on one of the secret programs—Military Intelligence Service-X (MIS-X)—which specialized in "escape and evasion."

The soldiers created equipment and communication strategies to help U.S. pilots who were shot down avoid capture or to help U.S. military POWs escape from German prison camps in Europe.[10]

When Shoemaker wrote that Fort Hunt was the site of this clandestine program, to nearby residents, Fort Hunt Park seemed to be the most unlikely place for such an operation. Located on the George Washington Memorial Parkway between Mount Vernon and the City of Alexandria, Fort Hunt is currently a popular picnic and recreation area, managed by the National Park Service. Before Shoemaker's book and the declassification of World War II information, the park staff only had some inklings of what took place there during the war. To learn more about the park's history, the staff contracted with Dr. Matthew R. Laird of Cultural Resources, Inc. to research and write a historic resource study on Fort Hunt Park. In this comprehensive study, titled 'By the River Potomac' (2000), Dr. Laird wrote about the site from earliest prehistory through to recent development of the park. He devoted a chapter to the World War II programs at the fort, using many of the recently declassified documents from the National Archives for this chapter, which alerted park staff to the existence of previously unknown documents that chronicled the secret operations at Fort Hunt during the war.[11]

As the park began to piece together its World War II history, park staff understood that the MIS-X program Shoemaker described was only one of the secret programs operating there during World War II. The site was not called Fort Hunt at the time but rather PO Box 1142, from its mailing address in Alexandria. Another program, Military Intelligence Service-Y (MIS-Y), served two functions. Soldiers interrogated high-value German prisoners and listened in on conversations around the fort through an elaborate electronic surveillance system. Early on, the U.S. Navy operated a similar program under the code OP-16-Z. Another division, Military Intelligence Research Service (MIRS), translated and analyzed captured German documents. It shared its findings in special reports and in several editions of the "Order of Battle of the German Army" (referred to as the "Red Book"), which became an invaluable tool for the Allied fighting forces in the theaters of war.

The programs were housed at Fort Hunt but each operated independently. In fact, most men in any one program had no idea what men in the other programs did. Later, after the war, another secret program, called "Operation *Paperclip*," was designed to entice high-level German scientists and engineers to come to the United States and lend their expertise to America's new conflict—the Cold War with the Soviet Union.

Many of the American servicemen who interrogated German prisoners, eavesdropped on German POW conversations, or translated captured German documents were the Jews described above. Two themes emerged from their stories. First, each soldier was adamant that he never used corporal punishment in his interrogations of German soldiers. They used dozens of tricks to gain information from the Germans who refused or were reluctant to answer questions, but they never resorted to beating the prisoners. Generally, they found that German prisoners were often anxious to cooperate, especially toward the end of the war or after the Nazi regime had surrendered. Many were disillusioned with the Nazi cause. Others wanted to be on the American side in what they perceived as the future conflict with the Soviet Union. And still others were simply tired of fighting and wanted the war to end.[12]

Second, while the soldiers at Fort Hunt were pleased with their contributions to the war effort, they revealed that during their service, they were constantly haunted by concerns for their families and friends left behind in Germany and across occupied Europe. Most had lost all contact when the war started, and many learned later that their loved ones had perished in the concentration camps.

This is the story of Fort Hunt, PO Box 1142, and the people who did so much to help the Allies win the war.

CHAPTER I

River Farm Plantation and Beyond

"I had rather be on my farm than be emperor of the world."

GEORGE WASHINGTON

The year 1759 was momentous in the life of George Washington. At the end of 1758, he had resigned his commission as colonel and commander in chief of the Virginia militia, completing the first phase of his military career. He had accomplished this by the age of 26. He was now ready to throw himself full-time into the business of running his Mount Vernon farm. His brother Jack had been managing the farm in his absence, and according to most accounts, the farm was in deplorable condition. He received a big boost both to his farming ambitions and to his personal life, when, at the beginning of the year, he married Martha Dandridge Custis, a wealthy widow, who brought money, slaves, and her affection into the union. Later in the year, he was elected to the Virginia House of Burgesses, which ushered in the beginning of his political career.[1]

When he took over management of his farm in 1759, George Washington was an agricultural novice. He had worked on farms, but he had never managed an operation like Mount Vernon. From the outset, though, he did everything conceivable to excel as a farmer. He ordered treatises on crops, equipment, and every aspect of farm management. Then he purchased the newest, most advanced farm implements and what were purported to be highly productive seeds from England or elsewhere. He never stopped researching to learn the most advanced farming techniques, gadgets, and seeds then available.

He also continuously experimented and tinkered, and each day he recorded his activities and observations in his diary. As an example, on September 6, 1788, he recorded his experiments with wheat crops. He was not happy with the "Cape wheat," because it was "shriveled and bad." The imported Harrison wheat, planted in another plot, was "large, but not full & plump."

On the other hand, local seeds produced big kernels and high yield. Even so, he bemoaned that a strain of white wheat, that he had acquired early in his farming career, was far superior to any other variety. While he was away fighting in the Revolutionary War, however, the seed was mixed with other varieties, diluting the pure strain and producing lower yields.[2]

Most farmers have always believed that success hinges on the amount of land they farm. Acquiring more land is the goal. That certainly was the case for George Washington in 1760, when, fortuitously, the land to the north of Mount Vernon, across Little Hunting Creek, became available. William Clifton, the property owner, was having serious financial difficulties, and his creditors were clamoring for their money. If Clifton could sell this land, he would go a long way toward satisfying his creditors. With the involvement of the creditors in the sale, the process was complicated, but with Martha's money, plus his tenacity—that would serve him well throughout his life—George was able to purchase the 1806 acres of land on Clifton's Neck, for £1,210.[3]

He owned the land, but much of it was encumbered by tenants, whose leases were still in force, which delayed his active farming on the land. Eventually, when the leases expired, or, in one case when he bought out a tenant, George Washington incorporated what he called "River Farm" into his plantation system. River Farm would become the future site of Fort Hunt (PO Box 1142) some 150 years later.

George Washington's overall estate, which would grow to some 8,000 acres, consisted of five separate plantations. Like most of his neighbors, Washington grew tobacco as his major cash crop, but he quickly learned the difficulties with this crop. At that time, tobacco was sold to brokers in London at a price they determined. Some years the price was good, some not, but Virginia growers were at the mercy of buyers in the London market. Tobacco was a labor-intensive crop, which was not a major problem for George since he and Martha owned many slaves. However, tobacco also required an abundant supply of water, especially early in the growth cycle, which sometimes was a problem, since Northern Virginia suffered occasional droughts. Finally, tobacco depleted soil nutrients. Farmers like George Washington knew this but not exactly why. We now know that the plants use more nitrogen, phosphorus, and potassium than other major crops.[4]

Washington understood that planting different varieties of tobacco gave him healthier plants. Solving that one problem, however, did not resolve the other issues with growing tobacco. In 1765, George wrote to his agent in London, saying that although he raised nothing "but sweet-scented tobacco," and that he was very "careful in the management of it," he and his fellow Virginians were unhappy "with such unprofitable returns."

In his frustration, George Washington started experimenting with other crops. In his 30 plus years at Mount Vernon, he grew over 60 different crops, everything from varieties of wheat and corn to ryegrass, hop clover, guinea grass, hemp, Jerusalem artichokes, field peas, and potatoes. He also planted special forage crops to feed his livestock, such as Siberian melilot and sainfoin, which were both in the pea family, and burnet, another forage crop, which, with its deep roots, served as a soil stabilizer. Corn and wheat were particularly important as cash crops, as feed for his animals, and as the main ingredients for his whiskey distillery.[5]

Each of the five Mount Vernon farms was managed independently. Slaves, with an overseer, were housed on each farm. Most worked exclusively on that farm six days a week; on Sunday, they mingled with friends or family on other farms. Washington expected his slaves to work hard, but he was opposed to whipping them as punishment. We would like to think that he was against this practice for humanitarian reasons, but it was mostly because he did not believe this provided any beneficial results. He fed, clothed, and housed his slaves, but in some cases, he would break up families to meet the labor needs of his farms.

George Washington's quote at the top of this chapter is very revealing. He looked at his military and political careers as duties and services to his country, but his passion was farming. He was happiest when, each day, he would saddle up and ride through his five farms, seeing how his experiments were progressing, making sure his fences were secure, checking his crops to make sure harvest was timed when the grain was at its peak of ripeness, and generally ensuring that everything was running smoothly. From time to time, George would sit down and develop management plans that served as guidance for the coming year and well into the future for each of his farms. The last plan he prepared was on December 10, 1799, only days before his death. In addition to the action plan, he listed the slaves on each plantation, their ages, their relationships to each other, and whether they were his or Martha's slaves. Fifty-seven slaves lived on the River Plantation, 30 belonging to Martha, 27 to George. They ranged in age from one to 80; 19 were children, 36 were workers, one was a cook, and one was listed as "past labor"—too old to work.

George Washington's program for River Farm was extensive and thorough. For the year 1800, he laid out what he envisioned for each plot; for the following three years, he sketched out general guidelines. River Farm was divided into eight plots, with about half in crops and the rest for pasturage. He was precise as to which should be planted in wheat, which in corn, which in rye or oats, and which should grow potatoes or turnips. Some of the pasturage should be open, other parts fenced. Runoff from rainstorms was a constant problem. He directed that "litter, straw, weeds, or [other kinds of] rubbish" should be scattered and planted to stabilize these areas. In his experimentations, he found that mud from the local streams served as a good nutrient for his corn crops. Animal manure, as fertilizer, produced bumper crops of potatoes. He also learned that gathering up residue from harvests into mulch piles made excellent fertilizer. Farm animals "ought to be kept well littered, and the Stalls clean; as well for the comfort of the Creatures that are contained in them; as for the purpose of manure" to be collected and used for fertilizer.

At the end of his guidance for the River Farm and the rest of his plantations, George Washington made it very clear that the plan he laid out was not optional. "There is one thing however I cannot forbear to add, and in strong terms; it is, that whenever I order a thing to be done, it must be done." He went on to say that if an "impracticality is discovered, why [the task cannot be done], a countermand, or change" must be suggested immediately. Further, if it was determined that the project was not completed, or for some reason "could not be done; either of these is unpleasant, and disagreeable to me, having been accustomed all my life to more regularity, and punctuality, and know that nothing but system and method is required to accomplish all reasonable requests."[6]

Clearly, Washington had every intention of implementing his annual workplan just as he had done for many years previously. But two days after putting his ideas on paper, on December 12, he mounted his horse and did something of which he never grew tired, which was to ride the circuit around his farms. The weather was dreadful, starting with snow early, changing into a cold and heavy rain. When he returned home, he dined with guests without removing his wet clothes. The next day, he had a sore throat but thought nothing of it and walked down to the Potomac River to scope out an area where he intended to build a fishpond. During the night, he awoke with an inflamed throat, woke Martha and complained that he was having difficulty breathing. In the morning of December 14, his symptoms grew worse, and his family physician, Dr. Craik, was summoned from Alexandria. While waiting for the doctors to arrive, Washington asked one of his men to bleed him, a barbaric practice that generally made the symptoms worse. When Dr. Craik and two other doctors arrived, they continued bleeding the patient—probably removing about five pints of blood. The youngest physician, Dr. Dick, recommended a new treatment, which we now refer to as a tracheotomy, to ease Washington's breathing. The other two physicians vetoed the procedure. As the day progressed, the great man grew worse and died. In his last minutes, George Washington had his finger on his wrist, feeling his pulse as his life ebbed away.[7]

George Washington's plans for the future of his River Farm and for the rest of his plantations were not fulfilled. Gradually, the land was divided among family members or sold to others, and Washington's carefully orchestrated management quickly deteriorated. By 1834, an observer visited the farms and wrote that "more widespread and perfect agricultural ruin could not be imagined; yet the monuments of the great mind that once ruled, are seen throughout. The ruins of capacious barns, and long extended hedges, seem proudly to boast that their master looked to the future." By 1850, the Mount Vernon mansion and surrounding farmland belonged to George Washington's great-great-nephew, John Augustine Washington III, who could no longer afford to keep the estate. But he also recognized its importance to the nation and offered it for sale to the federal government and the Commonwealth of Virginia. Neither was interested, but Ann Pamela Cunningham, a young woman from South Carolina, took up the torch to preserve Mount Vernon and started a national fundraising effort in 1853. Her effort was successful and by 1859 she had raised the necessary $200,000—an extraordinary amount for that day—to buy Mount Vernon. The Mount Vernon Ladies' Association of the Union has continued to manage Mount Vernon as a private operation ever since.[8]

Mount Vernon and its 200 surrounding acres were secure for posterity, but the land associated with the River Farm continued to pass through multiple owners. Change came in 1885, when Congress recognized that the coastal defenses nationwide were in deplorable condition. During the Civil War, in April 1862, a Union field artillery battery, set up on a sand spit across from Fort Pulaski in Savannah Harbor, Georgia, had easily breeched the masonry wall of the Confederate-controlled fort in a day and a half. The vulnerability facing field artillery or the armaments on modern naval vessels, plus the reality that most of these masonry fortresses were not well maintained, and in some cases were crumbling, concerned many members of Congress. They authorized President Grover Cleveland to appoint a commission to develop recommendations for new fortifications.

President Cleveland appointed the Board on Fortifications and Other Defenses, generally referred to as the Endicott Board, named for Secretary of War William C. Endicott, who served as chair. The board confirmed what Congress already knew: the nation's coastal defenses were inadequate. The Endicott Board submitted its report to Congress in 1886, recommending an expenditure of $127 million for new, state-of-the-art defenses at 29 locations at port entrances and in coastal areas. One area of particular concern was the harbor entrance to Washington, DC. Fortress Monroe and Fort Wool continued as the primary defensive structures at the mouth of Chesapeake Bay. Up the Potomac River on the Maryland side, just upriver from Mount Vernon, Fort Washington continued to stand but was of little defensive value. After the Civil War, the War Department had upgraded Fort Foote, built as part of the circle of forts surrounding the nation's capital, as the last line of defense to protect Washington, DC, but it was inadequate as well. Clearly, the Chesapeake/Potomac waterways needed significant defensive upgrades.

As the Endicott program moved from plan to implementation, the fortifications demonstrated the era's genius for military engineering. The primary weaponry consisted of breech-loading rifled artillery on disappearing carriages, firing six- to fourteen-inch shells. The rifled tube would sit on a carriage below a 20-foot-thick reinforced concrete parapet. Earthwork would slope down from the front apron of the parapet. When fired, the gun crew released a mechanism raising the rifle above the parapet on a hydraulic system. Upon firing, the recoil pushed the barrel down where it would lock, ready for loading. The whole sequence would take seconds. Fire-control towers triangulated and coordinated targets, so that the weapons achieved pinpoint accuracy. In addition to the disappearing guns, many coastal systems also included 12-inch mortars, and smaller rapid-fire weapons. Underwater mines (then referred to as torpedoes) rounded out the weapon system. These weapons were placed at the bottom of the estuaries and were electrically detonated.[9]

The board recognized that Fort Washington was still in an important strategic location and thus should remain and be rearmed with the latest Endicott system weapons. It recommended spending over $1.3 million on the fort, plus other defenses on the Potomac. The War Department concluded that the best location for an additional fortification was on the Virginia side of the river, directly across from Fort Washington, on land that had once been part of George Washington's river plantation. If the landowners were unwilling to sell the roughly 300 acres needed, the government had the authorization to condemn the land and pay up to $500,000 if necessary for purchase. The government condemned and acquired the necessary land in 1893. Plans for the new fort and its armaments were completed in 1896, and construction commenced in 1897. With delays, the major features of the installation were completed and operational in 1899. Fort Washington and this new fort would be the last line of defense against any enemy vessel that somehow made it through the defenses at the mouth of Chesapeake Bay. The weaponry from these fortifications, plus the minefield, were designed with so many overlapping elements, any enemy ship commander would rue the day he had decided to attack the nation's capital.

Fort Hunt was the name for the new fort. It was named for Brigadier General Henry Jackson Hunt, who had served in the Mexican War and the Civil War, when he was breveted major general as commander of artillery for the Army of the Potomac. His last post was as governor of the Soldiers' Home in Washington, DC. The principal armaments were three 8-inch rifles on disappearing carriages located in Battery Mount Vernon. These were complemented with two 5-inch rapid-fire guns on pedestal mounts—Batteries Robinson and Porter. Battery Robinson was named for First Lieutenant Levi H. Robinson, who was killed in an engagement in Wyoming Territory in 1874; Battery Porter was named for First Lieutenant James Porter, killed in the Battle of the Little Big Horn in 1876. A fourth battery, Battery Sater, was added later, completed in 1904 and named for Lieutenant William A. Sater, killed in the Battle of San Juan in the Spanish–American War in 1898.

More than 30 buildings filled out the fort complex, with everything from officers' quarters and enlisted men's barracks to a hospital, stables, a mess hall, recreation facilities (including a bowling alley), a power plant, and a guard room. The military was also able to re-use several buildings owned by the previous landowner. When Fort Hunt was fully operational, it was manned with the 47th Company of the newly formed Coast Artillery Corps. Manpower was never more than a company (80–120 men), and for most of the time, the commanding officer was a captain. On occasion, Fort Hunt would sponsor joint training exercises with other Coast Artillery Corps companies.[10]

The U.S. Army had no way of knowing this, but just when Battery Sater was completed and became operational in January 1904, the Endicott period Coast Artillery system had started down its road to obsolescence. On December 17, 1903, the Wright Brothers successfully flew their "Flyer" at Kitty Hawk, North Carolina. With the elaborate precautions military engineers had designed to protect gun batteries from naval attacks, the eventual ability of airplanes to drop bombs on the forts could not be overcome. By World War I, the guns from many Coast Artillery forts were shipped to Europe as railway guns or scrapped. Such was the case with Fort Hunt. The electronic mine systems, and the gun batteries associated with those systems, were still practical but not the rest of the armaments.

Fort Hunt was never fired on in anger. That was true of all Coast Artillery forts in the Continental United States, with one exception—Fort Stevens in Oregon—on June 21, 1942, when a Japanese submarine surfaced near the mouth of the Columbia River and lobbed several shells in the direction of the fort. Ironically, although these Endicott Period fortifications were quickly out-of-date, the presence of the substantial concrete gun emplacements remain and likely will continue as curiosities for generations.

With its armaments shipped to Europe, and with new defenses constructed on Cape Henry at the mouth of Chesapeake Bay, Fort Hunt no longer had value as a Coast Artillery fort. What does one do with a military installation that is only 20 years old and close to the nation's capital? At first, the buildings housed troops stationed in or near Washington, DC. For a brief time, Fort Hunt served as the Finance School to train enlisted men to work in the new War Department Finance Department. The school showed promise but never reached the goal of the desired number of trainees and was eventually discontinued.

In the 1920s and early 1930s, Howard University used Fort Hunt for summer Reserve Officers' Training Corps (ROTC) training. Some years, students from Wilberforce University in Ohio used the site as well. Students spent six weeks in the summer, stayed in the barracks, and trained with small arms.[11] Multiple proposals came to the War Department for the fort, in the form of federal or municipal government proposals, and others came from private entities to use the land and the facilities. The District of Columbia was interested in using the site to train National Guard soldiers; the U.S. Department of Agriculture considered turning the site into a plant experimental station. The City of Alexandria wanted to use the site as a park, including a bathing beach on the Potomac. One of the most intriguing proposals came in 1923, when the Roosevelt Military Academy in Englewood, New Jersey, thought about relocating to the Washington, DC area, and specifically utilizing Fort Hunt. Members of the school's board, including Colonel Theodore Roosevelt, Jr., son of the former president, supported the proposal. The negotiations ended when the school recognized that it would incur substantial expenses to convert the facility from a fort to a school, with no assurances that it could eventually own the land and facilities.[12]

At the same time the Roosevelt Military Academy ended negotiations for Fort Hunt, a new proposal surfaced that would become important to the future of the fort. In that year, the United States Commission for the "Celebration of the Two Hundredth Anniversary of the Birth of George Washington" was established by an act of Congress to commemorate the life of President Washington as farmer, soldier, and statesman. As one of its projects, the commission proposed constructing a highway that would connect the Memorial Bridge in Washington, DC to Mount Vernon. Not only would this provide a safe and scenic route to Mount Vernon; it would make Fort Hunt much more easily accessible. Construction started in 1929 and was completed in January 1932, on the eve of the anniversary of Washington's birth date.[13]

As construction of the Memorial Parkway (later the name was changed to the George Washington Memorial Parkway) was underway, the nation fell into the worst economic depression in its history. To deal with the crisis, President Herbert Hoover did far more than any previous president had done during an economic downturn. He immediately encouraged businesses to commit to spending $1.8 billion on new construction and repairs to existing facilities to increase employment. He pushed for a $160 million tax cut and doubled federal spending on constructing new buildings, dams, highways, and harbors. Then, in 1932, Hoover signed the Emergency Relief Construction Act, which loaned $300 million to the states for relief programs and $1.5 billion for public works projects. The programs helped, and, in 1932, it seemed that the nation was beginning to emerge from the crisis. In reality, these early efforts did little to ease the economic crisis. Between 1929 and 1933, the stock market lost nearly 90 percent of its value. Unemployment went from 3 percent in 1929 to 25 percent in 1933. During the course of the depression, average family income dropped by 40 percent; some 11,000 banks failed, and many Americans lost their life savings.[14]

In the early stages of the Great Depression, Fort Hunt continued as a former military installation that did not seem to have a purpose. Gradually, however, the fort played a greater and greater role, housing a program that would be a backbone in federal relief programs.

Following World War I, veterans started lobbying Congress for additional compensation for their service. In 1924, Congress and veterans agreed to a plan in which the government would invest funds, so that by the target date of 1945, each veteran would receive a one-time payment of about $1,000. The program made perfect sense when the overall economy was healthy in 1924, but as the grip of the depression became stronger and stronger, with many veterans out of work, they started a push to receive their compensation sooner.

In the spring of 1932, Walter W. Walters, from Burns, Oregon—a former sergeant in the war, whose small business enterprises had failed—organized a march to the nation's capital to lobby Congress to move up the "bonus" payment to unemployed veterans sooner rather than later. His call for a "Bonus Expeditionary Force" attracted veterans from the West Coast, who gathered in Portland and started their journey to the nation's capital. They rode in freight cars, hitchhiked, and walked; along the way, others joined, so that when the "army" reached Washington, DC, there were some 20,000 veterans, along with family members and other supporters. The marchers were allowed to erect makeshift shelters in three main camps and several smaller camps. One group stayed on Pennsylvania Avenue near the Capitol, around buildings that were slated for demolition. The largest group built its village east of the Anacostia River and south of the 11th Street Bridge, in Anacostia Flats (currently Anacostia Park). The third encampment, completely independent from Walter's group, was the Worker's Ex-Servicemen League, made up of American communist veterans. They were camped at 14th and D Streets in southwest Washington.

Since the veterans were unemployed, they were in no hurry to return to their homes. Conversely, Congress was in no hurry to consider or meet their demands for bonus money. As time stretched from days to weeks, District of Columbia Police Superintendent Pelham D. Glassford, who was a World War I veteran and sympathetic to the veterans, grew concerned about the health and sanitary conditions of the camps. The issue came to the attention of President Hoover, who directed Frank T. Hines, the Administrator of Veterans' Affairs, to create a 300-bed hospital for the marchers at Fort Hunt. The army, under the command of Chief of Staff, General Douglas MacArthur, quickly prepared and furnished Fort Hunt to serve as a hospital. This was one of the few positive stories from the march.

On June 17, 1932, the Senate defeated a bill passed by the House of Representatives that would have compensated the veterans. President Hoover intimated that even if the bill had passed, he would have vetoed the measure. He was concerned about showing favoritism to any particular group. With defeat of the bonus bill, and with Congress leaving town for its summer recess, President Hoover hoped to encourage the marchers to leave town as well. He set aside $100,000 to pay for transportation for the veterans to return to their homes. Instead, Waters' group and the communist veterans decided to remain in town. Their efforts were, for the most part, receiving public support nationwide. It was true that many people in every corner of the country were suffering, but many believed that World War I veterans, who had risked their lives in battle, deserved federal assistance. The longer they stayed, however, the more impatient President Hoover grew with their presence, especially the group staying around the abandoned buildings on Pennsylvania Avenue. The camp was an eyesore in the nation's capital, and the buildings were slated for demolition to make way for new federal buildings. Further, this shantytown and the similar makeshift collections of shelters around the country were being called "Hoovervilles," as a rebuke to the president's response to the depression.

Police Superintendent Glassford, who all along had not only been sympathetic to his fellow veterans' cause but had also provided materials to build their shelters as well as food, was now directed to force the Bonus Army to leave town. He gave the order for them to disperse by 10:00a.m. on July 28, 1932. Most veterans and their families complied with the order, but others resisted, and soon a riot broke out between the marchers and 500 District of Columbia police.[15]

General MacArthur had been preparing his soldiers for a contingency should the Bonus Army get out of hand at some point and require his intervention. He stationed his troops—the infantry and the cavalry, under the command of Major George Patton—on the Ellipse across from the White House, ready for action. MacArthur's aid, Major Dwight Eisenhower, advised caution and suggested that MacArthur should allow more junior officers to take command. The general ignored the advice, and at about 4:00p.m., Patton led his cavalry down Pennsylvania Avenue, followed by tanks and the infantry, clearing out everyone and everything in their paths. The army also destroyed the communist camp. Later that evening, MacArthur led his army across the Anacostia River and torched the shantytown on Anacostia Flats. Eisenhower would later say that MacArthur ignored specific orders from the president, passed on by Secretary of War Patrick Hurley, not to cross the Anacostia River. The future president wrote that, when he passed the order to MacArthur, the general "said he was too busy and did not want either himself or his staff bothered by people coming down and pretending to bring orders." Then years later, in an interview with historian Stephen Ambrose, Eisenhower said: "I told that dumb son-of-a-bitch [General MacArthur] he had no business going down there [across the Anacostia River]."[16]

President Hoover succeeded in removing the Bonus Marchers from Washington, DC, but at a great cost. Two marchers were killed and several were injured in the confrontation. The nation sympathized with the veterans and turned against Hoover. He was soundly defeated later in 1932. Although General MacArthur disobeyed a direct order, which helped precipitate Hoover's downfall, he went on to a glorious career as overall army commander in the Pacific theater in World War II.

"The Bonus Expeditionary Force" of 1932 was the best known but not the only effort of World War I veterans to secure their bonus payments. Early in May 1933, soon after Franklin D. Roosevelt's inauguration, another, smaller, veterans group came to Washington, DC. President Roosevelt (FDR) wanted to do whatever was necessary to avoid the confrontation and public relations nightmare of the Hoover Administration, but he also was opposed to providing a special bonus to veterans. His first action was to provide housing in barracks and tents at Fort Hunt for the 3,000 veterans. As soon as they arrived in the capital, they were bussed to the fort, which accomplished two things: the veterans were housed and well fed, and they were out of the limelight of Washington, DC. On May 16, first lady Eleanor Roosevelt visited the marchers, and her visit was reported in the *New York Times*. She had a rousing reception in part for her visit and in part for her comments to the veterans. "I will always be grateful to those who served their country," Mrs. Roosevelt said. "I hope we will never have to ask such service [in a war] again and I hope that you will carry on in peace times as you did in the war days, for that is the duty of every patriotic American."

Ever the consummate politician, FDR followed up on the first lady's visit by inviting the veterans to Washington, DC on May 19, where he addressed them in front of the White House. He was avoiding another problem from the first bonus march, when Hoover refused to meet with the veterans during their stay. In many ways, what FDR offered was far greater than the bonus they were after. He offered them jobs in the new—barely two months old—"Forest Army," more commonly known as the Civilian Conservation Corps (CCC). All but about 350 of the 3,000 veterans enthusiastically accepted the offer, enrolled in the CCC, and remained at Fort Hunt. The Veterans Administration paid for the remaining veterans' transportation home.

Ironically, FDR continued to oppose special payments to World War I veterans. When Congress passed the Adjusted Compensation Payment Act of 1936, he vetoed the measure, even though a majority of members of the House and Senate were, like him, Democrats. By a vote of 324 to 63 in the House and 76 to 19 in the Senate, Congress overrode the veto and appropriated almost $2 billion in payments to World War I veterans.[17]

The CCC, into which FDR allowed veterans to enter, was primarily designed for teenage and young, single men, aged 18 to 24 (later expanded to 17 to 28). Their age group was one of the hardest hit in the depression, with 25 percent unemployed and another 29 percent working part-time. Each enrollee received three meals a day, shelter, and clothing. They also received a small salary, of which they were directed to send most of the money home to support their families. Obviously, World War I veterans did not fit the general criteria to join the CCC. They were well past this age group, and most were married, but they were also unemployed and anxious to join. In the nine-year existence of the CCC, some 25,000 veterans were among the 2.5 million enrollees.[18]

The CCC camp at Fort Hunt was designated as NP-6, under the authority of the National Park Service, which, through a circuitous process now managed the fort after it was transferred from the War Department to the National Park Service by executive order in 1933. The men at Fort Hunt worked eight-hour days on conservation projects, which included building drainage systems or stabilizing streambanks; cutting, pruning, or planting trees; or on construction projects, such as building picnic shelters or restrooms. They developed a bird sanctuary near the fort and cleared and stabilized a lagoon on the Potomac River and built a road and parking area so that visitors could enjoy their handiwork. After work, they could engage in a variety of recreational activities. Then, after dinner, they could enroll in education programs or learn trades such as carpentry, auto mechanics, or other skills. The camp maintained a large library and the men could watch films in the camp theater. The men even produced their own newspaper called *Happy Days*.

Because of its close proximity to Washington, DC, the Roosevelt Administration loved to show off the Fort Hunt CCC camp to visiting dignitaries. Anthony Eden, the former foreign secretary and future prime minister of Great Britain, visited the camp in 1938 as he returned from Mount Vernon to Washington, DC. By far the biggest coup for the CCC camp came on June 9, 1939, when first lady Eleanor Roosevelt brought King George VI and Queen Elizabeth to Fort Hunt on their way from Mount Vernon to Arlington Cemetery. Mrs. Roosevelt was very moved by the respect King George showed to the young men she later recalled in her memoirs:

> The king walked with the commander of the camp towards the boys who were drawn up in two lines in the broiling sun. A large bulletin board had been put up with pictures of the various camps throughout the country, showing the different kinds of work done by the boys, but he did not stop to look at it then. As we went down the long line, the king stopped at every other boy and asked questions while the queen spoke to the intervening boys. ... He asked really interested questions, such as whether they were satisfied with their food, what they were learning and whether they thought it would help them to obtain work and lastly, how much they were earning.

Finally, the royal couple looked at the exhibit panels the boys had prepared for them. They asked to have copies made and sent to them.

The next day, in the newest edition of the camp's newspaper, *Happy Days*, the headline read: "King and Queen Get Chummy with Men at CCC Inspection," along with an image of the royal couple. The paper reported that the preparations for the visit were worthwhile because now each man could "compare experiences and fix the details in mind for the home folks." Within three months of the royal visit, Hitler invaded Poland, ushering in the beginning of World War II. Before long, many of the young men at Fort Hunt and other CCC camps would find work manufacturing war materials; others would join the military. Fort Hunt would change as well and become one of the most important, yet secret, facilities in the war effort.[19]

As the CCC men phased out of the program, and the CCC program phased out of existence, Fort Hunt took on a new role. The National Park Service owned the facility, but it had not functioned as a park. With the attack on Pearl Harbor on December 7, 1941, Fort Hunt quickly became important for several functions. For one thing, the National Archives needed a place to safely store its nitrate film. This early film material deteriorated rapidly and was highly flammable and toxic. It was important to find a safe storage location in the unlikely event that the archives might be attacked, but it was also a good idea to move the film away from the National Archives building to protect the health and safety of employees. The Archives Committee on Protection Against the Hazards of War looked for potential sites to store the nitrate film and decided that the abandoned turn-of-the-century gun emplacements at Fort Hunt would be perfect. Contractors renovated and attempted to waterproof the underground artillery magazines, erecting 45 storage vaults. The threat of toxic fires harming humans was removed, but the moisture that seeped into the magazines could not be controlled, and, eventually, the National Archives moved the film to another location.

The second agreement was with the War Department. On May 15, 1942, under a special-use permit with the National Park Service, the military established a "Joint Interrogation Center" at Fort Hunt, which stipulated that the War Department would occupy the site during the duration of World War II plus one year. Once the agreement was in place, construction commenced at a furious pace to accommodate the top-secret facility. Once the facilities were completed, access was tightly controlled. Anyone observing the comings and goings to the fort probably had a sense of its secret nature. In addition to the restricted access, cars and buses going to and from the fort had blacked-out windows, and much of the traffic came and went at night. As per the special-use permit, the War Department continued using the site after the war, and by the end of 1946, many of the temporary structures had been removed. Then, in January 1948, the military formally returned Fort Hunt to the National Park Service.[20]

After the war, the suburbs around Washington, DC were growing in population. The need and desire for open space was critical, and to private developers and the Commonwealth of Virginia, Fort Hunt seemed like the perfect location. The National Park Service did not go out of its way to entertain proposals, but they came in anyway. Private entities wanted to build golf courses or other recreational venues, including one company that wanted to build an equestrian center, including a large arena. Virginia, which wanted to develop a recreational facility in the fast-growing Northern Virginia region, proposed to turn the fort land into a state park.

Ultimately, National Park Service management concluded that the best use for the land was for it to develop its own park. The overall plan called for utilizing the trails developed during the CCC period, as well as picnic areas, ball fields, and general open spaces. The first large picnic pavilion, encompassing some 8,000 square feet, was proposed and built in 1963. Other picnic areas were added, and the park became so popular, a reservation system was implemented to reserve areas during the busy summer season. The park also started sponsoring a regular concert series on Sunday evenings during the summer.[21]

The gun batteries remained in place, in large measure because the cost of demolishing them would have been prohibitive. The gun platforms were open to the public, but the magazines were closed, because the National Archives had installed asbestos to fireproof the spaces for the nitrate film storage. The only other historic structure remaining from Fort Hunt's earlier military history was a non-commissioned officer's house near the park entrance.

Among the most popular features at Fort Hunt, or at any National Park site for that matter, are the ranger-led tours. The enthusiasm of park rangers and the high quality of the content make these tours the envy of parks around the world. One day, in the fall of 2005, Ranger Dana Dierkes led a historical tour of the park. She began as she always did by asking her audience to look around and to think about and describe what they saw. As was the usual response, the folks described the picnic shelters, the concrete gun emplacements—although most had no idea what they were or how they were used—and the large, grassy open areas. This technique always worked to engage the visitors. Then, she proceeded to give the tour in which she started with describing the indigenous people who stopped in the area and the history of George Washington's River Farm plantation as a part of Mount Vernon. Then she took them to the abandoned gun batteries of Fort Hunt. She made sure that her charges were careful as they navigated the concrete batteries, and she explained the significance of the fort as part of the rearmament of American coastal areas from around 1900. Then she described the CCC operation and the fort in World War II.

At this point, Ranger Dierkes did what she and her colleagues had been doing for months. She asked her group to imagine the fort as a bustling top-secret facility with buildings, guard towers, fences, and other structures, with security that was so tight, virtually no one other than the men stationed there knew what was going on. Not only were the men not allowed to describe what they were doing to anyone—not even to their families—but they were sworn to secrecy for the remainder of their lives. Then she asked her visitors to imagine that most of the men populating the site were high-level German prisoners, brought there for American soldiers to learn as much as they could from one-on-one interrogations and eavesdropping on their conversations. She noted that during the war, the site was almost never referred to as Fort Hunt, but rather by its codename of PO Box 1142. Further, she said that many of the documents related to the program had been declassified, allowing park staff to begin to solve many of the mysteries from that period. She noted that the "By the River Potomac," (2000) historical resource study, by historian Matthew Laird, and Lloyd Shoemaker's *The Escape Factory* (1990), were providing the foundations for the park staff's understanding of the World War II history of the fort.

Ranger Dierkes and her colleagues would end their tours by saying that the park staff hoped they could find men who were stationed there during World War II, so they could continue to build their interpretive scaffold. On this particular day, as Ranger Dierkes made her pitch about finding men stationed at the fort, someone in the audience mentioned that a former neighbor was a member of the team who was assigned to a top-secret program at Fort Hunt during World War II. Ranger Dierkes wrote down the contact information, passed it along to her supervisor, Vincent Santucci, and thus began one of the most important oral history projects in the National Park Service.[22]

The neighbor was Fred Michel, who was assigned to interrogating high-level German POWs at Fort Hunt. Park staff contacted Mr. Michel and his wife, Lucille, and on May 30–31, 2006, park historian Brandon Bies interviewed the couple, which turned out to be the first large nugget of a virtual gold mine of information.[23]

CHAPTER 2

Escape from the Nazis

"My dad and I walked slowly. Silently we watched as German soldiers marched down Market Street—my last impression of Höxter, Germany."

RUDY PINS

Before Adolph Hitler came to power in 1933, many of the young Jewish men who were eventually assigned to Fort Hunt shared early childhood experiences that were little different from those of other children. They had Jewish and non-Jewish friends; they attended school without restrictions, and they participated in a variety of activities, such as Boy Scouts. But when the Nazis came to power, and they started their concerted antisemitic campaigns, these young peoples' worlds were turned upside down. They could no longer attend school, nor participate in normal activities. They quickly became second-class citizens.

On March 14, 1938, one of these young men, fifteen-year-old George Weidinger, went to school as he did every Monday morning. His school was a technical high school—the *Real Schule*—in Heitzig, Austria, just outside of Vienna. On this particular day, he was called into the principal's office and was told he could no longer attend the school. "Why not?" he asked. The reason was shocking. He was informed that he was Jewish. He had no idea that his family had any connection to Judaism. Before George was born, his family had converted to Christianity and had not told him about the family's Jewish heritage.

What George Weidinger knew at this point in his life was that he had been raised and baptized in the Helvetic (Swiss) Confession Protestant faith. There was not a nearby church in his denomination, so he and his family attended the nearby Lutheran church, which was theologically closest to their church. He was required to take a religion class in his school, and the teacher was the Lutheran minister. To try to ensure that he would get a good grade, he made sure that the minister—his teacher—saw him in the church every Sunday. In addition, the woman who cleaned and cooked for the Weidinger family was a devout Catholic. She frequently took George and his younger brother to services in her church during the week. He thought he was as much a Christian as anyone in his community; in fact, he thought he was more Christian than most because he attended two Christian churches. When he found out his parents had converted to Christianity from Judaism years before, he was stunned.[1]

George Weidinger was only one of thousands of Austrians whose lives were upended in March of 1938. The Austro-Hungarian Empire and Germany were allies in World War I, though the Treaty of Versailles forbade the two countries—the Empire then reduced to Austria—from re-establishing the alliance after the war. There was widespread support in Austria and Germany to reconnect the two countries in some fashion in the 1920s and early 1930s. As unification was gaining support, however, the Austrian chancellor, Kurt von Schuschnigg, wanted Austria to maintain its independence. Instead, he was bullied into naming several top Austrian Nazis to his cabinet. He was further thwarted when a national vote intended to resolve the question of *Anschluss,* or "annexation," scheduled for March 9, was canceled. Finally, Schuschnigg was forced to resign on March 11, and with the prime minister out of the way, German troops marched into Austria the next day with virtually no resistance. On March 13, Hitler announced that Austria had been annexed by Germany. Almost immediately, Nazis, with support from many Austrians, started rounding up communists, social democrats, Jews, and other political opponents. Over 70,000 were arrested and imprisoned or sent to concentration camps.

Neither George nor his family were victims of this early purge, but, as George said, "not being able to go to school, the question was, what am I going to do with my time?" A man who operated an auto repair shop offered him a job, with no pay, so he could learn a useful trade. "My job was to get up at five o'clock in the morning and to wash cars," he said. "From there I would go to a parts store for bicycles and automobiles, and I would have to open the store." Just as he was beginning to feel comfortable with his new job, "the owner of the store told me that he took a job in Germany with the German Luftwaffe as a lubrication engineer." George asked what was going to happen to the business and was told, "You're going to run it!"

George Weidinger quickly found out what his new role as store manager meant. Not long after the Nazis moved into Austria, the SS hierarchy confiscated a mansion and a new Buick from a Jewish family across the street from the auto repair shop. One day, the leading SS officer and his chauffer came to the shop with the Buick and ordered George to change the transmission oil, adding that he needed the car back by 5:00p.m. that afternoon. George jacked up the car and drained the oil, but then realized that the replacement oil was frozen solid. When the German officer came back at 5:00p.m. the car was not ready. He threatened to send George's parents to a concentration camp if he did not fix the car immediately. George carried the large can of oil over to the officer's house, put it on the stove, heated the oil, brought it back to the shop and put it in the car. He later recalled that the incident "certainly was very, very frightening to me."

The Weidinger family was eventually able to secure visas to emigrate to the United States. George, his mother, and his brother left Europe in October 1939, and his father followed in December of that year. George's father was a World War I veteran and a successful and prosperous businessman in Austria, working as the principal sales representative for an American paint company based in Cleveland. Nevertheless, when the Weidinger family arrived in America and settled in Cleveland they had little more than the shirts on their backs. The paint company president had advanced the Weidingers $3,000 to help with the emigration and moving expenses, but he required the family to reimburse him for the advance. Within a short time, each family member found a job. George's older brother was an engineer; he secured a well-paying job, and, with his income, the family was able to repay the advance within a year. When George's father arrived in Cleveland, he found a job as a stockroom clerk for a building supply company, which was a substantial downgrade from his position in Austria. George said that at age 53, his father was the happiest man in the world just to be in the United States. George found a job at a lamp factory where he met his future wife, to whom he was married for over 65 years.[2]

Unlike George Weidinger, Rudolph (Rudy) Pins knew from an early age that he was Jewish. Rudy was born in Höxter, Germany, in April 1920 and attended the local Catholic school. One of his earliest memories was of his teacher, Miss Döring, coming to visit him when he had the chickenpox. He recalled that he was the only Jewish boy in the town, which made no difference to any of his friends. When he was eligible, he took and passed an examination that allowed him to enter the highly selective gymnasium school. He enjoyed school and was an excellent student, and his life was pleasant. His family vacationed near the Dutch border with other family members, where Rudy would go on hikes, go swimming, and enjoy everything the outdoors had to offer.

He neither knew nor much cared about politics. He occasionally heard the name Hitler, and he saw parades and demonstrations, but he did not see how any of this could possibly affect him. By 1933, however, things began to change. Rudy heard that Germans were boycotting Jewish businesses, and, as he and his family listened to the radio, they could not avoid the hateful language spewed by Joseph Goebbels. But, even as the Nazification of Germany was beginning to unfold, Rudy said everything at his school was perfectly normal. Normal, that was, until the spring of 1934, when his teacher took him aside and told him that he would not be allowed to go on a weekend field trip, because he was Jewish. As he would later say, "That was a big hit for a 14-year-old boy."[3]

By the spring of 1934, Rudy was beginning to understand the perils of being a young Jewish boy in Germany. His parents had been concerned for some time that the situation for Jewish people was becoming more and more precarious. They started researching programs that would allow them to emigrate, or at least allow their son to go to the United States. They found that the United States government had agreed to allow some 1,000 unaccompanied German Jewish children under the age of 16 to emigrate to the States. The program was politically acceptable in the United States because taxpayer dollars were not involved, and, in addition, children under the age of 16 would not pose threats to the tight employment market during the Great Depression. Moreover, by setting the number at 1,000 Jewish children, the government gambled that American nativist and antisemitic sentiments would not threaten the program. The principal private sponsor, the German Jewish Children's Aid Program, worked with national American Jewish groups to raise money to cover the expenses of travel and to help settle the children with American families. They also found Jewish families willing to sponsor children in their homes. From Germany, families like the Pins could apply for visas for their children at United States consulates, and if accepted, the children were sent to the United States to live with sponsoring families.[4]

Rudy Pins's parents took him to the American Consulate in Stuttgart, where they applied for him to join the program and where he was given a physical examination. He was accepted and would later say that his "feelings were very mixed—on the one hand, that was a big adventure." But on the other hand, "there was a sadness to leave my parents [though we hoped it would be a temporary breakup]." And finally, he "had a fear of the future."

As the big day for his departure approached, Rudy's parents did all they could to help him prepare for his experience in America—what he should expect, how he should behave, and other advice. When the actual day for his departure arrived, his mother could not go with him to the train station. "My dad and I walked slowly," he said. "Silently we watched as [German soldiers] marched down Market Street—my last impression of Höxter." Rudy had no way of knowing that this would be the last time he would ever see his parents.

Like most Jewish parents who sent their children to America, Rudy's parents had no doubt that they would be reunited soon. They believed Hitler and the Nazis were a temporary aberration in Germany. Soon, they thought, the German people would vote Hitler out of office, and then the Pins family could be together again after this brief separation. They, and others like them, had no idea how wrong they were.

Rudy arrived in New York as part of a group of 12 to 15 children, aged 10 to 16. Representatives from the German Jewish Children's Aid Program met him and the other children where their ship docked. Some of the children remained in New York, but Rudy and others boarded a train and headed west. When the train arrived in Cleveland, he got off and met his new family, who were very nice. As an additional bonus, the family had a son who was Rudy's age, but there was an immediate communications issue. His new family thought they would have no trouble talking to Rudy, because they were fluent in Yiddish. While the roots of Yiddish were early High German, its mixture with Hebrew, Aramaic, Slavic, and some Romance languages made it incomprehensible to German-speaking Rudy Pins. He would later joke that his new family might as well have spoken to him in Chinese for all of the Yiddish he understood.

Rudy started school immediately and quickly learned to speak English. After about six months, however, he was moved to live with another family. He later learned that his first foster family devoted so much time to helping him acclimate to the United States, they neglected their biological son, so either the program or the foster family decided to relocate him. During the 1930s, Rudy communicated with this family in Germany on a regular basis. As the political situation in Germany continued to deteriorate, however, and as communications from his family were more infrequent, his concern for his family grew more acute. After December 7, 1941, all correspondence with his parents ended, and he did not hear from them again.[5]

Günther Stern was born in Hildesheim, Germany, in 1922. His early life was pleasant. Günther's father sold fabrics to clients in the nearby towns, and, gradually, as his business grew, the family became economically comfortable by the early 1930s. The Stern family was active in the local synagogue. They attended services every Sabbath and their social life was closely connected to the local Jewish community. Günther attended the Andreas *Realgymnasium* (later: *Scharnhorstgymnasium*); he was a good student and enjoyed and participated in many sports. In the evenings, when the family gathered for dessert, his father would ask how he was doing academically, then chide him for frequently fighting with a class bully, complaining that he was not paying tuition for "dishing out or receiving body blows or black eyes."

Günther's comfortable life changed forever on January 31, 1933, when Adolf Hitler came to power. "Most of our teachers and most of my fellow students acted as though the Messiah had stepped into our midst." Gradually at first, then with accelerating momentum, Günther and his family experienced the frightening new order. Günther's teachers fell in line with the new Nazi school curriculum. One day, his teacher handed out razor blades to class, then wrote page numbers on the blackboard. He then directed the students to cut out the corresponding pages, leaving enough space to paste in new pages. "All positive achievements by Jews, other 'inferior races', and 'political deviants' were excised and replaced by historical distortions."

Günther said, "My father [Julius Stern] was an optimist and was hopeful that this all [the rise of Hitler and the Nazis] would pass." As things grew worse for Jews in Germany, Julius's philosophy was that the family should maintain a low profile and "resemble invisible ink." He wanted them to stay hidden and not make waves, hoping that soon they could reveal themselves as the true individuals they were. Although Günther's father's optimism for a brighter future continued, Julius and his mother, Hedwig Stern, wanted to keep their options open. They learned about the American German Jewish Children's Aid's "1000 Children" program, and immediately thought of sending Günther to live with Hedwig's brother, Benno, who had emigrated to the United States and was living in St. Louis. The problem was that Benno had fallen on hard times during the Great Depression. He needed to provide an affidavit to show that he had enough money to support Günther—money he did not have. Benno was creative, though, and he arranged for his friends to deposit money in his bank account to show that he had sufficient funds. The bank gave him the affidavit he needed, then he returned the money to his friends.

In 1937, and with a visa in hand, 15-year-old Günther emigrated to the United States. His father had arranged for a tutor to teach him English, so he was comfortable with the language when he arrived in the States. He later recalled that his uncle and aunt "were warm and welcoming, which made my transition easy." He quickly integrated into his new surroundings, became active in his high school's programs, in part because his teachers and fellow students were supportive and helpful. By his senior year, he was on the school's swim team and editor of the school's newspaper.

Günther, who later changed his name to Guy, did everything he could to bring his family to the United States. A couple of times he came close, but to no avail. Like so many of his fellow Jewish refuge soldiers, he never saw his father, mother, and two siblings again. He later learned that Julius and Hedwig Stern with their children, Eleonore and Werner, were deported to Warsaw in April 1942 and probably perished in the Warsaw Ghetto or in Auschwitz.

With the passage of time—Guy was nearing age 100 at the time of this writing—he could look back nearly 85 years to his early life in Germany. Even with the grief he and his family suffered, he recalled that his childhood "was especially useful in understanding the psyche of the enemy [German] soldiers" when he was interrogating prisoners during the war. He found it was also "helpful [to have his] interest and knowledge in regard to soccer. That sometimes made it easier to connect with a German POW."[6]

Jewish children in other parts of Europe did not immediately witness or experience the same growing antisemitism as many of Günther's future colleagues. One Jewish boy, Arno Mayer, who was born and spent his early years in the Grand Duchy of Luxembourg, recalled that the Jewish community in Luxembourg was divided between native-born Jews and Jews who had migrated into the Duchy from Poland, Lithuania, and other Eastern European countries. Many native Luxembourg Jews believed they were far superior to the new arrivals, whom they viewed with disdain. Arno learned acceptance from his father, who would chastise anyone who made fun of immigrant Jews. The dominant religion in Luxembourg was Catholic, but Arno Mayer observed that Jews were treated well and allowed to worship in their synagogues without any restrictions.

Arno Mayer was born in 1926. Nestled between France, Belgium, and Germany, Arno noted that Luxembourg was one of the most vulnerable places in Europe. With its small population and small size—slightly less than 1,000 square miles—plus no natural barriers and no standing army, Luxembourg has often been defenseless against any enemy who chose to attack it. Because of its defenseless position, the nation's posture has always been to pursue peace by any means possible. Arno Mayer learned this at an early age. As a young child, he visited the World War I Verdun battlefield, France, on a field trip. The message, presented in the site's interpretation, was that war was so terrible, nations should do everything in their power to ensure that the world would not engage in war again. This message stuck with him through the rest of his life.

Arno said he was a poor student, but he was a good athlete who excelled at soccer and cycling. He thought he would spend at least the rest of his childhood in Luxembourg, until everything changed suddenly on May 10, 1940. On that day, the Nazis invaded Luxembourg, Belgium, and the Netherlands. Arno's father received a tip from the French Secret Service that the Germans were coming and moved his family to France at 1:00a.m., before the Germans arrived. At that "traumatic moment," Arno said, "all of a sudden brought to end my lack of seriousness about life. For me, until then, life had been a vacation. Vacation was over." He decided that he would not be a problem for his parents. He immediately confessed several sins—like taking candy from a candy store—and he swore to his parents that he would be a model child.

From France, the Mayer family tried, but were unable, to obtain visas to travel to the United States. After several months and numerous unsuccessful attempts to secure the necessary papers, they made their way to North Africa, where they finally received their visas. Arno Mayer's grandfather had a cousin who owned a clothing factory in Mobile, Alabama. The cousin was politically connected, and arranged for visas through his local congressman, Frank Boykin III. The Mayer family arrived safely in New York. Almost as soon as the family disembarked from the ship, Arno's father ordered the entire family to dress in their finest clothes, so they could travel to Washington, DC, to personally thank Congressman Boykin for helping them obtain their visas. Arno recalled that the congressman was polite but had other things on his mind beyond meeting this immigrant family.

The Mayer family settled in the Washington Heights section of Manhattan, New York, and Arno started attending George Washington High School with many other immigrant children. When he went with a neighbor girl to register for school, the registrar looked at his name—Arno—and said no one could have a name like that. He asked where he got his name. Arno said his parents had visited Florence, Italy, before he was born and loved the place so much, they decided to name him for the Arno River running through the town. The registrar thought the story was preposterous and asked him for his middle name. He did not have a middle name but decided on the spot that he wanted his middle name to be Joseph. From then on, his name was Arno Joseph Mayer.

Among his school mates, future Secretary of State Henry Kissinger was one year ahead of him. Arno knew Henry Kissinger and one day asked him why he did not attend the wonderful live concerts that were frequently performed at Lewisohn Stadium on the campus of the City College of New York. Concerts only cost five dollars. Kissinger said he preferred attending sports events. Future United States Federal Reserve Chairman Alan Greenspan also attended the same high school. The school was the perfect place for Arno. The teachers were supportive, and he began to excel academically. Nearly everyone from the neighborhood in the school were refugees, mostly from Germany, and people began to jokingly call Washington Heights the "Fourth Reich."[7]

Whereas Arno Mayer struggled as a student early in his life, one of his contemporaries, Gunther Dienstfertig, was the opposite. Gunther was born in Breslau, Germany, in 1926 and showed strong academic promise, which was fulfilled when he was accepted and enrolled in the exclusive *Von Zawatzki Schule* in Breslau. His father was a lawyer who also served as chairman of the board of directors of a bank and chairman of several large corporations. He also was influential in the overall Jewish community in Germany. Not only was the elder Dienstfertig respected in the Jewish and business community of Germany, local non-Jewish politicians held him in high esteem. Nevertheless, as the 1930s progressed, and as Hitler and the Nazis became more vocally and more aggressively antisemitic, Mr. Dienstfertig concluded that things could only get worse for Jews in Germany. His concerns became reality when he witnessed the two-day reign of terror for Jews, commonly referred to as *Kristallnacht.*[8]

Kristallnacht—which means the "night of broken glass"—was a major turning point in the treatment of Jews by Nazi Germany. On November 9–10, 1938, Nazi storm troopers, the Hitler Youth, and others destroyed Jewish businesses, houses, and synagogues throughout Germany and rounded up and sent over 30,000 German Jewish men to concentration camps. The excuse for these atrocities was the assassination of Ernst vom Rath, a German official in the Paris Embassy, by a 17-year-old Jewish Polish boy. Shortly after *Kristallnacht,* the Nazi German government passed dozens of laws and decrees that deprived Jews of their property and livelihoods. Many enterprises were transferred to "Aryans" for a fraction of their value. Jews were barred from almost all jobs and Jewish children could not attend school. German Jews could not own cars or ride on public transport and could no longer attend theaters, cinemas, or concerts.[9]

Shortly after *Kristallnacht,* the head of the local police force advised Mr. Dienstfertig to take his family to America. His connections in the community would not be enough to protect him and his family. Mr. Dienstfertig was able to obtain visas to take his family to the United States in December 1938. The family settled in Kansas City, Missouri, and shortly afterward, the family name was legally changed from Dienstfertig to Dean. The senior Mr. Dean obtained a teaching position at the University of Kansas. Gunther did well in school, and his teacher suggested that he might want to change his name to John, thus his name became John Gunther Dean. John's academic brilliance continued in the United States, and he was admitted to Harvard at age 16.[10]

Kristallnacht was even more painful for Werner Moritz than many of his future Fort Hunt colleagues. He was able to relocate from Germany to

England in his mid-teens because his mother was an English citizen. He had made the necessary arrangements to emigrate to the United States along with this family, but, when he returned to his family's home in Frankfurt, with assurances both from the British and German governments that he could return to England without any complications, he quickly and tragically found that the promises were worthless. He arrived in Germany on November 9, 1938, the beginning of *Kristallnacht*. He was arrested and confined to a prison camp. After a month, he was released, with no explanation as to why he was arrested or released. "I went back to Frankfurt to say goodbye to my family," he recalled. It was "a terrible scene. I mean, you can't imagine. And now they couldn't come out. I couldn't get them out." The uncertainty of leaving his family behind was painful, but his parents insisted that he needed to take advantage of his opportunity.

Werner returned to England and shortly thereafter was able to secure passage on a ship to Halifax, Nova Scotia. When he arrived, he had enough money to buy a train ticket to Buffalo, but when he arrived there, he had only the shirt on his back and all of 30 cents in his pocket. Eventually he was able to make his way to New York City. He had worked in the fur business for his uncle in England and was able to easily secure a job in the fur and leather industry. When he heard the news of the Japanese attacking Pearl Harbor, he volunteered for the army the next day. He recalled that the recruiters "were amazed, but that's what I wanted to do. I was motivated." For his close calls with—but averting—disaster, Werner Moritz acquired the nickname "Lucky Moritz."[11]

Norman Graber was not quite as lucky. He was born in 1916 in Jasło, Poland.[12] His family moved to Vienna when he was a child. His father owned a high-end clothing store, and like many Jewish children, Norman had Jewish and non-Jewish friends and lived a comfortable early life. Things changed when Hitler came to power, and Norman's life took a dramatic turn for the worse. Two months after *Anschluss,* he was arrested and sent to Dachau concentration camp. He was never given a reason for his arrest, and he was the only one in his family sent to the camp. He observed that homosexuals and Seventh-day Adventists were treated as poorly as Jews in the camps. For a period of some 30 days, inmates were forced to subsist on virtually no food and just barely enough water.

He was held and forced to do hard labor in Dachau and Buchenwald for a year, then miraculously was released and allowed to emigrate with his family to the United States. Exactly how and why Norman was released is an unsolved mystery. His father was a World War I veteran who continued to have business and social contacts in Vienna, but Norman never knew the reason for his release. Norman was allowed to go to England, where he stayed for eight months. Then in 1940, he emigrated to the United States. His family went to the Netherlands, then on to the United States. Norman had an easy time finding work in tailor shops in New York City. Then, in April 1941, he joined the army.[13]

Walter Schueman was born in Frankfurt, Germany, in 1913. He graduated from high school in Germany and went to work for a wool importing company for six or seven years. Then he recalled that "in 1934, after I listened to all this stuff on the radio, I decided to leave and I applied for permission to leave and in 1935. I got a visa to the United States and I came here." When he was asked for his reasons for leaving Germany, he said that "number one, is I thought a war was coming. Number two was they announced that Jewish people would be kicked out, so I decided to leave before I was kicked out. It's as simple as that." He added that when he left, the Nazis were not actively oppressing Jews, but the antisemitic rhetoric was growing more intense. He came to the United States by himself, and, within three years, his family was able to join him.

Even though the United States was in the grips of the Great Depression when Walter arrived in New York, he quickly found work for an automotive wholesale business. From there, he went to work with a company tied to the Chrysler Corporation, that intended to start exporting automobiles, but that idea fizzled out. Schueman was restless and looking for new challenges, which came his way when he landed a job representing an American company that bought manufactured goods from Brazil. He was the company's representative in Brazil, purchasing items that would be sold in department stores like Macy's. He was creative and found new products that would be successful in the United States stores.[14]

Many of the men stationed at PO Box 1142 talked about their childhoods in Germany and how, when the Nazis came to power, everything changed. For most, they could no longer attend the schools of their choice, or, in some cases, they could not attend school at all. Dieter Kober had a slightly different experience; he was allowed to remain in school longer than many of his future Fort Hunt colleagues. In his school, starting in 1934, the emphasis shifted from a focus on academics to more physical activity as the beginnings of the Hitler Youth movement took shape. Every day the children had to run around the track in rain, sun, or snow, wearing shorts and t-shirts. Gradually, the emphasis shifted to more military activities as well, such as learning to handle and throw fake hand grenades. As the Olympic games were nearing in Berlin in 1936, the German youth were encouraged to compete in the events that maximized their skills. For Dieter, his best event was swimming, and he had become quite a good swimmer. As the time for participation in the major swimming event came around, Dieter's coach and teacher took him aside and said: "We don't believe that this is right, but we have been told that you cannot participate in this event." He said he was really shocked, and from that moment, he said to himself, "I don't want to stay in this country [Germany] and be a second-class citizen."

At age 16, Dieter found it relatively easy to leave Germany. He had relatives in the United States, and they were able to help him obtain the necessary visa for immigration. Even at his young age, he was already in the German military system, and he had to be released from that obligation, which did not take much effort. On a sad note, his parents remained in Germany, but, at the time, that did not seem to be a major issue. When he arrived in New York, he was able to attend and graduate from high school. However, when he tried to attend the City College of New York, he discovered that, since he was not an American citizen, he could not enroll. He had neighbors from Germany living in Nebraska and was admitted into the University of Nebraska School of Music. The one extra requirement was that he needed to join the ROTC program.[15]

Dieter Kober met and became a lifelong friend of Paul Fairbrook, another young German Jewish man, while they were both serving at Fort Hunt. Paul Fairbrook, whose name was Paul Schöenbach in Germany, had a very sketchy memory of his early life in Germany. In fact, he was fascinated that his memory of his German childhood was such a blur. "I lived in Germany for 10 years and I don't remember much about it," Paul would later recall. Paul was born in Borgsdorf, Germany—a suburb of Berlin—in 1923. His father had established a bank and became a member of the Berlin Stock Exchange. With his prosperity, the elder Mr. Schöenbach purchased a large house in the country and a fancy car. The first day Mr. Schöenbach drove his new car through a poor neighborhood in Berlin, the locals threw eggs and tomatoes at it. He traded in that car for a more modest one the next day.

Paul's sense was that the family did not suffer much in the way of anti-semitism; except, he did remember that he was kicked out of an organization called *Tierschutz*, which was similar to the Boy Scouts, because he was Jewish. One vivid memory for Paul came in 1933, when he and his brother were not allowed to enroll in the local school. His father was livid and announced to the family that Germany "is not a country in which I want to live." Shortly afterward, Mr. Schöenbach packed up Paul, who was 10, and the rest of the family and relocated to Palestine. Paul's father was able to take some of his money with him, and he hoped he could continue his profession as a banker, but he quickly discovered that Palestine needed young farmers, not bankers.

Mr. Schöenbach invested his money in a small factory to make excavation scrapers to build roads. The factory initially showed promise, but after five years, it failed. Now, the Schöenbach family, who were near the top of the economic ladder in Germany, was broke. It was now 1938, and Mr. Schöenbach wanted to take his family to America, but he needed cash. The family left Palestine and relocated to the Netherlands, and Mr. Schöenbach started pulling together his assets so the family could go to the United States. He had a painting that he knew was quite valuable. He sent it to an auction house in London, and it sold for a great deal of money.

Other than the cash from the sale of the painting, the family had few other assets. Mr. Schöenbach did, however, have a valuable stamp collection that he thought could give him some leverage in convincing United States immigration officials that he could support his family in the United States. Paul accompanied his father when he met with the agent from the United States Immigration and Naturalization Service, and he watched his father turn on his skills of persuasion. The agent was concerned that the family would not have enough money if they were granted visas to emigrate and asked, "How are you going to support your family with four children?" Without missing a beat, Mr. Schöenbach told the agent that the family would be fine with his stamp collection. His father pulled out a first-day cover with four unused stamps of the Zeppelin *Hindenburg* disaster (May 6, 1937), along with a catalog that showed that these stamps were worth $1,000. With that, the Schöenbachs received their visas and emigrated to the United States. When the family arrived in New York, Mr. Schöenbach, decided to Americanize the family name from Schöenbach, which in German meant "fair brook," to Fairbrook.[16]

Paul Fairbrook could not remember much about his early childhood in Germany, but another former soldier from Fort Hunt, Fred Michel, simply did not say much about his early life. Fred was born to a Jewish family in Germany in 1921 and emigrated to New York in 1936. He believed that his early life was uneventful because his father was a veteran of World War I, which, he believed, meant his family was treated better than most of his Jewish neighbors. He attended public schools and was enrolled in a gymnasium for high school. However, as Michel's family began to realize the sinister designs of the Nazi regime, Michel's father was able to secure the necessary papers to move his family to the United States, in part because, as Fred understood it, the elder Michel was a German war veteran.

Fred Michel and his family arrived in New York and settled in Brooklyn. The day after they arrived, he and his brother "went to school at PS 26," where they were enrolled in "English-speaking classes in order to quickly learn English." He said he was "also encouraged to read the funnies or the comics [newspaper comic strips] because that showed us both the illustration and the language and made it a lot easier for us to learn English." He passed the rigorous exam required to attend Brooklyn Technical High School—one of the elite high schools in New York—and later received an engineering degree from the City College of New York.[17]

From the descriptions of Fred Michel, Arno Mayer, and other German Jewish emigres who arrived in New York City, it is clear that the New York City school system and its teachers went to great lengths to help these children assimilate into American society as quickly as possible. Arno Mayer said that one teacher, Mrs. Orock, took a special interest in him and encouraged him to reach his academic potential. He continued to correspond with her long after he left high school. Henry Kissinger was not stationed at Fort Hunt, but his story was similar to other German Jewish children who came to New York. His family was so poor, he worked in a shaving brush factory during the day to help support his family and attended school at night. He was extremely shy because he was never able to lose his thick German accent, but he excelled in school. One of his teachers said Kissinger "was the most serious and mature of the German refugee students." She went on to say that she thought the refugee "students were more serious than our own [American children]."[18]

In his oral history interview, Fred Michel often referred to a colleague and fellow scientist, whom he frequently collaborated with at Fort Hunt—George Mandel. In addition to their science training, they had similar backgrounds and their fathers were World War I veterans. Mandel was born in Berlin in 1924, and he said his early life was uneventful. He had a large network of friends—both Jewish and Christian—and he did not recall any incidents of discrimination or antisemitism in his early childhood. George was a good student, but he did not like school very much. He remembered that the German education system emphasized rote learning, and corporal punishment was how the school system dealt with recalcitrant students. While George did not like school, he later admitted that he received an outstanding education in Berlin because his family was well-off financially and could afford to send him to the best schools. The elder Mr. Mandel was a banker and well respected in the community. Further, George's father's status as a decorated World War I veteran added to his prestige.

When Hitler came to power, Jewish and non-Jewish friends of the family told George's father that he did not have "to worry about a thing in Nazi Germany." Because he was a pillar of the community and a decorated veteran, he should not "worry and just keep going [about his life as if nothing was different]." This was the message from friends in Germany. From the other side of the Atlantic Ocean, however, the Mandel family was hearing a completely different story. George's extended family, who had emigrated to the United States years earlier, started warning the Mandels that the news they were reading in the *New York Times* was distressing. Germany was becoming a dangerous place for Jewish people. They begged the Mandels to leave Germany and come to the United States as soon as possible.

In 1935, Mr. and Mrs. Mandel visited their relatives in the United States and decided that, even with the assurances that they would be safe in Germany, it would be wise to relocate to America as soon as possible. Because George did not experience the increasing antisemitism many of his future Jewish colleagues at Fort Hunt had faced, when George's parents broke the news that they would be moving, he was not happy. He would have to leave his friends and his comfortable life in Germany. He was also worried that he would have a difficult time acclimating to his new home in America, because the only language he knew was German.

The Mandel family was able to transfer much of its wealth to the United States, so when the Mandels arrived in the United States, they purchased a house in Scarsdale, New York—one of the wealthy suburbs of New York City. Mr. and Mrs. Mandel wanted their children to have the best education available in the area, and they understood that Scarsdale schools were outstanding. George enrolled in Scarsdale High School; he quickly learned English, and the school system bumped him up a grade because of the excellent education he had received in Germany. He had complained about the rote education system in Germany, but he realized that it prepared him well for the American educational system. "I had a nice relationship with the teachers and with the students," he recalled. "I thought school could really be fun, in total contrast to what my old opinion was about German education." When he graduated from high school in 1941, George Mandel went on to attend Yale University.[19]

Henry Kolm was born in Austria, near Vienna, in 1924. His father was a doctor, who had served as a physician in World War I, and following the war, he owned and operated a small pharmaceutical factory in Vienna. When Hitler annexed Austria, Dr. Kolm and his family remained in Vienna, but within a year, his father sold—or essentially gave away—his business and moved the family to Prague, Czechoslovakia. Kolm's father thought the family would be safe in Prague, but not long after they arrived in 1939, the Nazis invaded Czechoslovakia. Later, Henry Kolm recalled that "we saw Hitler march into Vienna in 1938." Later, he saw the Nazis march "down the main street in Prague." Through his medical practice, Dr. Kolm had connections, and later in 1939, he arranged for the family to be smuggled into Luxembourg. "We were driven up to the woods and walked up a hill and crawled under the barbed wire, waiting for the German patrols to go by," Henry recalled, "down the other side of a hill into what was Luxembourg." Eventually, the family made its way to Paris. Then, late in 1939, it was able to sail to the United States.

The Kolm family arrived in New York in December 1939, and not long afterward, Dr. Kolm secured a position as a professor of medicine at Temple University in Philadelphia. Henry Kolm was happy. He finished high school in 1941 and worked in a garage in the evenings, earning enough money to buy his first car. After high school, he worked for an engineering firm and then joined the army.[20]

Like Henry Kolm, Peter Weiss was born in Austria. His father was an officer in the Austro-Hungarian Army in World War I. The elder Weiss's job was to requisition automobiles for the army, which was challenging in that he confiscated the vehicles from the wealthiest and most socially connected citizens.

Peter did not experience antisemitism as a boy. He had Jewish and non-Jewish friends, and he and his family were prominent members of the community. His grandfather owned the "biggest men's clothing store in Vienna. He had dropped out of the equivalent of high school and started out going from door to door, buying up old clothes for this big store." Peter's grandfather "read the entire *Brockhaus Encyclopedia* which is the German version of the *Encyclopedia Britannica*, from beginning to end, all 23 volumes. So, he was pretty much a self-educated man." Several days during the week, Peter's grandfather would meet with his non-Jewish business associates for a late-morning glass of wine. He was highly regarded in Vienna.

On March 12, 1938, with *Anschluss*, everything changed for the Weiss family. Peter was 12, and he and his fellow Jewish students—about one-third of the class—were told to go the back of the classroom. From there they were loaded on a bus and taken to another school. All of the students in his new school were Jewish. At about the same time, he was riding his bicycle and three older boys stopped him. He was certain they were planning to beat him up, but they let him leave and go home. With being forced to leave his school and fearing that he was in for a beating, Peter knew his world had changed, but another incident made him realize that his life in Vienna would never be the same. "I was walking with my grandfather," Peter recalled, "and a friend of his came walking towards us. My grandfather waved, but the man not only did not wave back; he crossed to the other side of the street. My grandfather, who thought Vienna was a wonderful place to live, was absolutely shattered with *Anschluss*."

Peter's father was Slovakian, and he moved the family to Slovakia (which had become part of Czechoslovakia after World War I), thinking they would be safer. What seemed a good idea was not, when the Germans rolled into Czechoslovakia in March 1939. The Weiss family moved to France, where, again, they thought they would be safe. When Peter was in school in Paris, he gained a better understanding of antisemitism. A classmate called him a "dirty Jew." Peter was so incensed he picked the boy up and threw him out of the classroom window. Luckily the classroom was on the first floor!

The move to France was not safe either. When the Nazis crossed the supposedly impenetrable Maginot Line, Peter's father was able to secure visas for the family to move to the United States. Everything was going well, until the family reached Portugal, from which they intended to secure passage on a ship to the United States. All of the ships were full, and if the Weiss family was unable to secure passage within the one-month timeframe on their temporary visas in Portugal, they would be sent back to occupied France. Peter's mother visited every shipping company in Portugal each day, and finally, one ship had a cancelation, and the family was able to travel to the United States on a small Portuguese ship, *La Magalhães*.

When the family arrived in New York, Peter was enrolled in Straubenmuller Textile High School. He was a smart young man, but his parents said that the "one thing they had learned from what was happening in Europe was that the intellectuals were the first people to be sent to the camps. So, they wanted me to have a trade." He went on to say that he "became the first graduate of Textile High to be admitted to Harvard."[21]

Unlike most of his colleagues at Fort Hunt, Edgar Danciger was born in St. Petersburg, Russia, in 1918. His mother was Russian; his father was Latvian. A year after he was born, his mother was able to escape the Russian Revolution and take Edgar to Riga, Latvia, where he lived until he was 15, when he left home and went to sea. By the time Edgar was 18, he had already lived what most young men would have considered a full life, but he had not experienced enough adventures yet and joined the Latvian army. He remained a soldier, until war seemed inevitable. He went back to sea, then jumped ship in Boston. He made his way to England, and while there, made five trips to help British soldiers escape the siege at Dunkirk. Eventually, he was a gunner on commercial ships fighting off German aircraft. When he finally settled in the United States and joined the army in 1945, his life of adventure changed to a staid office setting at Fort Hunt.[22]

Like Fred Michel, George Mandel, Henry Kolm, and others, Ernest Salomon's father was a veteran of World War I, but unlike the others, Ernest's father did not think his service in the war would protect him and his family in Hitler's Germany. He sensed that, before long, Jews would become targets for discrimination under the Nazi regime, and he started thinking of moving his family out of Germany.

The Salomon family lived in Düsseldorf, Germany, where Ernest was born in 1923. Like most Jewish German children, the first 10 years of Ernest's life was uneventful. He attended school; he had friends, and he participated in numerous activities. He was not aware that his father was thinking of taking the family away from Düsseldorf, and when the family relocated in 1933, Ernest did not later recall what his reaction was to the move. Mr. Salomon was able to settle his family in Belgium—its new home—with relative ease. The father worked on several projects in Belgium when the family lived in Germany, and he was able to convert his experience there into full-time employment. For seven years, life in Belgium was good for the Salomon family. Everything changed, quickly and dramatically, when, in May 1940, the Nazis stormed into Belgium. Ernest's father and uncle were arrested as German Jews and sent off to an internment camp. Ernest, along with his mother and his aunt were able to cross the border into France, where they thought they would be safe. But the French, in collaboration with the Germans, interned German-born women, so his mother and aunt were sent to a camp near the Spanish border.

Seventeen-year-old Ernest was a very driven young man. He made his way to the camp where his mother and aunt were held, put on his Boy Scout uniform, and convinced the commandant that he could do odd jobs around the camp. In so doing, he was allowed to visit his mother and aunt. This was only the beginning of his adventures. He learned that his father and uncle were being held in a detention center in the south of France, so he jumped on several freight trains and walked to the facility. Ernest, still wearing his Boy Scout uniform, talked his way into a job at this camp as well, and, within several days, he was allowed to see his father. Ernest was not exactly sure of the sequence, but either while still in the camp or shortly afterward, his father was able to purchase visas for the entire family to emigrate to Cuba for $5,000. Ernest, his father, and his uncle left the detention camp. Again, the details were a bit murky in Ernest's memory, but he was fairly certain his father bribed the camp commander to secure their release. Ernest guessed this, because the commander made it clear he never wanted to see any Salomons again. Ernest, his father, and uncle then boarded a train to the women's camp.

Working through his political and diplomatic connections, Ernest's father somehow was able to secure freedom for Ernest's mother and aunt. Next, the family boarded a train to Spain and secured passage on an old freighter, along with 1,500 other refugees, to Cuba. Shortly after embarkation, the freighter was stopped and boarded by sailors from a Dutch submarine, but it was allowed to continue on its journey. When the ship arrived off the coast of Florida, the crew threatened to illegally offload the passengers if they did not pay more money to continue to Cuba. Ernest and his family paid the extra money and arrived in Havana in the summer of 1941.

Between purchasing visas and paying for passage on the freighter, the Salomon family had depleted its savings. In Havana, Ernest started selling fruit door to door. His mother baked German cookies, which Ernest added, along with cigars, to his offerings. He learned Spanish and bought time on a radio station to advertise a French language program he had started. Between Ernest's earnings and the odd jobs the rest of the family secured, they set their sights on saving enough money to emigrate to the United States. They stayed in Cuba for one-and-a-half years and were finally able to secure United States visas. In February 1943, they flew to Miami and eventually settled in Pittsburgh—their harrowing adventures finally over. By living in Germany, Belgium, and Cuba, Ernest became fluent in German, French, Flemish, and Spanish. He quickly picked up English in Pittsburgh.[23]

The day after Ernest and his parents arrived in Pittsburgh, the local newspaper did a feature article on the adventures the family had faced coming to the United States. The real story, though, was that the first thing Ernest did when he arrived was to go down to the draft board and sign up to "go fight the Nazis." At the end of the article, Ernest said: "We will never go back to Europe. We had enough of that. There is only one country in the whole world that gives you freedom, and that is the United States." With his considerable language skills, enthusiasm, and energy, Ernest became a perfect candidate for the United States Army intelligence programs.[24]

Now these young German Jewish men had settled in the United States. They all shared common experiences. They had evaded Nazi repression in Europe. They were fluent in German, and, in some cases, multiple languages. They generally understood the nuances of German language and culture. In short, they had developed skills desperately needed by the American military establishment for winning World War II. Above all, they had personal reasons to detest Hitler and the Nazis.

CHAPTER 3

How Do You Fit a Fort into a Post Office Box?

"When we got a contract for a building, they usually gave you six months to decide [to] build it, and another six to nine months for construction. This thing [the Fort Hunt POW structures were] built in six weeks."

HOWARD NOTTINGHAM, CONSTRUCTION SUPERVISOR

At 2:00p.m. on December 7, 1941, the Washington Redskins football team was just starting its rivalry game with the Philadelphia Eagles in front of 27,000 fans in Griffith Stadium. Led by its star and future Hall of Fame quarterback, Sammy Baugh, the Redskins were hoping to keep their playoff hopes alive. The Eagles, at 2-7-1, were having a dreadful year; the Redskins were respectable at 5-5. The Washington team came from behind and won 21-7. The fans cheered on their team, not knowing that about five minutes before kickoff, the Japanese had begun their attack on Pearl Harbor in Hawaii. Although team management was aware of the attack, they chose not to inform the fans until the game was over. Several years ago, a sportswriter appropriately described this game as "the Most Forgotten Game Ever Played."[1]

The following day, on December 8, Alan Lomax, with the Archive of American Folk Song (now the American Folklife Center archive in the Library of Congress), sent telegrams to fieldworkers in 10 cities across the United States, asking them to collect "man-on-the-street" reactions of ordinary Americans to the bombing of Pearl Harbor and the declaration of war by the United States. These fieldworkers had been recording local folk music around the country during the depression, and Lomax came up with this brilliant idea to use the recording devices to hear what Americans thought about the tragedy while it was still very fresh in their minds. The staff captured some 200 interviews, and a large majority of the respondents said they were not surprised by the attack, although they were surprised by how, when, and where it happened. Most also said they would be happy to go and fight our enemies wherever they were. One respondent in front of a theater in Washington said he wanted to get on an "aeroplane" and fly over to personally get even with the Japanese. Another man, interviewed on the street in Washington with horns blaring in the background (all names of interviewees were redacted), said he thought he would be drafted soon. "I'm eligible. I'm in the 1-A classification [meaning that his name was at the top of the list for the draft] and it hit me pretty bad. I was expecting something to happen, but this, even when it did come along, well it does surprise me. I didn't expect it so soon." When he was asked who he thought would win the war, he responded, "Well, I believe that the United States will eventually win out." Some women were fearful of what might happen to their husbands.[2]

Americans who were old enough to process events in 1941 could recall exactly where they were and what they were doing when the Japanese attacked Pearl Harbor. The Jewish boys who had recently emigrated from Germany and other occupied countries were now young men and the attack on Pearl Harbor had profound impacts on most of them. Arno Mayer remembered that he was playing tennis on the public courts in New York "when a guy came running, saying: 'Pearl Harbor has just been bombed.' We thought the guy was crazy." Once he digested the news, he said his reaction might "seem a very bizarre one because we celebrated. Why did we celebrate? Because to us, that was the signal that the U.S. was going to get into the war. In other words, we were totally Euro-centric in the way in which we reacted to that particular event."

Paul Fairbrook was working as a room clerk at the Park Central Hotel in New York when he heard the news of the attack on Pearl Harbor. He said he remembered that day "very well, because well, shortly afterwards I took out the daughter of Linton Wells, who was a famous news commentator at the time," on a date that evening. But when the hotel manager found out, Paul was fired on the spot for fraternizing with a hotel patron. Ten years later, Paul returned to the hotel. The same manager who had fired him—a Mr. Miller—was still the manager. Paul Fairbrook gave him his card and said: "This is what I'm doing these days. I want you to know I'm the guy you fired 10 years earlier." Fairbrook was then the dean of the Culinary Institute of American, considered by many to be the top culinary school in the country.

Guy Stern was a working in a St. Louis restaurant. As he was riding to work with a fellow waiter, they heard about the attack on Pearl Harbor on the radio. When they arrived at the restaurant, the owner told them: "You fellows can turn right around. Nobody will come to my restaurant tonight."[3]

Werner Moritz was working in a leather clothing manufacturing company in New York, and on December 7, he went to the factory to work on the bomber jackets his company was making at the time, and while he was walking on Second Avenue, "a young lady passed me, said to me, 'have you heard yet?' I said, 'Heard what?' She says, 'The Japanese bombarded [Pearl Harbor].'" On Monday morning he quit his job and enlisted in the army. For Rudy Pins, the where he was and the what he was doing on December 7 was far less important than the tragic fact that, from that moment on, he did not hear from his family again.[4]

Rudy, Paul, and Guy would soon find out that they were caught in a strange military conundrum at the beginning of the war. Paul Fairbrook was the first to encounter the problem shortly after he lost his hotel job. He went to the recruiting office and tried to enlist in the Marine Corps but was told he was ineligible. Rudy Pins described their situation: "With the outbreak of World War II, I was still a German citizen, and I was classified 4-C, which was the classification for criminals, asocial elements, and enemy aliens." The last two words—enemy aliens—was the key phrase for this classification. Rudy, Paul, and Guy were hardly enemies of the United States—quite the contrary—but, in international law, a person with this classification was simply the citizen or resident of a country that was in conflict or war with another country. Germany was at war with the United States. In time, Rudy Pins's and others' status would change, but for the time being, Rudy was "still in limbo at the time," and he "continued to go to school." However, "suddenly, in 1943, my classification was altered to 1-A. And within a week, I was in the army."[5]

Unbeknownst to Rudy and his future colleagues at Fort Hunt, the United States military was making plans of which they would become integral parts. Even before the United States entered World War II, the War Department started to substantially upgrade its intelligence-gathering operations. It borrowed heavily from the British, who had established MI9 in 1939, primarily to assist its military personnel, mostly airmen, in evading capture, and if captured, developing means by which they might escape from POW camps. MI9 also included a section for debriefing former British POWs, who had escaped from captivity or had evaded capture; another section trained military personnel to gather intelligence behind enemy lines. Later, in 1940, the British created MI9a, later changed to MI19, to interrogate high-level German POWs. Located in a series of "cages" located at various places throughout the United Kingdom, these facilities housed skilled interrogators whose purpose was to coax information from German airmen, soldiers, and sailors.

Rather than upgrading its intelligence-gathering operation from scratch, the American Office of Naval Intelligence sent a team to study the British system between June and December 1941. The group recommended that the War Department create a program to interrogate prisoners using "trained officers to conduct such interrogations in a central interrogation center." Further, the program should consist of a single facility with both army and navy prisoners, and since the report was written by naval personnel, "Naval prisoners of war [should be held] in the custody of the navy only so long as is necessary to effect their transfer to army custody." Thus, navy personnel would conduct the initial interrogations, then transfer the POWs to the facility/facilities managed by the army. And, finally, "the Secretary of War [should] be requested to provide suitable Interrogation Centers ... from appropriations now available to the War Department."[6]

The War Department, for the most part, followed the recommendation from the naval intelligence report. Its intelligence-gathering program would consist of two centers—one on the West Coast—somewhere in the vicinity of San Francisco or Los Angeles to cover the Pacific theater and one on the East Coast—preferably within about 100 miles of the Pentagon—to cover the Eastern Theater. These centers would generally follow the British model to include one section, referred to as MIS-Y (Military Intelligence Section-Y), which would focus on interrogating prisoners and eavesdropping on conversations in the facility. Another program, called MIRS—Military Intelligence Research Section—would translate and evaluate captured enemy documents. The staff at the East Coast center would produce a "Red Book," which was the order of battle for the German military operations, and a "Green Book"—the order of battle for the Japanese military. Another East Coast section, MIS-X, was the escape and evasion section. It would create documents and equipment to aid American airmen to avoid capture if their planes were downed in Europe. This office hid radios, money, maps, and other communication or escape tools in innocent looking baseballs, cribbage boards, or other items, that were included in packages or parcels that prisoners were allowed to receive under the Geneva Convention. MIS-Y also established an encrypted communication system to communicate with American prisoners.

Finding the West Coast interrogation center was relatively easy. The army settled on Byron Hot Springs Hotel, located in Eastern Contra Costa County, California, between the Bay Area and Stockton. The location was suitable; the facilities were ideal—the main structure was a four-story hotel—and the price was right. The owner, Mae Reed, offered to lease her property to the army for $250 a year. One of the officers involved in the search for a facility said that her "motives are patriotic," because she had lost her son in World War I. In its heyday, the healing waters, mud baths, and relaxing atmosphere had attracted such notables as Clark Gable, Mae West, and Charlie Chaplin, but now it would house Japanese POWs. Its official wartime name was Camp Tracy, and its code was PO Box 651.

The hotel rooms that would house Japanese prisoners were modified with dropped ceilings to hide the concealed listening devices. One army officer understood Japanese culture and found the hotel appealing because he thought the various baths, or what the Japanese called *onsens*, might prove a useful tool for "softening up" the POWs. In addition to the baths, Japanese chefs prepared their meals. Lieutenant Colonel Alex Corbin, who wrote the comprehensive history of Camp Tracy and who, at the time, was an officer in U.S. Army Intelligence, analyzed the interrogation methods at the camp. "My thoughts are that if you start off at [a severity of one], you can always ramp up," he said. "But if you start at 10, you can't expect to start getting nicer and expect to get information."[7]

For the most part, the Americans did what they could to keep the intelligence-gathering process as humane and friendly as possible. In addition to the amenities, the U.S. military went one step further to make the Japanese comfortable. The primary interrogators were Nisei Japanese-Americans (A Nisei is a person born in the United States whose parents were emigrants from Japan). The Nisei interrogators were not only fluent in Japanese; they understood the nuances of Japanese culture, and thus were ideal for the job. On occasion, Nisei also roomed with Japanese POWs, posing as prisoners, for the purpose of gaining their confidences. They did what they could to draw out important information that would be picked up by the monitoring system. The fact that these Japanese-Americans were willing to serve in this capacity was extraordinary, because many of their family members had been forced to leave their homes and businesses, and were being held in Japanese internment camps (officially called "relocation centers" by the U.S. government) during the war.

While Japanese POWs were generally comfortable with their Nisei interrogators, the American military was not entirely at ease with the arrangement. For nearly every interrogation, the Nisei interrogator was accompanied by an Anglo-American who had at least a basic understanding of the Japanese language. Louis Al Nipkow was one of the army officers who filled this role. Nipkow was born in Japan to a Swiss father and a British half-Japanese mother. He lived there for 17 years, but for the most part did not associate with very many Japanese children. He lived in an enclave made up mostly of European and American families. He said he understood Japanese fairly well but was neither adept nor comfortable speaking the language. Thus, in his case, having a Nisei interrogator do the bulk of the questioning was ideal. Nipkow said that Japanese POWs were held and interrogated at Camp Tracy for up to 10 days but no longer. When finished, they were transferred to POW prison camps, such as Angel Island in San Francisco Bay. For each interrogation, the commanding officer "would tell us what they wanted to know," Nipkow said. Then his job was to relay the questions "to the Nisei which was parlayed to the prisoner. ... It was pretty lax."[8]

That any Japanese soldiers and sailors surrendered to the Americans and were ripe for interrogation was surprising. Ancient Japanese cultural traditions—including *bushido*, the way of the warrior, formalized in the *Senjinkun* (the pocket-sized military code booklet issued to Imperial Japanese forces)—emphasized that soldiers and sailors should "never live to experience shame as a prisoner." Suicide was preferable to surrender. Members of the Japanese military did surrender, however, and those who did were generally willing to share what they knew with American interrogators. One sailor, who jumped off a sinking aircraft carrier during the Battle of Midway, was rescued at sea and shared his knowledge of the design, structure, armaments, and capabilities of Japanese naval vessels. Another sailor, rescued from a submarine near the Aleutians, described the characteristics of the new Japanese waveless torpedoes. A soldier revealed the location of the building in which aircraft engines were manufactured in the Mitsubishi airplane factory complex in Nagoya—which was successfully targeted by American bombers. Many soldiers, captured in the battle of Iwo Jima, warned that, if United States forces attacked the Japanese home islands, soldiers and civilians would fight to the death to protect their homeland.[9]

Camp Tracy was fully operational in December 1942, and it continued to function until September 1945, although starting in 1944, more and more Japanese prisoners were transferred to Fort Hunt for interrogations. After 2000, when the secret documents collected from Camp Tracy and Fort Hunt were declassified, staff from the Japanese public television station NHK traveled to Washington, DC to the National Archives, combed through the interrogation files, and identified the Japanese POWs at Camp Tracy. When the crew returned to Japan, they tracked down many of the POWs who were still alive and featured them in their film *Secret Interrogation Center Tracy: the Top Secrets Revealed by Japanese Prisoners of War*. Some shared the secrets they had shared with their American interrogators.[10]

Selection of the East Coast intelligence location was relatively easy as well. Swannanoa, an Italian Renaissance Revival villa built in 1912 by millionaire and philanthropist James H. Dooley on the border of Nelson and Augusta Counties, Virginia, and 125 miles from Washington, was one possibility. Marwood, a 1926 French Neoclassical mansion in Potomac, Maryland, built by Samuel Klump Martin III and inspired by Château de Malmaison (a country estate in France built for Napoleon Bonaparte), was another.[11] Marwood was in a general Washington, DC suburb. Both would have followed the British model of bringing prisoners for interrogation to secluded country estates. While these two estates would have presented some advantages, the most desirable location turned out to be Fort Hunt. Many of the facilities that would be needed for the center were already there, and it was a straight shot, only 12 miles on the Memorial Parkway, to the Pentagon.

Major General George V. Strong, the Director of Military Intelligence for the War Department, made the formal request to establish Fort Hunt as the interrogation center in a May 6, 1942, memorandum to General George C. Marshall, War Department Chief of Staff. Strong noted that Fort Hunt was the most desirable facility, located in the ideal location. There was a potential complication, however, in that it belonged "to the National Park Service of the Department of Interior ... used by a CCC camp." Nevertheless, "the Chief of Engineers [stated] that provision [could] be made at Fort Belvoir to accommodate the CCC unit, thereby releasing Fort Hunt for an Interrogation Center." The CCC camp was not actually an issue, most of the men had left the camp. The camp had officially closed in March 1942. With that issue out of the way, "the sum of $221,000 [would] be required to construct the desired facilities at Fort Hunt and to provide for the accommodation of the CCC activities at Fort Belvoir." Then, General Strong recommended "that the attached letter from the Secretary of War to the Secretary of Interior [should] be signed and dispatched."[12]

In the letter, the Secretary of War impressed upon his counterpart, the Secretary of the Interior, the urgency of moving quickly, and on May 15, 1942, the War Department obtained a special-use permit, allowing the army to establish a "Joint Interrogation Center" at Fort Hunt. The permit was granted for the duration of the war plus one year. The "old powder magazines and antiquated gun emplacements" were excluded, because the National Archives had a separate permit to store its nitrate film there.

While the Secretary of the Interior and the National Park Service understood the importance of cooperating with its fellow agency, the provisions of the permit made it abundantly clear that it did not give the army carte blanche to do whatever it wanted with the facility. First, the military needed "to preserve and protect all objects of a geological and historical nature ...

[as well as] wherever possible, [also protect] structures, roads, trees, shrubs and other natural terrain features." Second, the permittee needed to protect the area and buildings from fire and vandalism and provide equipment and personnel for fire suppression. Next, although the War Department would need to erect additional structures and facilities, "the exact location of such structures [needed] to be determined by the Superintendent, National Capital Parks, and the proper Army authorities." Finally, at the conclusion of the permitted period, "all buildings and other structures except those of a strictly military technical character erected by it on land covered by this permit shall be transferred to the Department of the Interior or shall be removed by the War Department and the site restored as nearly as possible to its condition at the time of the issuance of this permit, at the option of the Secretary of the Interior."[13]

The army was able to utilize the early military buildings—some dating back to the early 1900s—as well as the structures erected for the CCC program. In addition, by the end of May, the army had the necessary funds at its disposal for the construction program. The timing to erect adequate facilities to house, monitor, and interrogate prisoners was critical, because the navy anticipated that the first wave of German POWs would be arriving soon from a captured U-boat. The army brought in Howard Nottingham, one of its lead engineers, to manage the erection of the new POW complex. It would be located to the southwest of the older fort buildings and was referred to as "Enclosure A." It was designed to be self-contained, with space for up to three POWs per room, plus additional facilities for solitary confinement. Interrogation rooms, a kitchen, a guard room, the control officer's quarters, along with offices of the intelligence personnel and an area for the technical equipment, were the main features of this compound. Two cyclone fences, separated by a 15-foot grassy area, surrounded "Enclosure A." Guard towers were located at the four corners of these fences.

Nottingham had supervised multiple projects at Walter Reed Hospital, Andrews (Air) Field and other military installations in the Washington, DC area, and he was ordered to complete construction—from start to finish—in two months. He arranged for crews of federal employees to work three shifts, around the clock, as his construction team. When construction started in early June, there were no plans or specifications, just sketches and general guidelines. The work was completed by July 22, 1942, or in just six weeks, which seems extraordinary, but at the same time, the federal government was achieving amazing building feats, such as erecting the Pentagon—still one of the largest buildings in the world for interior floor space—in 16 months (from 1941 to

1943). Plans and specifications for the new Fort Hunt structures were prepared after construction. A week after completion, the buildings were furnished, telephones were operational, and listening devices were ready for installation in prisoner quarters and interrogation rooms. The new state-of-the-art recording equipment came a little later.[14]

With existing structures and new constructions, there were 87 buildings in the fort, with everything from enlisted men's and officers' barracks and mess halls, recreation buildings and a swimming pool, to maintenance and storage facilities. It had grown into a bustling small town, which was now called "PO Box 1142." By 1944, so many POWs were coming through the fort that another prisoner compound, "Enclosure B," was added closer to the main fort compound and just south of old Battery Mount Vernon. The design was different, with the structures erected in a cross design, but the facilities within were similar to the other prisoner compound.[15]

Perimeter fences and guard towers were included in the prisoner compound. Soldiers were brought in as guards/military police, but they did not receive any special training for their duties. Most were sent to the fort without any understanding of their new assignments as guards and were expected to learn their new responsibilities on the job. One such guard, Victor Hacker, had minimal experience with guard duty in his previous posting in Panama, with no special training as a military policeman before his assignment at Fort Hunt. Victor said he did not recall ever wearing a helmet and, rather than being armed with machine guns in the guard tower, he carried only his 45mm pistol and a shotgun loaded with buckshot. The guard towers were equipped with spotlights, but guards typically did not man the towers after 9:00p.m. They might stay a little longer if interrogations of prisoners went into the evenings.[16]

Fort Hunt and its sister facility, Camp Tracy, were classified as "Temporary Detention Centers," not POW camps. To most casual observers, the distinction might have seemed trivial, but in the realm of international law, the classification was important. The Geneva Convention of 1929 contained nearly 100 articles, detailing the humane treatment of POWs. They could not be held in war zones; they could not be used as human shields; they had to receive good food, clothing, and shelter; and camps were inspected by the Red Cross.

Regarding interrogation of prisoners, the Geneva Convention stated that "no physical or mental torture, nor any other form of coercion, may be inflicted on prisoners of war to secure from them information of any kind whatever. Prisoners of war who refuse to answer may not be threatened, insulted, or exposed to unpleasant or disadvantageous treatment of any kind." The War Department believed it was abiding by the definition of the Geneva Convention. It considered Fort Hunt and Camp Tracy temporary, and when U.S. intelligence personnel had completed their work, prisoners were transferred to regular POW camps.[17]

When PO Box 1142 was operational, and for the duration of the war, it was never intended as a place to hold large numbers of prisoners. Early on, survivors from German U-boats were the primary POWs. In some cases, such as *U-67*, sunk in July 1943, with three survivors, or *U-68*, sunk in April 1944, with one survivor, accommodating and interrogating these German sailors was manageable. But the 49 survivors of the 51-man crew of *U-162*, sunk in September 1942, had to be split into three different groups for interrogations.[18]

As the war progressed, more and more of the POWs were from German land forces. Whether or not these men came through PO Box 1142 depended on several factors. In the war zones, German-speaking American intelligence soldiers—in many cases former German Jewish refugees—were the first-level interrogators. Often, they were seeking information that could immediately benefit the Allies. What was a German division's next move? During the war, Germans often built factories underground, so another line of questioning might be where a certain factory was located. Probing a little deeper, the Americans might sense that a German may not only know where a factory is located but what was produced there and how. This POW might be identified as an ideal person for more in-depth interrogation. This German might well be transferred to a place called Pine Grove Furnace, Pennsylvania.

Pine Grove Furnace was located about 120 miles from Fort Hunt in a remote location about one-half hour north of Gettysburg. As its name implied, Pine Grove Furnace was historically an iron smelter, started in 1787 and operating until 1913. In 1933, the federal government established a CCC camp, for the primary purpose of restoring the environmental destruction caused by the nearly 150 years as an iron smelter. In its new role, between May 1943 and November 1945, some 7,000 German POWs were processed through the facility. Busloads of 20–50 Germans would come to the camp, where they were evaluated for further disposition. If it was clear that someone was a radical Nazi, he was usually segregated from the others, so he would not threaten or intimidate other prisoners. Once the initial assessment was completed, individuals were either sent to POW camps scattered around the United States or to PO Box 1142. Intelligence interrogators would screen prisoners, and if one appeared to have valuable information, he was either sent to Fort Hunt immediately, or placed in a queue for transfer later. Thus, Pine Grove Furnace became both a transfer point or a holding facility for Fort

Hunt. Toward the end of the war, Japanese prisoners were processed through Pine Grove Furnace as well.[19]

The German Jewish soldiers at Fort Hunt, Pine Grove Furnace, and in the war zones knew very little about serving in the armed forces and nothing about interrogating enemy soldiers or translating and interpreting captured documents. Their dedication to the cause went a long way toward their success, but they needed training. The War Department recognized the necessity for extensive training and established a facility for that purpose at Camp Ritchie, Maryland.

CHAPTER 4

Military Institute of Total Confusion

"Somebody changed [Military Intelligence Training Center] and made it Military Institute of Total Confusion – MITC. And that in many ways it was. It was the strangest collection of people, but I found a great number of them exceedingly pleasant."

WERNER ANGRESS

Camp Ritchie was a former Maryland National Guard facility, located in the Catoctin Mountains, close to the future site of Camp David and not far from Gettysburg National Military Park. The site combined the features of being remote but was also relatively near the Pentagon—just 75 miles away. The purpose was to train American soldiers in every phase of intelligence gathering. From its opening in June 1942 until it closed in June 1946, over 15,000 men cycled through Camp Ritchie, and of that number 2,200 were Jewish refugees, mostly from Germany and Austria, with a sprinkling from Czechoslovakia, Poland, and elsewhere. Seventy-five percent of the trainees were sent to North Africa or Europe; the remainder went to the Pacific theater or remained stateside. Most of the latter group were assigned to PO Box 1142.

Training varied as to what and where the assignment would be. Before their specialized training, members of each class were required to take an eight-week course that included interpreting aerial photographs, hand-to-hand combat, counterintelligence, military intelligence, communications, and other general courses. Beyond these basic courses, since most trainees would be sent to Europe or North Africa, the initial training included a heavy concentration on every conceivable aspect of the German military establishment. Most spent hours learning the intricacies of interrogating prisoners. Many were trained to translate and evaluate documents. No matter what subject matter they learned, the criteria common to all were that the men needed to be quick studies and creative. They worked hard, spending seven days on, one day off, and often many hours into the night.

Everyone, no matter his future assignment, was required to study, and in some cases, memorize parts of the "Order of Battle of the German Army,"—"Red Book," designated as such because it had a red cover. Unlike what the title implied—a detailed, chronological discussion of German military engagements— the "Order of Battle" instead listed every organization in the German military in detail, along with perceived strengths, weaknesses, and trends that might impact future operations. A similar "Green Book" was prepared and updated for the Pacific theater. Both were frequently updated, and most of the soldiers who prepared and constantly revised the Red Book were trained at Camp Ritchie, then transferred to MIRS at Fort Hunt, where they evaluated and translated the volumes of captured documents brought to the fort to facilitate the frequent updates.

Trainees complained about the time they were forced to spend studying and memorizing the Red Book, but when they later put their training into practice, they understood the value of the effort. "Most useful!" This was Guy Stern's reaction when asked the value of the Red Book in the field, 75 years after the conclusion of the war. He went on to say that "if you showed a prisoner that you knew more about his own outfit than he himself, he thought, 'Why should I hide anything?'"[1]

One of the most demanding courses of study was the interrogation section. At the beginning of the war, and before Camp Ritchie was fully functioning, the army's and the War Department's School for Interrogation of Prisoners of War functioned at Fort Bullis near San Antonio, Texas. The curriculum focused on the post-World War I German army, the German Military Order of Battle, German opinion and psychology, geography and map reading, and interrogation techniques. To further refine the training program, the department brought former army major Sanford Griffith to Fort Bullis to deliver a series of lectures, followed up with the preparation of confidential papers on interrogations. Griffith was an interrogation expert from World War I, and since that time he had refined his thinking about that special craft. His insights and straightforward presentations proved invaluable. He believed that interrogations were in the realms of both science and art. Most interrogations— probably 75 percent—"in the army falls into the category of science. There remains 25 percent which must be regarded as an art. The unusual prisoner will require the unusual interviewer and delicate handling." In many instances, the "art" part of the interrogation produced the most valuable results.[2]

Griffith compared Germany in World War I with World War II. Some comparisons were obvious. Tanks and aircraft were coming into their own in World

War I; now they were deadly tools in the German arsenal. Communications had been spotty; now, they were mostly instantaneous. Some were not so clear. The gulf between German officers and enlisted men was significant in World War I, and while the relationship between both had improved in World War II, the breech between Nazi Party members and the Wehrmacht (the unified military forces) was enormous. Finally, whereas leadership, strategy, direction, garnering resources, and much else were often fragmented in the first war, because Hitler was in absolute control of almost everything in World War II, many of these functions operated more efficiently.

Griffith proposed a framework for interrogations of Germans in World War II. First, the interrogator should do whatever was necessary to put himself in the prisoner's shoes. The goal here was to create a relaxed atmosphere. The next two objectives related directly to the Nazis. Nazis were not, nor should they be, considered supermen by the interrogators. Most came from the same backgrounds as American soldiers. They were farmers, businessmen, teachers, and factory workers before the war and likely would return to the same professions after the war. Also, it was perfectly natural to hate the Nazis for a variety of reasons but carrying that hatred into the interrogation room would create a hostile environment with no positive results.

The next group of Griffith's recommendations dealt with Germans as individuals. People like to talk about themselves; getting a prisoner to talk about himself can often provide valuable intelligence, but the interrogator needed to also recognize that his subject survived the battlefield's death and destruction and would likely have accompanying fears and anxieties. Assuring him that his captivity would not cause him physical harm would go a long way toward building trust. Probing religious beliefs could be beneficial as well. Most Germans were terrified of the Gestapo and in constant fear of saying or doing the wrong thing or having religious beliefs that were contradictory to what was acceptable in Nazi Germany. Confirming that their religious beliefs would not bring them harm could be useful.

The final recommendation fit within the realm of art, rather than science. An interrogator never wanted to reveal what information he was seeking from a POW. If the interrogator followed the steps above and gained the trust of the prisoner, the German might have then created a story—maybe part fact and part fiction—that he thought would please the interrogator. This might create a puzzle, but with prompting and patience, the prisoner may well fill in the missing pieces.

Griffith emphasized the importance of good listening techniques. Rather than cutting the POW off when he started to ramble, it was better to keep him talking, then edit out the superfluous material later. Similarly, it was advisable to let a prisoner complain. The interrogator should not "look for repentant Nazis," because the prisoner probably was not going to switch to being an anti-Nazi overnight. If simply allowed to talk, however, he could reveal some of the problems he perceived with the Nazi system. Along this line of questioning, Griffith offered insights in what he perceived as weaknesses in the Nazi system and how those might be exploited during interrogations. One was his observation that Nazis had huge egos. If the interrogator just let them spew their venom, maybe something useful would come out. There was also a myth that Nazis would rather die than be captured. Since, instead, they were prisoners, they preferred life to death, and that fact alone offered advantages for interrogators.[3]

Converting Griffith's theoretical observations into a training program that would prepare American military personnel to interrogate prisoners was the job of the trainers at Camp Ritchie. One of the first instructors in interrogation techniques at Camp Ritchie was Master Sergeant Paul Kubala. He came to the United States from Germany as a teenager in 1924, and, according to his daughter, he was fluent in five languages. He already was an enlisted man in the army at the beginning of the war, and with his German heritage and his language skills, he was an ideal candidate for the army's interrogation program. By July 1942, Kubala was promoted into the officer ranks as a lieutenant, and during much of the war years, he moved between tours of duty as an instructor at Camp Ritchie and as an interrogator at Fort Hunt. He also served in the European theater. Kubala interrogated more than 2,700 Germans during the course of the war, and by 1945, he had reached the rank of major.[4]

Thanks to George Frenkel, another early instructor at Camp Ritchie, we have a window into the interrogation training program. In many ways Frenkel was ideal for this role of instructor. He started his service at Fort Bullis, which introduced him to the interrogation program. Then he was transferred to Fort Hunt in August 1942, as one of the earliest soldiers assigned to PO Box 1142. While there, he worked in the monitoring program, listening to and transcribing interrogations and conversations around the fort. Although he had not personally conducted interrogations, he understood what was required for the training program from his training at Fort Bullis. He made sure that the beginning of the program was a living hell for each recruit, to see if he could handle the pressure that came with the interrogating of "hostile prisoners." For most, eventually, with more and more practice, they became more comfortable with their roles as interrogators.

Trainees learned their new skills by interrogating German American "prisoners" posing as German soldiers. These pretend POWs used every trick imaginable to intimidate and frustrate the trainees and thwart the interrogation process. Frenkel described how the interaction with a fake German soldier nearly drove one trainee interrogator out of the program. "In German," he said, "a cannon or a gun is a '*kanone*,' but they also have a funny word for a field kitchen, and that was '*Goulash kanone*.'" Literally translated it would mean a "beef-stew gun" or "beef-stew cannon," or, with a little imagination, it could have been beef-stew shot from a cannon! Most Germans, even natives who spoke German as their primary language at the time, would have been perplexed with the idiom for field kitchen, because it was a military term. "The make-believe prisoner managed to get this interrogator into the business of cannons, but he first already antagonized his [trainee] interrogator by refusing to give him his name and serial number. ... The interrogator got very mad at this make-believe prisoner and said ... 'I don't want to know what your name is.' So, a certain hostile atmosphere had already been established." Frenkel continued, saying the prisoner started to talk about "these *Goulash kanones*, which were of no military interest at all." Next, the prisoner created a scene in which "artillery pieces were standing on top of a hill, and the Goulash was flowing down the hill," which, of course was total nonsense.

There were two important lessons here. First, future interrogators needed to learn German military jargon, and second, they needed to learn "not to get rattled" no matter what was thrown at them. They also needed to control their underlying anger against the men who had taken over their homeland—if they were German refugees—and possibly were responsible for the horrific treatment meted out to their loved ones. Ultimately, some potential interrogators never could overcome the intimidation nor master the military jargon. They were part of the 40 percent who washed out at Camp Ritchie and transferred elsewhere. Those who survived became more and more comfortable with everything the German actors and Camp Ritchie staff threw at them and moved on to their intelligence assignments.[5]

The German American actor who intimidated the poor trainee was part of a much larger group of actors who portrayed German soldiers in numerous scenarios at Camp Ritchie. One soldier later reported that he was afraid he had made a wrong turn somewhere and had accidentally stumbled onto a secret Nazi cell in Maryland when he went to the camp. Another soldier, Dieter Kober, later recalled that when he arrived at Camp Ritchie, he had just endured a long train ride without food and was starving. He thought for a moment that he was hallucinating when he entered the mess hall and saw table after table of German soldiers eating there as well.[6]

Behind the entry gate, German soldiers—or what looked like German soldiers—were marching in perfect order. German military vehicles—tanks, half-track trucks, and other equipment, made from cardboard—were scattered throughout the camp. Even a German village, created as if it were a movie set, was on the property as well. And if all of this was not enough, rallies were held in the camp auditorium, but not just any rallies: a German American, who looked remarkably like Adolf Hitler, including a pasted-on mustache, railed on with the same bombastic rhetoric as the real *Führer*. His followers would enthusiastically approve, giving frequent *Sieg Heil* salutes. Every conceivable piece of captured German military equipment was scattered around the camp, and trainees were required to identify each piece and its use. Weapons, from large artillery pieces to small arms, were fired, so trainees could identify if what they heard in the war zone was enemy or friendly fire.[7]

The men who were trained at Camp Ritchie and were later stationed at Fort Hunt shared their memories of the former. Some thought the training was valuable; others thought it was a waste of time, and most had mixed memories—good and bad. Paul Fairbrook was an early trainee as a member of the seventh class, arriving there in April 1943. One of the first exercises, required of Fairbrook and other trainees, consisted of dropping them off in the middle of the night with a compass and azimuth. Using these navigation tools, his job was to return to the camp. "Of course, I was a German Jewish wise guy," Fairbrook recalled. "I knew that I didn't have to do that. I could just follow a street. And so, I found a street and I followed it. And I never got to where I was supposed to go, and I got punished for it." His performance on that exercise likely precluded any assignment to an operation in which he would parachute behind enemy lines to gather intelligence. Next, he went through the program interrogating German-speaking American soldiers posing as German prisoners. Eventually, the program at which he was the most adept was MIRS, with an assignment to Fort Hunt. Paul Fairbrook enjoyed his time at Camp Ritchie, especially the camaraderie with his fellow soldiers. Most were German Jewish refugees, like him, and for most, this was really the first time they were able to associate with men from the same ethnic background. He spent three or four months at Camp Ritchie, then was transferred to Fort Hunt.[8]

Walter Schueman, who was later stationed at Fort Hunt, offered the most detailed description of the training he and his colleagues received for the MIRS program at Camp Ritchie. He started his program there in the spring of 1943. "The student body consisted of two colonels, two majors, two captains, a flock of lieutenants, and two privates, him [the other private], and me. And the course lasted four weeks. It was a six-day cycle. It started on a Sunday and all the information had to be learned by heart, all the information, and every afternoon, there was a quiz, and every Friday, afternoon there was a four-hour quiz." At the end of the four-week course "there was an all-day quiz." Shueman was sure he had flunked the test, but instead he "passed it which was a big surprise to me because I was the only non-college graduate in the whole class." Before long, in July 1943, he was sent to PO Box 1142.[9]

When George Mandel arrived at Camp Ritchie in 1944, a German counter-offensive—the Battle of the Bulge—was underway. "The idea was that we would be sent to Germany or to Europe because we spoke German, [and were] able to know what captured German prisoners would be saying," He recalled. "We could communicate with them and we could ask questions ... as to where was the fortification? Where were the machine guns? Where was the large portion of the military establishment? And so forth." Mandel understood there was a need for German-speaking interrogators in Europe, but what he did not know at the time was that there were new dangers, particularly for native Germans like him. As part of the German offensive, German soldiers, who could speak perfect English, were dressed in American uniforms, with the purpose of infiltrating American forces. Since many of the German American soldiers retained their native accents, they faced the danger that they could be mistaken as German impersonators. Once the German spies wearing American uniforms were identified, they were summarily executed by firing squads.

Because of the German counter-offensive, George Mandel was certain that he would be sent to Europe, based on the interrogation training. Another possibility was that he might be assigned to a scientific research project, with his science-based education at Yale. "But to my great surprise, while a lot of my colleagues and friends did go to Germany," he said, "I was sent to a place near Washington, and it didn't have a name. They said, 'You'll know when you get there.' And this turned out to be [PO Box] 1142. ... I'd never been to Washington. So I thought this would be exciting. I thought that I'd probably never be able to see Washington again. And so I thought this would be sort of an interesting experience." He had no way of knowing that what seemed like a temporary stop in Washington, DC would end up his home for the next 60 years.[10]

The military recognized the potential predicament for German American soldiers and devised a test to determine if they were friend or foe. The questions were like, what is the Windy City? Who won the World Series last year? That test was perfect for most native-born Americans, but unfortunately, many German immigrants were recent arrivals to the United States who did not identify Chicago as the Windy City and did not know who won the World Series, or even what it was. Some of the German Americans were arrested and temporarily held, but most were quickly released. One, however, was not so fortunate. One night, he had to leave his tent to relieve himself. The guard asked him for the password for that night. He gave the correct password, but with his heavy German accent, the guard thought he was one of the German impersonators and shot and killed him.[11]

Arno Mayer thought the training he received at Camp Ritchie was, for the most part, a waste of time. Like Paul Fairbrook, soon after he arrived, he was dropped off in the woods in the middle of the night with only a compass and was directed to find his way back to camp. Unlike Fairbrook, he did what he was supposed to do and made it back none the worse for wear. While Mayer said the training was not useful, he made the best of his time there. He met two men—Leslie Willson and Peter Weiss—who were in the same class. They were assigned to Fort Hunt and remained friends after their service ended. Weiss was a student at St. Johns College in Annapolis, which used a unique "Great Books" curriculum. "I remember one Saturday, instead of going for hot dates," Mayer recalled, "we would sit there and discuss Machiavelli's *Prince*. Now, where else in the U.S. Army would you do that? That was my first contact with something classical in political literature." He was at Camp Ritchie when President Franklin D. Roosevelt died, and to him and most European Jews, his death was tragic. German POWs were being held at Camp Ritchie at the time, and their reaction was quite different and disturbing to Mayer. "There were whoops of joy at the death of FDR [from the German barracks]. … FDR, for us coming from Europe, was a god." Mayer's assessment of his time at Camp Ritchie was that he did not "remember any instruction in interrogation … [but] the whole thing was a hoot in my judgment. We learned nothing."[12]

Peter Weiss recalled how he was selected as a candidate for training at Camp Ritchie. "I was at Fort Sam Houston in San Antonio. One day I was called into the colonel's office, and the colonel said, I understand you speak German.' And, I said, 'Yes, Sir.' And he says, 'Say something in German.' And I gave him the first line of a poem that was by Goethe. He said, 'That's good enough. You're going to Camp Ritchie.'" He recalled meeting Arno Mayer, but he did not mention introducing Mayer and others to Great Books. His memory of the full curriculum at Camp Ritchie was a bit foggy, but he did remember how much he enjoyed the photo interpretation courses. He also took a course in military intelligence, but, when he left Camp Ritchie, he did not know where he was headed, which turned out to be Fort Hunt.[13]

Unlike most of his colleagues at Camp Ritchie, Leslie Willson was neither Jewish nor German, but he had shown an amazing aptitude for languages, especially German. Most of his fellow trainees at Camp Ritchie did not mention the physical requirements of their training. Willson not only mentioned the training; he was determined to master parts of it, even though it might have nothing to do with his future assignment. One task was to swing from a rope over a large trench. Willson had done this multiple times, but one time he "had a carbine around my shoulder. And it was too tight. ... And when I jumped, my fingers didn't reach one another, and I smashed into a low barricade, broke some teeth, and had to go the hospital." He essentially was on a soup diet for a week. He said he was not very strong, but he was determined to master rope climbing. "I'd go out after supper and practice climbing a rope. So I'd improve my rope climbing."

Willson said the training was very compartmentalized. "Some people were doing translation and reading texts about new ship propellers [in] use by the Germans. Other areas [focused on] language and area training." He said the training was supposed to last for nine months to a year, but his lasted for six months. When he completed his training at Camp Ritchie, "they put us on a bus and started driving. Didn't tell us where we were going, [but] we drove up to the Pentagon." Even "our officer didn't know where we were going." The officer asked for directions at the Pentagon, and the bus ended up at PO Box 1142. When the bus pulled up to the gate of Fort Hunt, one of the young men leaned out and asked where they were. The guard replied, "nowhere!"[14]

When a new soldier arrived at Camp Ritchie, one of the first things to greet him was the sign above the camp entrance that read "Military Intelligence Training Center." Most trainees thought the army was not very smart to give away a secret facility with a sign saying: *"Here is a secret facility!"* Soldiers had fun with another sign on the headquarters building with the initials "MITC," which stood for the name of the camp. The joke was that the initials really meant "Military Institute of Total Confusion"!

One soldier must have thought that was not a joke when he left the camp. As a teenager, Ernest Rosenthal emigrated first to the Netherlands, then to the United States, where he lived with relatives. When he was drafted in 1942, he was sent to Fort Hale in Colorado for training, which prepared him for the 10th Mountain Division. He was an excellent skier, so the assignment made perfect sense. As much as he enjoyed his assignment, he felt that he was much better suited for army intelligence, since he was German and spoke fluent German, among five languages. The military wisely accepted his offer and sent him to Camp Ritchie in 1945. He completed his training as a member of the 27th class in April 1945, but in a bizarre twist, he was sent to Kiska in the Aleutian Islands to interrogate Japanese prisoners. Of the five languages of which Ernest was fluent, Japanese was not one of them. To him, the joke that Camp Ritchie was the "Military Institute of Total Confusion" was reality.[15]

Ernest Rosenthal believed leaving his assignment with 10th Mountain Division and volunteering to service in military intelligence would be his greatest contribution for the American war effort. Many other German Jews who had been forced out of their homeland had different views. Men like Hans Spear had one goal and that was to join the American military, go to Europe, and kill Nazis. Instead, he was assigned to the medical corps. He had the highest regard for medics, because they risked their lives on a daily basis, but, as a medic, Spear could not achieve his goal of shooting Germans. When, however, the army learned that he was fluent in German, his next assignment was at Camp Ritchie. He would still not be able to fight on the front lines, but with this assignment, he understood that his potential contribution was invaluable. He said that "in six months the army could train a soldier to shoot a gun or throw a hand grenade, but in six months [or six years] no one could learn to speak German like a native." As an added benefit, by interrogating German POWs, he felt like he was making an important contribution that ultimately could help save American soldiers' lives.[16]

Learning how to interrogate prisoners was part classroom training, as described by George Frenkel above, and part intuition and common sense. With time, American soldiers developed their own techniques. Most realized that once a German started talking, they did not want to do anything that would shut off the oral spigot. Taking notes during the interview could be disruptive, so most just listened and jotted down their notes after the interrogation was over. Two universal principles were common to all German prisoner interrogations, whether on or near the battlefield or at interrogation facilities such as PO Box 1142. POWs were far more responsive if they were being interrogated by someone who was either at or near their same military rank. American interrogators wore uniforms without insignias of rank, then put on the proper identification markings for each prisoner. Sometimes a private became a major for the purposes of interrogating a German major. The other principle was that Germans were almost universally terrified of being turned over to the Russians for any reason. If a prisoner refused to answer questions or was evasive, the interrogator might say something like: *"You don't want to talk to me? How about I turn you* over *to the Russians? I'm sure they will be interested in something you have to offer."*

Two German Americans trained at Camp Ritchie created perhaps the most elaborate scenario for posing the Russian threat. Guy Stern and Fred Howard frequently worked in tandem, interrogating prisoners in Europe. Fred was the good cop; Guy was the bad cop. The interrogation of a reluctant German would go something like this: "I see that your division was involved in the Battle of Smolensk [in Russia], when you were on the Eastern Front," Howard asked a high-ranking German officer. Then he would probe to find out more about the German army. If the officer refused to answer, Howard would say, "Look, I gave you a chance to answer, but since you refused, I have no choice. I am required to take you over [to] the Commissar Krukov." Commissar Krukov was actually Guy Stern, who had a separate tent and was dressed in a Red Army uniform with dozens of medals covering his tunic. The crowning touch was the picture of Josef Stalin hanging in the tent, signed "to Commissar Krukov" from Stalin himself. In German, with a very thick Russian accent, Guy Stern would lay into the German with constant threats that if he did not tell him what he needed to know, "Commissar Krukov" would have no choice but to transfer him to a Soviet prison camp. Some Germans were wise to the deception, but the ruse frequently worked, and the German would tell Stern what he needed to know.[17]

Some of the Camp Ritchie soldiers were embedded with combat troops in the European theater as interpreters and interrogators. For these men, the training at Camp Ritchie, requiring them to find their way back to camp with a compass as well as combat training often came in handy. Such was the case with Werner Angress. Werner was a German Jewish refugee who left Germany in 1937, settled first in Amsterdam, then on to the United States in 1939. He trained at Camp Ritchie, then was sent to the European theater. He parachuted into Normandy on D-day with his company as a member of the 82nd Airborne Division. The plane came under attack and the pilot veered far off course, so when the men jumped, they were miles away from their designated landing zone. Angress's company tried to get its bearings, but after nine days, the men were captured by a German patrol. Werner had a potential problem: because he was Jewish and fluent in German, with an innocent slip he could have been in serious trouble. They were held for two weeks, and in that time, the Germans did not discover Angress's identity. In fact, he was actually on friendly terms with the German officer in command. In a twist of fate, after two weeks, American forces overran the Germans, and Werner was now the interrogator rather than a potential interrogee.

Werner and several of his German American colleagues were interrogating German POWs in early December, and it became clear that Hitler was planning a huge counter-offensive. They reported their findings up through the chain-of-command but were told there was nothing to worry about. Of course, there should have been a great deal to worry about; on December 16, 1944, the German army launched the Battle of the Bulge.

At the height of the battle, Werner circulated among the various companies of the 82nd Airborne, trying to find German prisoners who could give him information of what might happen next in the offensive operation. One evening, he found an Allied machine-gun battalion dug in on top of a hill. He quickly realized the danger, because the men were under constant attack from snipers. After midnight, SS Nazi zealots charged up the hill directly into the machine-gun fire, not hesitating as their colleagues were mowed down all around them. In the heat of the attack, Werner went from interrogator to warrior, firing at the enemy as rapidly as possible. Werner saw the American captain and his lead sergeant turn and run away from the battle. At that moment, a young Jewish American lieutenant in the foxhole yelled that he was in charge. Angress reported that the young officer held his men together and repulsed the attack.[18]

Most of the men who spent time at Camp Ritchie had something positive to say about their time there. For some, particularly the German Jews, the camp provided the first time in the United States that they had the chance to meet and associate with people who were like them. Most, even those who joked about the camp as the place of "total confusion," could find at least a nugget of training that had value. Everyone at the time complained about having to study and memorize sections of the Red Book, but the men who were assigned to the battle zones could quickly see how critical that volume was to their assignments. From a pure military perspective, Camp Ritchie was a success story. In a very short time, the War Department built an intelligence training program that had not previously existed. Many believed the training they received at Camp Ritchie was valuable for the next phase of their military service at PO Box 1142. Guy Stern summed up his experience at Camp Ritchie, and many agreed with him that "nothing at [Camp] Ritchie was superfluous."[19]

buildings—were damaged or destroyed. He also knew which German ships were damaged or sunk. The last series of questions was often the most important. In the case of Seaman Mycke and other German sailors, the Americans wanted to find out about any new designs, weapons, or anything else that improved the U-boats. They also wanted to find out about the crews and the officers to see whether morale was high or low, whether the captain was competent or incompetent, and how well everyone was doing their jobs. These questions were important, not necessarily for answers from an individual interrogee, but for their cumulative value. If most Germans said or suggested that morale was low, or that commanders were not well liked, it could indicate that the Allies were winning the psychological side of the war.

Seaman Mycke brightened when the interrogator asked about his commander. He said the entire crew loved Captain Rudolph Lemke, who was killed along with five other crewmen in the attack on the U-boat. Ultimately, the interrogator did not get much from Mycke, not because he was cagey, but rather because it appeared that he simply did not have much information to share. A year or two later, his interrogation would likely have been much shorter.[3]

While Mycke's interview was not directly useful to the Allied war effort, parts of his story provided valuable insights into the interwar period. Those years in Germany were economically brutal, but when the Nazis came to power, Mycke and many others had an opportunity for work—in his case, with the navy. Also, there is no reason to think that he was bluffing when he said that prisoners of war were treated very well. His statement that Germany only wanted peace and went to war to protect its borders appeared to be sincere as well. The Nazis went to great lengths to convince the rank-and-file German people that everything they were doing was just. Mycke, for one, seems to have believed what the Nazi propaganda machine pumped out to the German people.

Seaman Mycke was an early prisoner interrogated at Fort Hunt. In time, interrogators were able to ascertain, often within minutes, whether or not a prisoner might have anything useful to share. While a later interrogation of someone like Seaman Mycke might well have been much shorter, some prisoners had data that was so valuable, American interrogators might spend weeks or even months gathering whatever information they had to share, often approaching the questioning from different perspectives. One such German prisoner spent nearly nine months at PO Box 1142. He was neither a German soldier, a scientist, nor a member of the Nazi Party. Moreover, he came to the fort after the conclusion of World War II. But the knowledge he imparted might well have been the most useful any prisoner provided.

This prisoner's name was Gustav Hilger. He knew more about the inner workings of the Soviet Union than any other German and quite possibly of anyone living outside of Russia at the time. The summary of his interrogation, written in 1945 (declassified in 2006) said that Hilger was "a living encyclopedia on Russia and Russians." It went on to say that "Gustav Hilger has probably more right than any other German today to speak with authority on German-Russian affairs during the past 25 years." If that was not enough, the report quoted Josef Stalin, who said the "German heads of state and German Ambassadors to Moscow came and went, but Gustav Hilger remained."[4]

Hilger was born in Moscow to German parents. His father was a German businessman working in Russia. Gustav spent his childhood and early adulthood in Russia and served as chief of the economic desk in the German Embassy in Moscow from 1923 until he was relieved of his duties in 1941 when Germany attacked Russia. From his post in the embassy, he was convinced that the Soviet military was far better prepared for warfare than Hitler or German Foreign Minister Joachim von Ribbentrop believed. Although Hilger strenuously argued against Operation *Barbarossa*—the German invasion of Russia—his advice was ignored, the invasion went ahead, and ultimately, the decision was disastrous for Germany. Hilger was expelled from the Soviet Union. Although he was no longer in Moscow, through his numerous connections, Hilger kept up to date on affairs in Russia during the war. Then, because of his experience, his contacts, and his vast knowledge of Russia, the interrogators at Fort Hunt concluded that "his views on possible future trends of developments [in the Soviet Union] seem, therefore, to deserve close attention."[5]

Only recently—as secret documents have been declassified—have we come to appreciate the tremendous contributions Gustave Hilger made to the United States during the Cold War. In addition to the information gained from interrogations at Fort Hunt, Hilger wrote numerous papers on the Soviet Union, Stalin, and relations between Hitler and Stalin. He described the Russian distrust of international security organizations, and he analyzed the psychological background of the Russian people. On the latter topic, he said that "the discontent of the peoples of the Soviet Union with their present rulers is so deep-seated and so great that they would support every effort from abroad which would appear to them as fit to free them from the hateful regime." He added that military action alone would not achieve this end, but that "skillful psychological warfare [was] absolutely necessary and must be conducted simultaneously [with military action]." His recommendation was partially responsible for the CIA developing an anti-Soviet psychological operation.[6]

Hilger was granted permission to live in the United States with his wife, working for the State Department, then he returned to West Germany in the 1953 as Counselor to the Foreign Office. He continued advising the American and West German governments on Russian affairs until his death in 1965.

Not only did Hilger provide volumes and volumes of information to interrogators at Fort Hunt; he was, quite possibly, the most well-liked German there as well. John Gunther Dean, a young German Jewish soldier stationed at Fort Hunt, who later had a distinguished career as an American diplomat, recalled that "Gustav Hilger was the most knowledgeable man about a country we knew relatively little. He was a fine gentleman. People came from all over the U.S. government to talk with him. ... He held very balanced views. Hilger represented what I thought was good in the German people."[7]

Rudy Pins, another German Jewish soldier who interrogated Hilger, recalled that the German started teaching him Russian. Pins visited Hilger and his wife in Washington, DC, where they socialized, enjoying vodka and caviar. Hilger did not drive, so Pins would drive him around on weekends. On one occasion, Hilger asked if they could visit Fort Hunt. Nearly all of the buildings were gone, and the hut that served as Hilger's residence had been converted into a restroom.[8]

In the four years Fort Hunt functioned as PO Box 1142, some interrogations provided scant information—such as with Seaman Johan Mycke—or a wealth of data—as in the case of Gustav Hilger. Most fell somewhere in between. In many ways the process of gathering intelligence was akin to fitting pieces into a complicated puzzle. One American sailor, Angus Thuermer, shared how American interrogators started fitting the pieces of the puzzle together. Thuermer participated in the early interrogations of German sailors at Fort Hunt, and in many ways, he was an ideal man for the job. He was born in Illinois and showed a remarkable aptitude for languages—especially German—at an early age. He graduated from the University of Illinois, then went to Germany to further his studies in the German language. He worked for the Associated Press in Berlin and observed first-hand the rise of the Nazis in Germany. He witnessed fire-bombings of a synagogue and Jewish-owned businesses on *Kristallnacht*. He described the chilling experience of seeing Adolph Hitler eye-to-eye as the chancellor slowly passed him in his car. Further, Thuermer was in Germany when the United States entered World War II, and he, along with about 100 other Americans, was held prisoner for five months before the United States government arranged for his release. Shortly after his return, Thuermer joined the United States Navy, and because of his understanding of the German language and his knowledge of Nazi Germany, he eventually was sent to Fort Hunt to interrogate prisoners.

One German, Captain Klaus Heinrich Bargsten, was particularly memorable to Angus Thuermer. Bargsten was the captain of *U-521*, which was sunk by the American sub chaser *PC-565* about 100 miles east of Cape Hatteras, North Carolina, in June 1943. What made Bargsten's capture fascinating was the way in which he was apprehended. The periscope operator on his sub saw a ship in the distance. Bargsten went topside to have a better look, and a freak wave slammed the hatch cover shut and knocked him overboard. The American sub chaser fired on and sank the *U-521*. Bargsten was the only survivor.

Bargsten provided some useful information, such as a list of U-boats that either had sunk or were severely damaged in non-combat accidents. He reported that the Germans were becoming so desperate for U-boat commanders that, rather than putting candidates through the normal rigorous training program, they were quickly pressing watch officers—normally the third level of command—into captains. (Generally executive officers, those second in command, were in line to become captains.) Thuermer observed that most of the German sailors were not dedicated Nazis, nor were they enthusiastic about the German war effort.[9]

Angus described how he and his colleagues would use gathered information in later interrogations. From the Bargsten interview, the Americans might start asking questions like: "*What do you think about having a former watch officer as your commander?*" German sailors would wonder how their interrogators would know that. The interrogators learned other tricks as well. For example, they might know that the Germans had developed a certain type of torpedo detonator—say detonator #6. They would ask if the German sailor knew about detonator #7. The prisoner probably did not know anything about detonator #7, and maybe it had not even been developed yet. The purpose here was twofold: the question would make the German wonder how the Americans knew so much, or, if indeed there was now a detonator #7, the prisoner might reveal its characteristics.

The Germans maintained brothels and made them available to soldiers and sailors. Each sailor kept a card for each visit, listing the establishment's number and the name of sex worker he had visited. Angus Thuermer described how interrogators used these cards. They might ask a question like: "Is Maria still on the job down there?" The German might respond with, "Wait, what do you mean?" Thuermer continued, saying that the interrogator might go on and say something like, "[Maria] at bordello Number 4?" The Germans would think: "My gosh, those bums [the Americans] know everything. They know the names of the prostitutes." Anything that could catch a prisoner off-guard was more likely to provide something useful.[10]

One U-boat commander was, in many ways, the most memorable and most tragic of all German prisoners. Captain Werner Henke believed that German Aryans were superior to all other races. However, to him, Hitler and the Nazis did not fulfill his ideal of that superiority. In his view, without Hitler the Germans could win World War II, but with him, they would likely lose. Captain Henke had become a legend as a highly decorated German U-boat commander. He had sunk 28 ships, with a gross weight of nearly 180,000 tons. His luck ran out in April 1944, however, when his *U-515* was sunk and he and his surviving crew members were captured. He was sent to Fort Hunt in May, where he was interrogated for over a month. According to the interrogation reports, Henke was one of the most arrogant, sullen, and bitter captives they had encountered. His conceit carried over to his command; his men grudgingly admired his ability but disliked his overbearing strictness and unbounded conceit. In addition to his political views, in which he said the German government under the Nazis was "only temporarily bad," he provided some useful intelligence. He reported that recent German naval innovations, such as more sophisticated radar and a new automatic 37mm gun, would improve U-boat operations.

Henke was also paranoid. He believed that if he was turned over to the British—the bulk of the ships he sank were British—he would be hanged for war crimes. He was so fearful of his potential fate, on June 15, 1944, he essentially committed suicide by running to the perimeter fence of Fort Hunt, started scaling the wire, and was shot by one of the camp guards. He was the only German prisoner killed trying to escape.[11]

By the time Henke met his end, the program at Fort Hunt had changed. Many prisoners were now land-based soldiers, and the interrogators were different as well. Early on, interrogators came from a variety of backgrounds, but by the middle of 1944, more and more interrogators were young German Jewish men who had emigrated to the United States in the 1920s—1930s as boys (described in Chapter 2). They continued to put the pieces of the puzzle together. With their understanding of the nuances of German language and culture and their passion for defeating Hitler and the Nazis, they were critical to the success of the programs at PO Box 1142. Ironically, though, because, many were classified as "enemy aliens" at the beginning of the war, their service in the program at Fort Hunt was delayed.

One young man classified as an enemy alien was Rudy Pins. When the war broke out, he was living with his foster family and in his sophomore year at Case Western Reserve University in Cleveland. Pins was not concerned about the war or what it might mean for him. During the summer of 1943, however, things changed. The U.S. War Department and the Office of Strategic Services changed the classification from enemy alien to eligible for recruitment or the draft, recognizing that Germans Jews could offer important strategic advantages, especially in gathering intelligence. Also, in 1941, the German government had declared that Jews were no longer citizens, meaning they were no longer citizens of any country.

Rudy Pins was now eligible for the draft, and in July 1943, he was drafted. He would later say that most of his friends were already soldiers, and he "was happy to be one too." He was sent to Camp Abbott in central Oregon for basic training. He had never met the men at the camp before. "Most of them hadn't even finished elementary school," he later recalled, and "some had hardly any schooling" at all. Ethnically, they were American Indians, Hispanics, and "'hillbillies' from the Appalachian region of West Virginia, Kentucky, Georgia, and Alabama." Although not educated, Pins quickly saw that they were smart, "learned quickly and became good soldiers." Pins was also popular because he volunteered to write letters home for his fellow recruits.

Not long after Pins completed his basic training, the army recognized his fluency in German, as well as an apparent aptitude for interrogations, and sent him to PO Box 1142 in 1944. He was stationed there for over two years. Because of the length of his stay at Fort Hunt, his observations of the operation there were invaluable. He said that during the war, the average time German prisoners spent there averaged a week to ten days. Some stayed longer and others were in and out very quickly. After the war, some, especially former German generals, stayed longer.

Pins and his colleagues used the same general interrogation template developed shortly after the creation of PO Box 1142, but they became much more efficient. Pins said he could determine in ten minutes whether a prisoner would have any useful information or not. If not, they were quickly transferred to other POW camps. Before he would ask these questions, however, Pins would toss out a few ice-breaker questions, much like the ones asked of Seaman Mycke earlier, like where they were from, how was their family, and so forth.[12]

Most German prisoners who came through PO Box 1142 were transferred from the war zone directly or indirectly to Fort Hunt, in many cases after they were processed through Pine Grove Furnace in Pennsylvania. On occasion, a prisoner in a regular POW camp was identified for potentially providing useful information and sent to Fort Hunt. Some of the trainees from Camp Ritchie were assigned to POW camps to identify potential candidates for further interrogations. Camp Breckinridge in Kentucky housed a large contingent of anti-Nazi prisoners, who, in most cases, came from countries overrun by the Nazis and were forced into military service. Some, however, were Germans who hated Hitler and the Nazis. One such prisoner, Gustav Sader, was transferred from Camp Breckinridge to Fort Hunt in September 1943. Once his interrogators—Herbert R. Sensenig and Arthur N. Sharp—verified that he was indeed a disgruntled German soldier, the information he provided was deemed extremely valuable.[13]

Sader was jailed in 1935 for anti-Nazi activities and afterwards was engaged in anti-war efforts. Partly from his own observations, but also from reports from his brother, he shared what he knew about factories, products, morale, and other affairs in Essen, Germany. He said morale in Essen was very low. The Germans had imported Ukrainian workers to work in the factories. The Ukrainians worked hard and for low wages, which caused resentment among German workers. The young people of Essen defied the regimen the government prescribed for "Hitler Youth," roaming the streets, hiking in the mountains, engaging in petty theft, and even attacking local military patrols. They called themselves the pirates or the "Roving Dudes," and they generally made a mockery of what the Nazis believed was the future of the *Herrenrasse* or *Herrenvolk* (the master race).

As far as German military technology was concerned, Sader said the Germans had analyzed the metal alloy used in downed American aircraft and were using the same materials to build German airplanes. German artillery was bouncing off Allied tanks, so German engineers had developed a soft, hollow lead nose on artillery shells that would spread on impact and cling to a metal surface before bursting. He thought the shells contained thermite, which would ignite to generate extremely high temperatures. Sader noted that the Russians cleverly protected their tanks against thermite shells by covering them with a layer of concrete, to which the soft nose of the projectile would not adhere.

One of the major manufacturing companies in Essen was the Krupp manufacturing division that made crankshafts for U-boats. Sader reported that in October 1942, an Allied bomb had destroyed most of the Essen factory, killing over 200 employees. The facility was moved from Essen to Berndorf, south of Vienna, where, as far as Sader knew, it was still producing crankshafts for U-boats, along with plane parts and other materials.[14]

Gustav Sader was a valuable source of information because he had such a strong antipathy toward Hitler and the Nazis and was happy to reveal everything he knew. Some prisoners had valuable information but were less forthcoming with what they knew. Corporal Walter Koehnlechner fell into this category. Early on in his interrogation, he made his feelings of loyalty to Germany known, when he said that Hitler and the German army had overrun Poland because of "the wonderful genius of our *Führer* that he always pounces upon the enemy at the right moment." Nevertheless, Corporal Koehnlechner could provide important intelligence because he had been on the Eastern Front and had some familiarity with the Russian military. He also knew about the recently developed German Mark VI Tiger tank. To benefit the most from Corporal Koehnlechner's knowledge, a highly skilled interrogator in the person of Captain Paul Kubala was chosen to question the German.[15]

The interrogation took place in February 1943. The Americans were piecing together what they knew about the Tiger tank and were eager to learn as much as they could about this colossus, which was by far the largest tank in the German arsenal. At first, the German was cagey, pretending he did not know much about the Mark VI. But Captain Kubala could be crafty as well.

"Do you believe that this VI is just as strong as the Russian tank?" Kubala asked.

Koehnlechner responded, "yes, definitely. It is heavily armored. There is nothing that can beat the 88mm cannon."

"Great Scott, that is a heavy gun. Does it diminish the speed of the tank to some extent?" Koehnlechner told him the gun did not affect the tank's speed and Kubala added, "the 88 [must have] a terribly long barrel."

Koehnlechner said, "the barrel is at least four meters long."

Kubala was able to extract that the tank used iron rather than rubber tracks. Then he probed a bit deeper to try to find how much the Tiger weighed. The Americans had estimated that it weighed about 60 tons, which Kubala suggested to Koehnlechner (the Tiger actually weighed between 54–57 tons).

The German probably was not familiar with the overall weight and said, "all I can say is that they are far better than the others. Besides, their armor is much thicker."

"Would you say the armor plate was 4 or 5cm. thick?" Kubala asked.

"I have seen the shell of a 75mm. gun being hurled at one of those tanks and not succeeding in penetrating it. It merely pierced the armor plate."

"This ought to confirm my guess that the armor plate is at least 5 or 6cm thick."

"No, more than that. The minimum thickness ought to be 12cm."

When Captain Kubala believed he had extracted as much information about the Tiger tank as he could, he shifted gears and asked the German, "What is your opinion about the Russian war?"

"Here is my opinion. If the Americans or the British had been our opponents, the war in Russia would have been decided long ago.... When we can fight against the Americans or British, we consider it a stroke of good luck. In the worst case, fighting against them would not be half as bad as fighting against the Russians."

Although the United States and the United Kingdom were allies with the Soviet Union in World War II, their marriage was a marriage of necessity and far from a partnership of love or convenience. British Prime Minister Winston Churchill summed up the relationship when Germany invaded Russia on June 22, 1941. In a radio address to the British people that evening he noted that he had been an outspoken opponent of communism, and still was, but given the current circumstances, and given the fact that the British and Russian people were fighting a common enemy, he would support the Soviet war effort in any way possible. In private, Churchill's military leaders advised their boss that they believed the Germans would destroy the Soviet Army within six weeks. Churchill strenuously disagreed and reiterating that defeating the Nazis in any conceivable way was paramount, he said: "If Hitler invaded hell I would make at least a favourable reference to the devil in the House of Commons."[16]

Corporal Koehnlechner confirmed that Churchill was correct. Not only were the Soviet soldiers capable of fighting the Germans; in his view, they were superior in combat to their British and American allies. In their public utterances, British and American leaders expressed the full support of their Russian ally, but in private, they did not fully trust each other. Further, along with the lack of trust, the United States did not know very much about the Red Army. Few German prisoners from the Eastern Front became available for interrogations. Thus, Corporal Koehnlechner became a valuable asset.

The German said fighting with Russia was brutal and neither side treated POWs well. He said he had met SS comrades "who were taken prisoner and released after two days. They were mutilated in the most terrible manner." He admitted that Germans were not too kind to the Russian prisoners either. Although the German POW clearly hated the Russians, he grudgingly complimented Russian tank technology. He said the T-34 tank's steel tracks were wider and more maneuverable in mud than German tanks; plus, the Russian tank's cannon could be elevated to a high enough angle to fire on oncoming aircraft. The Russian treatment of prisoners was well known. Americans knew some of the characteristics of Russian tanks, which was confirmed by Koehnlechner, but his personal observation of their capabilities was very useful. This information and the report that Russians were covering their tanks with concrete—provided by POW Sader—were pieces that helped the Americans understand more about their current allies and future adversaries.[17]

In the years PO Box 1142 was in business, 3,451 prisoners passed through the system. Some stayed for months, others for days. A large majority of prisoners were Germans, but Austrians, Italians, and Hungarians also passed through Fort Hunt. Toward the end of the war, Japanese prisoners were transferred there as well. Most prisoners were transported to Fort Hunt at night, in buses, vans, or cars with blacked-out windows.

The best insights into the political leanings of the Germans are snapshots, compiled from the anecdotal perceptions of the soldiers who conducted interrogations during the years 1944–45. Overall, they believed that 51.2 percent of all prisoners were anti-Nazi. The rest were either pro-Nazi or their political inclinations could not be determined. A further breakdown showed that 64.5 percent of officers were pro-Nazi and 35.5 percent anti-Nazi. Enlisted men were 55.1 percent anti-Nazi and 44.9 percent pro-Nazi.

PO Box 1142 interrogators also observed German morale, or more precisely whether German prisoners thought their side would win the war soon after, then two months after, and finally three months after the Allied invasion of Normandy on D-day in June 1944. They based their observations on a survey they gave to German prisoners. In June 1944, 55 of 112 Germans were convinced their side was going to win the war. In August, only 27 of 148 thought they would come out on top. Then, in September 1944, just 5 of 67 Germans thought they would win the war. Granted, the sample size was tiny and the controls that would make the survey more scientific were not in place, but there was a tangible sense—at least at Fort Hunt—that the Germans were beginning to sense that they were not invincible.[18]

Looking at the interrogation transcripts and the recollections of the American interrogators, there were three general phases of interviews at Fort Hunt. The first group who came through the fort—like Seaman Mycke or Corporal Koehnlechner—were generally more guarded in their answers. Some offered useful information without a great deal of prompting; others had to be prodded for information, and still others clammed up and provided nothing. The next group, captured toward the end of the war—such as the ones in the survey above—were often more forthcoming with information. This group wanted the war to end, and when it was over, they wanted to be on the side of the United States. The final group came through PO Box 1142 after the war. Many were scientific, political, or military leaders who could see that the postwar world would be divided between two dominant spheres—the United States and the Soviet Union. Either the United States government was anxious to recruit them, or the Germans were willing to take whatever steps were necessary to not only align with the United States but also to remain there and contribute to the American Cold War effort. Gustav Hilger was part of this group. For this latter group, some, for various reasons, were ambivalent as to where they wanted to be when the war ended. Perhaps their families were in precarious locations—such as in areas controlled by the Soviet Union—or maybe they were not sure whether they favored the Russian or American side as the Cold War was unfolding. For this group, if they had valuable expertise, such as understanding the physics of rockets, the Americans tried to convince them to stay in the United States.[19]

When German Corporal Walter Koehnlechner said in his interrogation that the German soldiers feared fighting the Russians far more than fighting the Americans or British, was this only his impression or was this substantiated by other German POWs? Or, when Gustav Sader said the overall morale among Germans in Essen, Germany, was very low and that the German youth in that town were running amok, was he describing things as they really were, or was he expressing the views of a disgruntled German soldier? With practice, American interrogators became skilled at ferreting out the answers to these questions.

Also with time, many interrogators developed specialties, which proved useful for interrogating prisoners who appeared to have information to share in those areas. For example, Rudy Pins's expertise ranged from knowledge of German history to the Nazi Party and its military establishment. When he interrogated prisoners, he would probe deeply into the political situation in Germany. Was the populace growing restless with Nazi rule? Was there a movement to overthrow Hitler and his henchmen? Was there a shortage of food or other basic necessities? On the military side, he would try to find out about commanders, troop movements, and armaments. Was this or that general competent? Was the army forced to use foreign conscripts to fill the ranks? How many, and where were they stationed? Then, did the Third Reich have any new weapons? If there was a new tank, how large were the guns? What kind of mileage did it get? And how many were being produced?[20] Often Rudy or his colleagues would gain general information. Then, if they uncovered something that justified more specific inquiry, they would turn the prisoner over to someone with the expertise in that area.

As an example of how this sharing of expertise with prisoners worked, late in the war, Rudy recalled that he interviewed several German jet pilots. He asked them how long they had been flying jets, which units they were in, where their airfields were located, how much jet fuel was required per flight, and other general questions. But, for the design, engineering, flight characteristics, speed, armaments, and other technical questions, Pins recommended turning these prisoners over to scientists. One of the scientists might well have been George Mandel, another German Jew.

Mandel's special expertise was chemistry, but, in time, he became comfortable asking questions about more technical issues, such as German jets and jet engines. In short order he became one of the experts on jets at Fort Hunt. Once he learned about the technical capabilities, flight characteristics, speed, and everything else about German jets, he came to the chilling conclusion that had the Nazis developed these machines at the peak of their manufacturing capabilities, the war could well have ended very differently. These airplanes were far superior to anything the Allies had in the air.

George Mandel had entered Yale University as a chemistry major in 1941 at age 16. When the war started, he was too young to join or be drafted, and later, he was deferred because the military was anxious to have as many science majors as possible finish their degrees so that they could contribute their expertise to the war effort. He graduated from Yale in 1944, just before he turned 20. Shortly thereafter, in August, he was inducted into the U.S. Army. Most of his friends from Yale who joined the army or were drafted were sent to Oak Ridge, Tennessee, to work for a company called Kellogg. Mandel knew about Kellogg's Cornflakes but assumed what his friends were doing was something different. He later said, that, yes indeed, "they were not making cornflakes," but instead were working on the atomic bomb.

The U.S. Army recognized that George Mandel not only had tremendous value as a scientist; he had the added bonus of being raised in Germany. He was first sent to a three-month refresher course in German language and culture at Ohio State University, then to Camp Ritchie in Maryland. After his training at Camp Ritchie concluded, George Mandel went to PO Box 1142. He would later recall that only a few of the Germans he interrogated were chemists. In his case, that was not a critical issue. He started interrogating other scientists late in the war, and he quickly understood that they were anxious to share whatever they knew, even going so far as to act as tutors to explain in as much detail as necessary what they knew. They could see that the war would end soon, and most were terrified of being sent to the Soviet Union, so it was in their best interests to share what they knew with Mandel and his colleagues.

One German scientist described his responsibility of enriching uranium. Mandel would later say that he could not understand why anyone would bother to enrich uranium, but as he probed deeper, he learned that the Germans had been working on developing a nuclear bomb. This was critical information that needed to be passed along to the Pentagon—immediately! He had no way of knowing that the Germans were not close to developing a nuclear weapon, but the simple fact that they were developing the critical ingredient for a nuclear bomb was important information.

While interrogating another scientist, Mandel learned about proximity fuses. The Allies had developed proximity fuses—which could detonate an explosive shell when it was close to or in the proximity of a target for maximum effect—but the Pentagon wanted to better understand the German uses of the devices. Mandel discovered that the German development of these devices was further advanced than those in the United States.

Proximity fuses were formidable, but, in addition to jets and jet engines, what truly frightened Mandel and others was the German rocket program. The V-1 and V-2 rockets played havoc in England, starting in 1944.[21] An estimated 10,000 rockets were fired on England, with over 2,000 reaching London. Over 6,000 people were killed, and an additional 17,000 were injured. Allied bombers successfully destroyed the German rocket-launching facilities at Peenemünde, but what was even more important was the location of the plans and documents that detailed the rocket design, guidance systems, fuel, armament, and other technical data. Americans and the British were desperate to learn as much as possible about rockets, as quickly as possible, because they could see potentially devastating results if the Russians had a head start on the technology. George Mandel learned a great deal about the rockets from his interrogees, but not where the critical design and development documents were located.[22]

It was up to another interrogator, whose name we do not know, to find where the rocket plans and the formula for the rocket fuel were located. A German scientist revealed that the documents were in a salt cave, and an elderly salt miner was the only person who knew the location. The miner led them to the mine, buried deep underground. U.S. engineer battalions dug out the mine and found the plans encased in armor plating. The Russians were in hot pursuit of the plans as well and might well have found them first.

Henry Kolm reported the coup of locating the hiding place for the V-1 and V-2 plans; he also described several of the discoveries resulting from the interrogations at Fort Hunt. Before he arrived at PO Box 1142, Henry Kolm graduated from Simon Gratz High School in Philadelphia in 1941, and shortly thereafter, he enlisted in the army. He thought he would soon be drafted and wanted to try to get a jump on his first choice of joining the Air Corps. He went to basic training in Georgia, a language program at Rollins College in Florida, and several additional assignments, until a general recognized his aptitude for language—especially German—and arranged for his transfer to Camp Ritchie. He was hoping he would be selected to parachute into a clandestine assignment in Europe, but instead was sent to PO Box 1142.

He recalled that during his time at Fort Hunt, the Pentagon posed specific problems and asked the interrogators to use their skills to find solutions. For example, Allied bombing missions successfully destroyed railroad stations and railroad yards, but overhead surveillance showed that the day following a successful bombing run, German trains appeared to operate as if nothing had happened. Why was this? From their interrogations, Kolm and his colleagues learned that the Germans were no longer using the stations or yards to load and unload equipment. Instead, they were making the transfers where roads crossed the tracks. The advantage for the Germans was that there were numerous crossings that they could vary from night to night. But once the Allies started focusing on these sites, they began to have more success in their bombing runs.

Another problem for the Allies was the failure to destroy U-boats when they were in harbor. The Germans generally housed the U-boats in enclosed pens in harbors, not visible from the air. Overhead surveillance located the hiding place for the submarines housed in Hamburg. Bombers obliterated what they thought was the concrete bunker covering the pen, along with the submarines housed there. But, like the trains, submarines were coming and going as if nothing had happened. Interrogators learned that the Germans had cleverly built a wooden platform that looked like the concrete bunker. The real submarine pen was several hundred feet inside of that wooden platform. On the next bombing run, the Allies aimed for the real concrete bunker, housing the U-boats, and had far more success.

Kolm learned that the Germans had a large ball-bearing plant in Schweinfurt. He passed this along to the Pentagon and it was destroyed on a subsequent bombing run. Combining his interrogations with research, he was able to pinpoint where the power produced by the dams on the Rhine and Ruhr Rivers went. With this information, he was able to direct bombing not only of the dams but of the substations that delivered the power. Toward the end of his time at Fort Hunt, Kolm became an expert on Russian T-34 tanks, which was useful for the Cold War. He realized that because of their design—low profile and wide-track base—plus their ease of repair and the low production cost, they could potentially cause problems for the Americans later.[23]

Kolm's directive to learn as much as he could about Russian tanks expanded on the questions interrogators had been asking since the establishment of PO Box 1142. American interrogators continued to focus on finding chinks in the Nazi war machine to bring a quick end to the war but learning about Russia became more and more important. George Salomon, who arrived at PO Box 1142 shortly after D-day, reported that he had one job and one job only, which was to interrogate German prisoners for the purpose of finding out as much as he could about Russia and Russians. Salomon joined the army in 1944, and because of his mastery of several languages (German, French, Flemish, and Spanish), he was immediately sent to Camp Ritchie. The commanding officer tried to persuade George to enroll in Officer Candidate School, but when he found out that he would need to make a commitment for an additional six months, he opted to remain an enlisted man. By the time he arrived at Camp Ritchie, the training had changed. Now, most of the men were officers, and they were being trained to go to Europe. Salomon said that of the trainees in camp, he was the only enlisted man and only one of two not sent to Europe. He was sent to PO Box 1142. When he arrived there, his commanding officer told him to "forget everything they taught you about interrogations (at Camp Ritchie)," because the subjects he would be dealing with at Fort Hunt were smart, high-level people.

The smart, high-level people coming through Fort Hunt, as the war was drawing to a close, led to a shift in interrogation techniques. Multiple interviews were more common. Salomon reported interrogating German POWs over several days, and the procedure would look like this: he would conduct the interview, then listen to the recording and read the transcript, then hone his approach, then interview the German again, and, in some cases, again and again. In addition to Salomon's charge to focus on gathering information about the Soviet Union, his specialty was metallurgy, particularly copper and zinc refineries. Based on the interrogations, he drew maps showing the locations of refineries. Then he provided data on production, factory equipment, staffing, and any other pertinent information. Once he and his commander concluded that he had gained as much as possible from an interrogee, he would often pass him along to another interrogator with a different specialty.[24]

Whereas George Salomon was assigned to interrogate POWs to learn about a specific topic, other soldiers at Fort Hunt were assigned to devote their energies to interrogating specific people. Such was the case with Fred Michel. Michel graduated from City College of New York in 1944, with a degree in engineering, and shortly after graduation, he was drafted into the army and sent to Camp Ritchie for training. When he arrived at Fort Hunt, his first interrogee was Dr. Carl Hellmuth Hertz. Hertz was captured by United States forces in North Africa in 1943, and because of a bureaucratic fluke—he should have been sent immediately to Fort Hunt—he was sent to a POW camp in Oklahoma, where he languished for nearly two years. Eventually, he came to the attention of army intelligence and was transferred to Fort Hunt late in the war. Hertz was one of the most important and accomplished physicists in Nazi Germany, but he was a member of a family that was even more distinguished. His father, Gustav Ludwig Hertz, was a Nobel Prize winner, along with James Franck, for physics. His uncle, Heinrich Rudolf Hertz, conclusively proved the existence of electromagnetic waves and is memorialized in the terms kilohertz and megahertz.

Hertz made it clear from the outset that he would provide any information asked of him. For this, he received special privileges, such as relative free range of the fort and the opportunity to sail on the Potomac. Most of what he had to offer was stale, since he had been out of touch with the most current German research while incarcerated, but his network of fellow physicists in Germany and Europe was enormous. He knew their areas of expertise, and which ones were likely to work for the United States after the war, so his information proved invaluable during the Cold War. Hertz spent nine months at Fort Hunt, and during that time, he continuously warned Fred Michel and anyone who would listen that the United States needed to be prepared for the Soviet Union and the Cold War.

Carl Hellmuth Hertz very much wanted to stay in the United States, but his father had ended up in Russia at the end of the war, so the younger Hertz was considered too much of a security risk. He emigrated to Sweden and became a professor at Lund University. While there, he invented the inkjet and the echocardiograph. Hertz and Michel stayed in contact after the war, and in the 1960s, Hertz came to Washington, DC, for a conference. Fred Michel and his wife picked Hertz up from the conference, drove him to Fort Hunt—which he requested to see—then on to Charlottesville to show him Monticello and the University of Virginia.[25]

The second scientist Fred Michel interrogated and the circumstances that brought him to Fort Hunt is one of the most extraordinary stories at the end of World War II. Late in 1944, a special German commission determined that a submarine should be refitted to carry Germany's most important technological and military innovations to Japan. Torpedo tubes and mine-laying shafts were removed or altered; the keel was hollowed out, and every inch of potential space was prepared for the precious cargo, along with the capacity to carry enough fuel for a six- to nine-month voyage. The spaces were filled with reams of technical drawings, the newest electric torpedoes, a disassembled but complete jet, including its engine, the newest model of a glide bomb, and 1,200 pounds of uranium oxide. All other spaces were filled with lead and mercury. The human cargo was valuable as well, including Major General Ulrich Kessler of the Luftwaffe; Kay Nieschling, who was designated as the new liaison officer between Germany and Japan; Heinz Schlicke, a specialist in radar; and a specialist in infra-red and other technologies. Two Japanese experts were also on board— Lieutenant Commander Hideo Tomonaga, a naval architect and submarine designer who had come to Germany in 1943, and Lieutenant Commander Shoji Genzo, an aircraft specialist and former naval attaché. There were other experts on board as well. Johann-Heinrich Fehler was the captain. The ultimate destination for the sub and its cargo was Japan.

After several test runs in the North Sea, *U-234* started on its journey on April 15, 1945. Captain Fehler varied between traveling submerged, with the snorkel—that provided air to the diesel engines—and on the surface. On May 4, while sailing on the surface, he intercepted a message from American and British radio stations announcing that German Admiral Karl Dönitz, the acting chief of state after Hitler committed suicide, had surrendered. Days later, on May 10, Fehler received a message from Admiral Dönitz ordering all German ships to surrender to the nearest Allied port or ship. Thinking both messages might well be hoaxes, Fehler continued on the planned journey, but when he contacted other German ships and found that the messages were real, he started planning for the best option for surrender. He decided to surrender to the Americans. The two Japanese naval officers committed suicide and were tossed overboard, along with some of the navigation equipment and radios. Then, on May 14, *U-234* was spotted by and surrendered to the USS *Sutton*. An American crew took charge of the ship and sailed it to the naval base at Portsmouth, New Hampshire.[26]

Although the war was over, the German officers were transferred to Fort Hunt for interrogations and debriefing. Dr. Heinz Schlicke became the responsibility of Fred Michel. Like Hertz, Schlicke was anxious to do what he could to help the Americans in what he saw as an inevitable war with the Russians. He reported that he was part of the submarine entourage for the purpose of establishing a radio link between Germany and Japan that could not be intercepted by the Americans. He also offered to write a textbook on everything he and the Germans knew about microwave technology. With this, and the potential that his expertise would prove invaluable, Schlicke was encouraged to remain in the United States.[27]

Not long after the *U-234* docked in Portsmouth, Henry Kolm and several other soldiers from Fort Hunt drove to New Hampshire to escort the entire German crew to PO Box 1142. Kolm served as the translator for the American military, both on board and on the trip to Virginia, under heavy MP guard. After all, as Kolm said, "they were Nazis." Before they left Portsmouth, Kolm chatted with and became friendly with Captain Fehler. The captain gave him a tour of the sub, and when they were alone, Fehler said that General Kessler had ordered him to ignore the surrender order and redirect the ship to Argentina. Kolm filed this away as something either he or whoever interrogated Kessler should ask about at Fort Hunt.

When Henry Kolm arrived back at Fort Hunt with the German prisoners from *U-234*, he, Rudy Pins, and others were assigned to interrogate General Kessler. The German, of course, denied ever saying that he had directed the U-boat captain to divert to Argentina. Instead, he cooked up the story that he had planned to jump ship in Florida, surrender, and collaborate with the Americans against the Japanese. The issue of whether he ordered Fehler to divert course and sail to Argentina was not important in and of itself, but it put Kolm and the other American interrogators on guard for the general's possible deception.

More important was the question of which German general had ordered the bombing of Amsterdam after the Netherlands had surrendered to the Nazis. Whoever ordered the bombing was likely guilty of a war crime. Kessler said he had not given the order, but instead it was Major General Heinrich Aschenbrenner. Kolm arranged with his superiors to have Aschenbrenner transferred from another POW facility to Fort Hunt to check his story. In a separate interview, Aschenbrenner denied giving the order as well.[28]

Both generals were placed in the same room with listening devices concealed in the ceiling. Maybe now Kolm and his colleagues would get to the truth. Instead, both Germans started arguing as to who had seniority over the other, and neither would reveal who, or if either, had ordered the bombing. Both men may well have suspected that someone was listening to their conversation.

Without a resolution on a possible war crime, or whether Kessler ordered Captain Fehler to redirect *U-234* to Argentina were less pressing matters than any information Kessler could provide to help with the ongoing war with Japan. Rudy Pins recalled that Kessler was arrogant and hostile when he arrived at Fort Hunt but quickly became "quiet and amiable," and started providing useful information. Kessler's directive from Germany was to share the new technology with Japan. He was the ideal officer for this role since he had developed a relationship with the Japanese military over several years.

Kessler was a survivor, who recognized that any information he shared not only would be a huge help in the American war effort but might lead to favorable treatment after the war. First, the *U-234* mission was critical both to Germany and Japan. Germany wanted to continue the war with its Axis ally by providing its newest and most potent weapons and weapons delivery systems. Second, sending this cargo by way of submarine was the only practical transportation method. Japan had vetoed sending anything by air, since it would require flying over the Soviet Union. Kessler revealed that Japan's objection to the Russian air route was because Japan and Russia had been secretly cooperating, laying plans to potentially join forces against the United States. Kessler could not provide documentation to substantiate his claims, but the United States military considered that his information had potential merit.[29]

The men at Fort Hunt interrogated the entire crew of the submarine. Fred Michel talked to the Luftwaffe pilot, whose primary purpose was to supervise the assembly, then demonstrate and train Japanese pilots on the crated jet airplane on board. An anti-aircraft artillery expert had been sent to instruct the Japanese on the newest models of anti-aircraft guns. Then there was Kay Nieschling, a German navy commander who was scheduled to become Judge Advocate General for German personnel in the Far East. Rudy Pins interrogated him and realized that he was a radical Nazi, who likely would never change and so was a source of little information.

The information American interrogators gained at PO Box 1142 was crucial to the Allied war effort. They provided the location of a strategic ball-bearing plant; they learned that the Germans were loading and unloading trains at crossings rather than rail yards; they found out that the Germans were masking submarine pens by building fake coverings some distance away. These and other discoveries were critical as the Allies planned their bombing runs. These interrogations gave the United States government a boost at the beginning of the Cold War with the Soviet Union by learning the inner workings of the Soviet military and government from German documents and diplomatic expertise. Further, by finding the plans for the V-1 and V-2 weapons, United States intelligence experts quickly ascertained their critical importance. It became a paramount objective not only to learn as much as possible about the rockets but to somehow ensure that the rocket experts should stay out of Russian hands. One of the biggest prizes, however, came from the surrender of *U-234* at the end of the war. These most recent German technological advancements, as well as the experts who understood how they worked, were invaluable to the United States.

Further, PO Box 1142 provided the opportunity for a group of young, smart, and talented Jewish immigrants to contribute their skills to the war effort. Their knowledge of the language and nuances of German culture, fortified by their incentive to defeat Hitler, enabled them to excel at their jobs. They were skilled at coaxing information from German POWs, but many still had family in Germany, with whom they had lost contact. Often when they were interrogating German prisoners, they had two thoughts: what was happening with their families in Germany, and, if they were on a battlefield with the fellow on the other side of the table, his and their main objective would be to kill or be killed. However, when they were able to focus on the POWs as individuals, many later reflected that the Germans were simply doing the same job they were doing, which was defending their country. This helped them focus on their job at hand.

CHAPTER 6

More Than One Way to Skin a Cat

Russian American soldiers Alex Schidlovsky and Alexander Dallin "would dress in Russian uniforms and they would attend the interrogations. We would play good cop, bad cop. If you want to talk, okay you can go to a nice POW camp in Fort Meade. Otherwise, you could go to the Soviet Union. And guess what they preferred?"

RUDY PINS

In 1941, as America's involvement in the war in Europe seemed imminent, the nation's military leaders debated as to how, or even if, they should eavesdrop on enemy conversations. Interrogating prisoners was accepted practice for Americans in the midst of a war but listening in on private conversations, reading private letters, or generally snooping on enemies was quite another issue. Secretary of War, Henry Stimson, was particularly concerned with the practice, having earlier said that "gentlemen don't read each other's mail." On the other hand, General George C. Marshall, U.S. Army Chief of Staff, was concerned that intelligence-gathering operations in the American military were in a deplorable state. When the American team, which the general had sent to learn all it could about British intelligence operations, returned in late 1941, it recommended that an eavesdropping feature should be central to the American intelligence-gathering program. The findings and recommendations led to the establishment of the monitoring program at Fort Hunt.[1]

Thus, when the War Department started planning the facility at Fort Hunt, a centerpiece was a secret surveillance system, allowing American soldiers as monitors to eavesdrop on every conceivable conversation of German POWs. High-tech microphones were installed in the German quarters and throughout the camp. A building referred to as the "Honeysuckle" building was the nerve center for listening to prisoner conversations, where an average of 12 Americans would man the listening posts. Normal hours for eavesdropping were between 7:00a.m. and 10:00p.m.; however, if it appeared that a particularly fruitful conversation might extend later, monitors would continue listening. Tape recorders—even reel-to-reel—were not yet available, but when a monitor thought a dialogue might reveal something important, he would record the conversation on machines that looked like record players, on discs that looked like vinyl records. If, indeed, one or both prisoners involved in a conversation said something significant, a monitor would produce a transcript from the recording that either he, or a colleague would use in follow-up interrogations. If a conversation produced information of immediate relevancy that could affect Allies fighting in war zones, the transcript was sent to the Pentagon.[2]

The monitoring program worked best when monitors in the Honeysuckle building eavesdropped on conversations immediately after interrogations. A conversation between two German roommates, not expecting that anyone was listening to their conversation, might go something like this: *"When the Americans talked to you today, did they ask you about the new anti-aircraft artillery we are using?"* With luck, the other POW might say something like, *"Oh, do you mean the new triggering mechanism?"* If the listeners were truly lucky, the prisoners might go on to describe that mechanism in more detail. Even if the exchange did not offer such details, the interrogator would know to follow up on anti-aircraft artillery with the next verbal exchange. Following up on conversations like the one above was one of the most useful tools of the monitoring system.

Another eavesdropping technique proved to be even more successful. The U.S. military recruited German soldier and sailor POWs to serve as "stool pigeons" (shortened to SPs) to bunk with recently arriving German POWs or to befriend them in the recreation yard. The perfect match would place a Luftwaffe pilot SP with another pilot, or a U-boat SP sailor with another U-boat sailor, but the best SPs were quick studies in whatever areas of expertise their targets possessed. They were also good actors. Some came from countries overtaken by the Nazis, who were pressed into service and more than happy to do whatever they could to get even with their oppressors. Many, however, were Germans willing to turn against their native land. The latter group knew they were traitors, and by aiding the Americans, they knew they were putting their lives in jeopardy. After an extensive vetting process to determine that, yes, indeed, they had switched loyalties, they would take on their new roles as SPs.

The Americans started recruiting SPs with the earliest U-boat prisoners. Twenty-eight volunteered, and, in many ways, they were ideal for the job. They were valuable for gaining information from their fellow sailors; as they gained experience, they were quite adept at coaxing intelligence from German ground troops as well. Lieutenant Count Maximilian Coreth was an SP recruit from the German navy. As his title of "count" implied, he came from wealth and privilege in the Austrian aristocracy. His father, Count Carl Theodor Coreth, opposed the German annexation of Austria, was jailed as a political prisoner, and, although the elder Coreth was released after several weeks, his son could not forgive the Nazis. When the younger Count Coreth was taken prisoner from *U-172*, it seemed that he was a loyal German officer. He was second-in-charge as the executive officer of the submarine. To his captors' surprise, he jumped at the opportunity to become an SP as revenge for his father's imprisonment. He came to Fort Hunt in 1944 and served as an SP and later as an interrogator. His expertise and language skills were particularly valuable when *U-234* surrendered to the Americans (described in Chapter 5). He understood most of the systems on board, and he was able to converse with the crew and learn about the new innovations. For his service, Coreth was allowed to remain in the United States after the war, and later became a United States citizen.

Werner Drechsler was one of the most valuable SPs at PO Box 1142. Like Count Coreth, Dreschler had a bone to pick with the Nazis. His family members were communist sympathizers, and his father was shipped off to a concentration camp for his political beliefs. Drechsler was a crew member on board the captured *U-118* and made it clear early on that he would be happy to serve as an SP. He came to Fort Hunt in late summer 1943, and, for seven months, was one of the stars of the SP program. He used two aliases, and he perfected the two important attributes for an SP: he was a quick study and an actor who could well have won an academy award. Unfortunately, Drechsler's service came to a tragic end. At the conclusion of his service at PO Box 1142, Drechsler was transferred to a POW camp—primarily for U-boat prisoners—in Papago Park in Phoenix, Arizona. The U.S. Navy had promised to provide him protection there, but, immediately after his arrival, several of his former crewmates from *U-118* recognized him and spread the word that Drechsler was a turncoat. They convened a "kangaroo" court, convicted, and murdered him. The seven ringleaders responsible for Drechsler's death were tried in a U.S. court-martial proceeding, sentenced to death, and hanged at Fort Leavenworth, Kansas.[3]

While disgruntled German soldiers and sailors were perfect as SPs, German-born American soldiers were ideal as monitors. They played two roles: in many cases, they would conduct an interrogation, then follow up by listening to prisoner-to-prisoner conversations that followed; they might also hear something in a conversation between two prisoners that seemed promising and follow up by digging deeper into the subject in an interrogation.

George Weidinger described the monitoring system. Each monitor was assigned three prisoner cells to monitor during an eight-hour shift. During most shifts, little of value came from the prisoners, so one of the most difficult parts of the monitoring work was its tedium. Monitors could sit around for hours on end, listening to silence much of the time, or conversations about the weather, the food, or other routine topics. They had to be careful to not daydream, however, because if they were not vigilant, something important could slip through the cracks. Not all conversations were recorded, so another responsibility of a monitor was to sense when his subject might say something important, at which time he would push the button to record the conversation. They also had to be aware of the possibility that prisoners might be feeding them false information. Sometimes the SP could be useful here. He could be placed in a room where a prisoner was suspected of feeding false information into the system, gain his confidence and ask the prisoner in the exercise yard or somewhere out of earshot of the bugging equipment, something like, "*I know what you were saying when we were in our room was false. Did you do that thinking our conversations are being overheard?*"

George Weidinger monitored hours and hours of conversations and did not recall any particularly significant revelations. Others reported the same experiences, but there were exceptions. One day, Werner Moritz and his fellow monitors heard two Germans talking about a place called Peenemünde. At first, they thought little of the conversation, except one of the Americans had a sense that something important was about to be revealed in this dialogue. They continued to listen, then the German officer said to his bunkmate: "Don't you worry. We're going to win this war because we have this Peenemünde situation. We have these V-1s and V-2s. That's going to change the war completely." Moritz and his partner stumbled onto what was a major potential intelligence coup. They immediately passed along what they had learned up through the chain-of-command, but, tragically, their report did not reach the right people in time. Any chance was lost to do anything to stop the rockets and potentially save thousands of casualties.[4]

In addition to German refugees, American-born soldiers, fluent in German, were tremendously valuable as monitors. Since English was their primary language, their reports from monitoring sessions often required little editing. Such was the case with Leslie Willson. He was born in 1923 in Texhoma, in the Texas panhandle, straddling the border of Texas and Oklahoma. In high school and at Amarillo Junior College in Amarillo, Texas, he demonstrated a high aptitude for languages, especially German. The army recognized his talent for language, and following his intelligence training at Camp Ritchie, he was assigned to Fort Hunt. Willson's specialty was understanding German equipment, especially transportation equipment. He could quickly convert German—in some cases complex and technical German terms—into well-crafted and easy-to-understand English. He was so good at this, sometimes he was asked to translate German into English for other technical subjects. Willson maintained a diary of his experiences at PO Box 1142, and between this contemporary source and his recollections years later, he provided helpful information on how the monitoring program functioned, especially how monitors and interrogators shared information to maximize intelligence gathering.[5]

The U.S. military hierarchy believed that the monitoring program at Fort Hunt was a great success. The after-action report, analyzing the MIS-Y section of the intelligence-gathering program, concluded that "whatever moral scruples may have served to impede development of this activity [the monitoring program] in the past have disappeared in the face of a war waged by an enemy, both brutal and unscrupulous." It went on to say that "failure to make use of 'listening-in' devices would be to allow the Nazis a decided advantage. [With] the bombing of cities or the use of submarines against merchant shipping, 'eavesdropping,' however repulsive it may be to standards of civilized conduct, is a potential 'new weapon' in modern warfare." It concluded by saying that "the systematic 'monitoring' or of 'listening-in' on the conversations of knowledgeable prisoners of war is an accepted feature of [American military intelligence]."[6]

In reality, how effective was the monitoring program at Fort Hunt? Chapter 5 discussed the incident in which German Generals Kessler and Aschenbrenner were placed in the same room and carefully monitored, hoping they would reveal valuable intelligence. They argued but revealed nothing valuable. Were they truly just arguing, or did they suspect their conversations were monitored? The problem with their conversation was a problem that would persist through the duration of PO Box 1142. Germans, particularly German officers, seemed to have sensed that they could not let their guard down in the camp. Someone might hear anything, anywhere.

Sixty years after the closure of PO Box 1142, two former German POWs, Franz Gajdosch and Anton Leonhard, described their experiences as prisoners at Fort Hunt. Both were enlisted men, and both agreed that they suspected that their captors were listening in on their conversations. One tip to Leonhard was that one day he was jumping on his bed and immediately a guard came into his room. The only way anyone could have heard the noise was if his cell was wired with listening devices.[7]

There were no official records as to which intelligence-gathering technique was more effective—monitoring or interrogation. Rudy Pins, who served at Fort Hunt longer than most of his colleagues—as an interrogator and a monitor—anecdotally estimated that he and his colleagues spent 65 percent of their time in the Honeysuckle building monitoring conversations around the fort, and about 35 percent on interrogations. Rudy went on to say that he believed that only about 20 percent of the most valuable information came from the monitoring program. The rest came from interrogations.[8]

More recently, Sönke Neitzel, the noted German historian, analyzed the 100,000 pages of interrogations and 40,000 pages from eavesdropping transcripts from Fort Hunt, which are housed in the National Archives. His research showed that the transcripts from the monitoring program had value well beyond their immediate importance during the war. He gained important insights into the impressions of German soldiers' views on the nature of warfare. He observed the hopes and fears and concerns and the day-to-day lives of these prisoners. He also noted that they openly discussed the horrors of war, including topics such as rape, death, and killing. Neitzel shared the material with psychologist Harald Welzer and they concluded that the vast volumes of material from PO Box 1142 and World War II were relevant to war in general. Further, these transcripts were valuable as well to our understanding of perceptions and how warfare affects soldiers in modern conflicts, such as in Iraq and Afghanistan.[9]

As Sönke Neitzel discovered, transcripts from the monitoring and interrogation programs utilized forests worth of paper, which created a huge potential logistical nightmare for managing the files. How crucial was the information? Did it need to be placed in the hands of commanders in the war zones as quickly as possible? Or did it need to be filed in such a way that it could be retrieved at a moment's notice? An estimated five thousand interrogations and notes from thousands of hours of monitoring were accumulated at PO Box 1142, and the man who created a filing system that was efficient, secure, and accessible at a moment's notice was Wayne Spivey. Wayne Spivey was born in rural Georgia in 1920 and moved with his family to Atlanta, where he graduated from high school. He joined the army not long out of school and showed a strong aptitude as a clerk. His superiors were impressed with his abilities, and early on selected him to create and manage the filing system at PO Box 1142. He arrived at Fort Hunt, just as it opened for business in July 1942 and remained until late 1945.

Spivey set up a system that worked with remarkable efficiency, starting with the first collection of interrogation documents that came to PO Box 1142 from North Africa, not long after he arrived at the fort. He organized and annotated the materials, then set up a cross-referencing system, by identifying subjects, then creating a database as a finding aid. He quickly understood that summaries of the files were invaluable, and he insisted that these extracts were essential for each file. When the interrogation and monitoring program was underway, Wayne put the interrogation excerpts in binders, organized by the interrogation number. Anyone who needed to look at an interview with a certain individual, could find it by its number, by who was interrogated, or by the date in which it was conducted. The excerpt was sometimes sufficient, but the entire file was easily accessible. If someone needed information on a place or topic, the database provided easy access to that as well. For example, there was a section for Stuttgart, as well as subsections under that category. Anyone who needed information about something specifically within the large general category of Stuttgart could refer to the extracts, which would summarize the contents of specific files within that category.

Sometimes Spivey would be asked to pull files for topics he knew nothing about. At one point there was a demand to find everything related to atoms. He did not know until much later that this request probably related to atom bombs, but at the time, that really did not matter, because in his usual efficiency, he quickly pulled the necessary files and prepared them for transmission to the Pentagon.[10]

* * *

For 60 years, Wayne Spivey could not discuss his filing system at Fort Hunt; George Weidinger could not say anything about the monitoring program, and Rudy Pins, Werner Moritz, and Leslie Willson were sworn to secrecy as well. When they could finally talk about their experiences, the one message they wanted to make abundantly clear was that they did not physically torture any German prisoners at PO Box 1142. This is a recurring theme throughout this study, that was emphasized so often by so many veterans of Fort Hunt, it bears repeating. They subscribed to the adage that you can catch more flies with honey than you can with vinegar; they believed that they gleaned far more from prisoners by playing chess or table tennis, or by taking them to nice steak dinners at fancy restaurants, than by using any form of physical torture.[11]

The two former German POWs mentioned above, Franz Gajdosch and Anton Leonhard, confirmed that they were treated well. Leonhard was an enlisted man in the German army who was captured during the Battle of the Bulge in 1945. In his initial questioning in England, he revealed that he was a guard at the notorious Gusen Mauthausen concentration camp in Austria. The Americans wanted to determine if Leonhard was potentially a war criminal, and, more importantly, they wanted to learn more about the prison camp. Within 30 minutes, his interrogator learned that Leonhard was a guard who escorted prisoners from the camp to a factory that produced Luftwaffe airplane wings. He remained at Fort Hunt for only a couple of days, then was transferred to a POW camp. But, although he was only at PO Box 1142 for a short time, and although his interrogation was brief, he confirmed a couple of issues. He said he was interrogated by a Jewish soldier who spoke perfect German. When asked how he knew his interrogator was Jewish, he said he just knew, even though the man neither gave his name nor his religion. He also said he was treated well.[12]

The second prisoner, Franz Gajdosch, was from Slovakia. He was a sergeant in the Waffen-SS panzer division and was captured during the German counter-offensive following D-day. His interrogation lasted several days, and he was grilled on the tank operations—the number of tanks, the commanders, the tank divisions, and the armaments. Then he was asked about what he knew of the partisan operations in Slovakia. He was forthright, recalling that his interrogator "asked me everything and I was telling him the whole story of my life and unit and everything." He provided some useful information but nothing of great consequence. In his National Park Service interview, he was complimentary of his treatment. Gajdosch said he was encouraged to learn English—an opportunity he enthusiastically embraced. He was allowed to remain at Fort Hunt initially and in the United States after the war, not so much because he had provided so much valuable information, but because Czechoslovakia was then behind the Iron Curtain. For his cooperation, he began working in the camp, starting as a dishwasher in the mess hall and moving up to bartender in the officers' club—a skill he translated into his profession after the war.[13]

If the Americans did not use corporal punishment, what, if anything, did they use to gain information? One practice that started with Seaman Mycke continued, and that was to offer prisoners a cigarette soon after the interview began. There were also a wide variety of games and recreational opportunities. One activity, new to the Germans that they thoroughly enjoyed, was the game of horseshoes. It seems amazing that Americans would let Germans throw horseshoes, potentially lethal weapons, but this suggested that prisoners and their captors developed mutual trust that made each comfortable with the other.

There also was a rewards system. If a prisoner was particularly forthcoming with information, he might be taken to a fine restaurant in Washington, DC.

Other Germans might prefer sailing on the Potomac. Some loved films and would be treated to either watching movies on site or at a movie theater in town. Others, especially high-value prisoners, were allowed to stay in private huts.

Ernest Salomon described yet another reward. One general wanted more than a meal. He wanted a woman and made it clear exactly what that meant. Salomon took him to a high-class brothel in Washington, DC. While he was waiting for the general in the lobby, the police raided the facility, which had the potential to create a huge problem for Salomon and his general. Among the customers, however, there were senators, congressmen, and diplomats. When the policemen realized that they would be involved in dealing with a potentially huge political scandal, they threw their hands up and, according to Salomon, said: "Forget it."[14]

Taking a German general to a brothel was on the extreme end of accommodating POWs. Most were happy with much less. "You gained their confidence," George Weidinger later recalled, by telling "them the war was almost over." Then, "[we would say] you guys are losing, so you might as well cooperate." He went on to say, "Play chess with them. Take them shopping. Invariably they'd start talking." In some cases, food, cigarettes, liquor, or shopping sprees alone would not suffice. The "soft" approach was preferable, but if that did not work, there were other ways to gain information.

* * *

Throughout the existence of PO Box 1142, hardcore Nazi POWs often were anything but helpful. For the latter group, just because army personnel did not use physical torture, this did not mean that their hands were then tied. They used several clever tricks short of physical torture to coerce the Germans to talk.

The first method was to blindfold the German, then lead him to the abandoned early 1900s Coast Artillery gun batteries and lock him in a damp, cold, and dark powder magazine under the gun platforms. He was kept there for hours, sometimes all day, but according to several former soldiers, never overnight. If, somehow, the Americans could convince the German that he might be kept there for an extended period, this intimidation method would sometimes convince the prisoner to reveal information.

The most effective coercion, however, was to frighten the POW, that if he continued to refuse to cooperate, he would be shipped off to the Soviet Union. Trainees at Camp Ritchie learned the value of incorporating this threat into interrogations. Soldiers stationed at Fort Hunt loved to tell stories of how this technique worked. If a prisoner showed any hesitation in his answers, he was threatened with being sent to Russia. Former POW Anton Leonhard confirmed that interrogators used this technique on him. At the beginning of his session, he was hesitant in his answers and was told if he did not reveal everything he knew, he would be sent to Russia.[15]

Two Russian American soldiers, Alexander Dallin and Alex Schidlovsky, who both spoke fluent Russian, were stationed at PO Box 1142 for the purpose of scaring Germans into talking. They were conspicuous around the fort in their Red Army uniforms and were always available if needed. If time in the underground powder magazine, or other forms of intimidation did not work, and the German POW still refused to answer any questions, the next step might well include the threat to have "Ivan" escort them to the Soviet Union. Then one of the Russians would come into the room; the technique worked for some, but not all. For those who still refused to share information, they were sent on to Fort Alva in Oklahoma or another undesirable POW camp for the remainder of the war.

Between the two Russian Americans at Fort Hunt and Guy Stern who pretended he was Commissar Krukov in Europe, and many other similar scenarios used by British and American Allies during the war, the success rate of coaxing German prisoners to talk with the threat of being sent to Russia if they did not was extremely high. Guy Stern said that in using this technique, 80 percent of German prisoners would start telling what they knew.[16]

In at least one occasion, Henry Kolm described an incident in which a German soldier came as close to receiving physical or psychological torture as anyone at Fort Hunt. Kolm described a shadowy character, who was in and out of Fort Hunt, by the name of Herbert (sometimes referred to as Rolf) Arndt. According to Kolm, Arndt was a double agent, who was working for the United States, but whom the Germans thought was working for them as well. Kolm also said that Arndt had been the president of a German bank in Africa, and during the war, the Nazis killed his wife and children. With that, he had an intense hatred for the Germans and wanted to do whatever he could to get revenge. Or at least that was the story. Kolm added that Arndt "was very shrewd, very tough, [and] very ingenious."

Arndt had indeed been an international banker, but because of his involvement in several illegal agricultural deals, he was arrested and sent to Buchenwald concentration camp where he was incarcerated for about two years. He was drafted into the German army in 1942 and captured by the Americans in 1943. He was sent to Fort Hunt in August 1943. The story about his family and his role as a double agent might or might not have been true.

He was interrogated at PO Box 1142 and quickly made it clear he would be happy to volunteer as an SP. He assumed multiple aliases and interrogated and/or bunked with more than 40 German prisoners. According to Henry Kolm, Arndt reserved a special level of hatred for the Waffen-SS, and on one occasion, while he was at PO Box 1142, he heard that a Waffen-SS officer refused to talk. Arndt got wind of the refusal and said, "I'll make him talk ... just let me handle it." He took the German to one of the abandoned gun emplacements, placed him in a small powder magazine and locked the steel doors. One of the Russian American soldiers—Dallin or Schidlovsky—was his accomplice. Through a hole in the steel door, he ran the hose from a vacuum cleaner, and asked the Waffen-SS officer: "Are you ready to talk now? Because if you're not, we're going to gas you." No answer. Arndt turned on the vacuum in reverse so the dust and dirt would shoot into the confined space. He knew that the Germans would gas prisoners to get them to talk. Arndt opened the door and let the prisoner come out and said, "Well? Are you willing to talk to us now?" Still nothing. Arndt told his "Russian" accomplice, "Ivan, more gas." And the Russian said, "Yes, okay," and this time they filled the chamber with so much dust, the German really thought he might die. Then he talked.

Henry Kolm said that was the only time he heard of that kind of treatment. Another soldier stationed at Fort Hunt, Bill Hess, confirmed the story with a variation. He said the German was sprayed with a pesticide. He confirmed that one of the Russian Americans was involved as well. Hess said that although he was not in the camp when the incident happened, it was common knowledge among the American soldiers stationed there. He added that Arndt, or whoever was the main perpetrator, was reprimanded for his actions and told to never do that again, because it violated the Geneva Convention.[17]

* * *

Another source for gathering intelligence was the partnership between divisions within PO Box 1142. The soldiers stationed in MIRS reviewed and analyzed thousands of captured German documents, and, from time to time, would find nuggets of information that related to POWs held for interrogation at the fort. John Kluge, who was the officer in charge of MIRS described how this partnership worked. On one occasion, Kluge's group uncovered documents showing that a German sergeant in custody, from the 10th Panzer Division, had visited several houses of prostitution. They also determined that when this German sergeant was drunk, he was talkative, and as he got drunker, he would say how much he regretted going to prostitutes. Eventually, according to Kluge, "he spilled the beans." His guilt made him feel that he needed to provide information, and as a result, he revealed that the 10th Panzer Division would travel on a particular route. His description was so precise, it was almost as if he had drawn a map. The information was quickly passed along to the Pentagon, then to Europe, which proved invaluable in bombing the 10th Panzer Division.

One of the most prized documents captured by the Americans was the *Reichstag* phone directory. Kluge described how this source came in handy for interrogations. The interrogator would confront a prisoner by saying he knew that said prisoner had called a particular person on a specific line. The prisoner would be stunned and ask how he knew that. The response was that the Americans had bugged every phone in the *Reichstag* and were able to listen in to every conversation. This was another mode of potential intimidation, and, if nothing else, would make German prisoners wonder how much information the Americans really had.

Kluge described another incident, in which one of his MIRS men found a picture of high-ranking German officers who attended General Erwin Rommel's daughter's wedding. The image was in an obscure small-town German newspaper. One of the officers in the picture was being held and interrogated at Fort Hunt, and, in this instance, Kluge took the first shot at interrogating the officer. "Look, we saw you there. We saw you there," Kluge recalled. The officer was surprised, and asked, "How did you see?" Without missing a beat, Kluge replied "Well, we had somebody [a spy] there." In the image, the officer was talking to a general, so Kluge added that the spy reported that he "saw you talking to General so-and-so. He was there, too." Of course, the whole story was fabricated from this newspaper picture. If nothing else, it probably made this officer wonder how far the Allied intelligence tentacles reached.

As an officer, John Kluge socialized with the German officers at Fort Hunt. He would play bridge with them and drive them around Washington, DC, both to soften them up for interrogations and to give them "believable misinformation." Sometimes he would have some fun. While driving one German around, they drove by the Pentagon and told the German general, "That's the Pentagon." The German was duly impressed, then Kluge added, yes but "that's the Annex. The real Pentagon is underground, much larger."[18]

* * *

Toward the end of the war, several of the European Jewish soldiers assigned to Fort Hunt were so young, both in age and appearance, it was clear they would not exude the desired gravitas to convince German soldiers that they had earned the necessary rank to serve as interrogators. These young soldiers did, however, play important roles in the intelligence-gathering process. They were called morale officers. They served two functions: they would listen in to conversations on the monitoring system, but more importantly, they would do what they could to ensure that high-value Germans were happy. This might mean they would serve them food or drinks, play sports in the recreation yard, take them to movies or dinner, or even shopping.

John Gunther Dean, who was 18 when he arrived at PO Box 1142—but looked much younger—was assigned to the duty of morale officer. His youthful looks were deceiving. He was a very smart young man, having dropped out of Harvard to join the army. He was sent to Fort Belvoir and was training to join the Corps of Engineers, but when the army recognized that he was fluent in German, he was sent to Fort Hunt. He later recalled that when he was given his assignment, he was driven to a location in Alexandria, Virginia, and given a nickel to call a certain number. He was directed to follow whatever instructions he received from the phone call. He called the mysterious number and was directed to wait where he was and that someone would pick him up. A short time later, a car picked him up and drove him to Fort Hunt. He arrived in October 1944 and left in August 1946.

As with most morale officers, Dean monitored conversations in the Honeysuckle building, but his primary duty was to make German prisoners comfortable with their captivity. As a monitor, he simply listened to conversations. Other morale officers might also make recordings and prepare transcripts. The one conversation he later recalled was when two German were discussing splitting an atom. At the time, the conversation seemed strange, but later he understood that they were discussing elements of nuclear fission. He also was valuable as a morale officer, because he was a good athlete and played sports with the POWs. Among his other duties, he also took them to dinners in Washington.

Dean would later reflect on his experiences at PO Box 1142 and their impact on his later life. He appreciated that he and his colleagues always worked within the law to gather the intelligence they needed. He also valued how everyone worked together and "felt good about doing it. Everybody was an American, whether you were an American of one year's standing or a Mayflower descendant."[19]

Arno Mayer, another morale officer, was barely out of high school when he was drafted into the army. He spent time at Fort Dix in New Jersey and Fort Knox in Kentucky, but when his superiors realized that he was fluent in both German and French, he became an ideal candidate for PO Box 1142. He went through the training program at Camp Ritchie and was then transferred to Fort Hunt in July 1945. During the time Mayer spent at Fort Hunt, the war with Germany ended, and the prospect of a conflict with the Soviet Union was real, so the American military establishment wanted to tap into the experience and talent of German scientists. As a morale officer, Mayer's job was to provide prisoners with reading materials, liquor, and anything else within reason. He spent time at Fort Hunt but was also shuttled to Fort Strong in Boston Harbor. Toward war's end and afterwards, Fort Strong was a major site for processing German scientists, like Wernher von Braun, into the United States.

Not only did the hierarchy at PO Box 1142 want to keep German scientists contented; they did not want any American soldiers to offend them. One day, Mayer overheard a group of scientists talking and heard one say that the biggest mistake Hitler made was going after the Jews. Since Mayer was Jewish, he took offense at this comment and felt compelled to chastise the German for singling out Jews in his comments. Mayer's superiors overheard the conversation through the monitoring system and reprimanded him for confronting the German. Mayer's job was to go to whatever lengths to keep the Germans happy, not to antagonize them.[20]

Mayer had a chance to redeem himself a little later. In October 1945, four German scientists reported to their American handlers that life for their families in Germany was dire, and they asked if they could buy food and clothing for them in town. Mayer was assigned the task of taking them on their mission. Mayer took them to Lansburgh and Brother Department Store, a store he picked because it was owned by Jews. The Germans bought cocoa, coffee, sugar, and other food supplies. Then they moved over to the women's section. Speaking in German, with Mayer as their translator, they asked to purchase women's underwear. The saleswoman asked what size. This was a problem, because the Germans were used to metrics, whereas American sizes were in inches. But the scientists were prepared; they pulled out their slide rules and converted from centimeters to inches. One scientist asked specifically if he could purchase women's long woolen underwear. In the translation, Mayer was able to explain that it was cold in Germany, where the underwear was to be sent. Next, they asked for brassieres, and again they pulled out their trusty slide rules to determine the correct sizes.

Mayer was wearing his army uniform, but without insignia, and two of the Germans were wearing long leather coats and Tyrolean hats. Before long, the military police showed up and started to arrest everyone, because the store clerks, no doubt, thought these Germans had evil intentions. Mayer called PO Box 1142 and quickly straightened out the mess, and his German charges were able to make their purchases and send their gifts to their families in Germany. Mayer said the German shopping spree cost U.S. taxpayers about $500.[21]

Mayer's and Dean's jobs were to keep the Germans comfortable, but that did not stop soldiers at Fort Hunt from having some fun. In early March 1946, Arno Mayer and Leslie Willson needed to get to Union Station in Washington to catch a train to New York. Both had leave, and Mayer had lined up a couple of hot dates in the Big Apple. "We had strict instructions not to do any hitchhiking on the [Memorial] Parkway ... because we would give away the location [of Fort Hunt]," Mayer later recalled. It was "raining cats and dogs; the bus is late," and because it was Sunday, "who's going to pay any attention? We started thumbing ... [and a] very, very elegant car came along and stopped, and there were three women in it." Leslie Willson picked up the story from there. "As we got in, one of the ladies, I think the driver, asked us what Arno was taking along, because he had a box." She asked: "'What do you got in that box?' And he said, 'The atomic bomb.' And she looked wide eyed for a minute. And then she said, 'No, you're kidding.' And he said, 'No.' So she said, 'Well, I know you are.'" The banter continued on the way to Union Station.

On the train trip to New York, Mayer and Willson started comparing notes and agreed that they heard one of the women referring to her husband as General Eisenhower and another woman kept calling her Mamie. Willson picked up the story from there. "When we got to New York, I called *Time* magazine and asked them what [General Eisenhower's wife's] name was. [The woman there said her name was] Mamie. I thought oh my God, it was Mamie." Mayer continued, saying, "We were nervous as hell, because we weren't supposed to hitchhike, and certainly I wasn't supposed to make a joke about secret work and an atomic bomb. We became rather glum. It wasn't funny any longer." Willson came up with the brilliant idea that they "should write [Mrs. Eisenhower] a letter and check with her by thanking her. ... So, we wrote a little letter thanking her for the ride and sent to in care of General Eisenhower at the Pentagon." At the time, the war was over, and he was the Department of War's Chief of Staff.

Four days later, they were called in to see their commanding officer. This was highly unusual and made both men nervous. Would they be reprimanded or worse for hitchhiking? Or was there something else? From there, Mayer picked up the story: "We got there [to the commander's office], and the guy was incredibly respectful of us, practically bowing from the waist and handed us this letter from General Eisenhower, which had been delivered by courier. [It] impressed the commander; it certainly impressed us," but not in a good way. "It scared the shit out of us. Then we opened the letter," and this is what it said:

War Department

The Chief of Staff

Washington

15 March 1946

Dear Sergeants Willson and Mayer:

Mrs. Eisenhower has been intermittently ill and always very busy. Consequently she asked me whether I could find the time to answer your very nice note written on the 11th of March. It is so unusual for anyone to take the trouble, later, to repeat their thanks for a casual ride that she was quite touched by your courtesy and wanted to make sure that your note was acknowledged. Both she and I look for opportunities to pick up smart looking soldiers not only because we like them but because we invariably learn something from them.

Sincerely Dwight D. Eisenhower (signature)

Rather than getting into trouble for hitching a ride into town, Mayer and Willson were the talk of the fort.[22]

The last part of General Eisenhower's letter that said "Both she [Mrs. Eisenhower] and I look for opportunities to pick up smart looking soldiers" rang true for Peter Weiss. He had a weekend pass and was going to Union Station to catch a train to New York. His mother had purchased a ticket for him to watch the New York Philharmonic Orchestra perform. He was hitchhiking on Memorial Parkway and a jeep with two women inside stopped to pick him up. "They asked what I was doing. I said I was stationed in a military post here. They asked me 'How did you like it?' and so forth. 'Do you have any complaints?' and I said 'Yeah. The food is pretty lousy.' And the one in the passenger seat said, 'I'll have to tell the general about that.'" Surprised, he asked which general that would be. She replied that the general was her husband: "General Eisenhower!"[23]

* * *

Did the Americans always get everything they wanted from every POW in the camp? Of course not. But it appears that most of the intelligence they obtained was valuable. Most experts agree that physical torture is not a reliable means of obtaining information. To avoid physical punishment, prisoners often tell their captors what they want to hear, not necessarily the truth. For example, near the end of World War II, after the atomic bombs were dropped on Hiroshima and Nagasaki, the Japanese tortured American Lieutenant Marcus McDilda, a captured American fighter pilot, to try to find out how many more bombs the Americans had in their arsenal. McDilda not only did not know how many bombs there were; he did not even know about the Manhattan Project, but to try to stop the torture, he said there were one hundred bombs, and the next targets were Kyoto and Tokyo.[24] There is no way of knowing whether this had any impact on ending the war, but, if nothing else, it likely made the Japanese wonder if his "confession" was truthful or not. More recently, in 2011, the United States Senate Intelligence Committee's 6,700-page report found that the CIA was not always truthful in its reporting of "enhanced interrogation" (a euphemism for torture). Moreover, the evidence showed that torture was not an effective intelligence-gathering technique.[25]

If any group had a motivation to torture their enemy, the German Jewish-American soldiers at PO Box 1142 fit that category. When he was 94, Rudy Pins summed up the feelings of many of his colleagues. "You don't get people to talk by beating them or waterboarding or anything of that nature," Pins said. "If you make life for certain prisoners fairly easy, they will relax [and tell you what you need to know]." Pins and his buddies had been forced to leave their homeland; most had lost family in the Holocaust, and some POWs, who came through the fort embodied all that was evil about the Nazi regime. Yet, they all did their jobs, did not resort to torturing their adversaries, and devoted their energies to winning the war.[26]

CHAPTER 7

The Books of Many Colors

"I had to really be on the ball to be in charge of the young, very intelligent German Jews under my command because they just absorbed knowledge like sponges and had great memories, which helped because you would be going over thousands of documents."
JOHN KLUGE

Gathering intelligence during World War II was a multifaceted operation. Interrogations in the war zone, at Fort Hunt, and elsewhere were one source; eavesdropping on prisoner conversation was another; and capturing, translating, and interpreting enemy documents were yet another source. Using captured enemy documents for military purposes was not new, but during this war, the Military Intelligence Research Section (MIRS) performed a critical function in the Allied war effort. With a large office of 85 or more soldiers stationed in London and a smaller office at PO Box 1142, MIRS processed 5,374 mailbags of documents, weighing a total of over 150 tons, between May 1943 and June 1945. The Germans were fastidious record keepers; so much so, the men in MIRS believed that captured German documents were, by far, the most useful intelligence-gathering tools. This attention to detail benefited the German military but ironically was also a boon to Americans analyzing captured documents.[1]

Early in the war, collecting enemy documents for processing was haphazard, but while American forces were still in North Africa, the importance of gathering and keeping German documents was instilled in the field commanders. Attached to many American units on the battlefield were an officer and three or four enlisted men whose primary responsibility was to collect as many enemy documents as they could. It was not their job to determine importance, but simply to collect official military documents, letters, orders, photographs, declarations, reports of troop movements, interceptions of transmitted messages, newspapers, individual soldier passbooks, and really anything that seemed to have German writing on it, leaving it to the men at MIRS to determine their value.

The documents were first gathered and processed in the London MIRS office. The mission here was to determine if a particular piece or collection of information might have immediate benefit for the Supreme Headquarters of the Allied Expeditionary Force (SHAEF). If it did, it was translated and passed along to the appropriate office. The London office also served as a clearinghouse for which captured German documents should go to Fort Hunt and which should go to various agencies in England. The volume of captured documents was substantial, but by the end of the war, the London office was not only able to process captured documents but also assist in preparing long-range studies on a variety of subjects.[2]

The mission of the Fort Hunt MIRS was to "exploit the documents for long-range intelligence purposes, circulate them to authorized agencies in the United States, and catalog and file them for permanent custody." The bulk of the work was conducted by 19 enlisted men, supervised by four officers—two American and two British—who came from a variety of backgrounds. They researched and prepared books, papers, handbooks, and other reports. To that end, the primary responsibility of the men at PO Box 1142 was to prepare and update the "Order of Battle of the German Army," commonly referred to as the "Red Book."[3]

The men assigned to MIRS worked in a large room and constantly shared information with each other. "Each of us had a desk and a little filing cabinet," Paul Fairbrook, one of the enlisted men stationed at Fort Hunt, later recalled, and each man had "a little box with cards in front of us. Those cards were very important, incidentally, because those cards were what we used in order to collect the information that would lead us to conclusions. The officers were over us, none of them used their authority." They did not need to because "we knew what we were supposed to do. And the reason we were successful is because we believed in what we were doing." Fairbrook went on, saying, "I was waiting for the next bag to come so I [could] get more information. ... When you've done research, it can be very exciting. And that's the way we felt."[4]

In addition to the military men, Philip Tucker, a civilian English professor, was assigned to the unit for the primary purpose of ensuring that the prose that came out of MIRS was well-crafted, clear, and immediately usable. Paul Fairbrook said that Tucker's tutoring was the main reason he was able to skip basic English composition classes in college and jump right into comparative literature classes. The men at Fort Hunt universally agreed that the professor's expertise was invaluable.[5]

No one knew the men at Fort Hunt better than their commanding officer, John Kluge. He had high praise for his staff, saying they "were primarily young, very intelligent German Jews who, because of their work there, were [able to receive their American citizenship.]" That was an advantage for them, but for Kluge, he "had to really be on the ball to be in charge of them because they just absorbed knowledge like sponges and had great memories, which helped because you would be going over thousands of documents."[6]

Lieutenant Charles Winick also praised the men who worked under him. "I was impressed with its quality [of the work of my staff]. I could see it and I realized that the people working on [the Red Book] were highly skilled editors, and professional in terms of information management. At a glance they could see connections that were not immediately visible."[7]

The men chosen to work in MIRS were a select group. John Kluge, who came to Fort Hunt as a lieutenant and was promoted to captain, was assigned to Fort Hunt in January 1943, and remained there until near the end of the war. Kluge was born in Chemnitz, Germany, in 1914, and came to the United States at age eight. His father was killed in World War I, and his mother remarried a German man who moved the family to Detroit. Kluge left home at age 14 and eventually attended Columbia University in New York, where he majored in economics and graduated in 1937. He joined the army, entered Officer Candidate School, and when the war broke out, he was shipped to the Aleutian Islands. When the army realized his German background, he went to PO Box 1142. His men considered him a good commander, not because of his knowledge of the German language, which most said was not the best, but because he recognized that if he left his men alone, they would produce high-quality work.[8]

Unlike many of the men he supervised, Charles Winick was not German but instead was born in the United States in 1922. Like his men, he was Jewish and, like some, grew up in a home where Yiddish was the first language. His parents were immigrants from Russia and Czechoslovakia. From an early age, he was interested in languages—English first—but he also studied French and German, as well as Latin and Greek, in high school and at City College in New York. Out of college in 1941, he joined the army in 1942 and was accepted into Officer Candidate School. His first duty as a junior officer was in military police, then, mysteriously, he was ordered to report to an installation in Alexandria, Virginia, which, of course, was Fort Hunt, in January 1945. At PO Box 1142, he supervised the compilation and preparation of the military personalities and High Command section of the 1945 edition of the Red Book. Later in 1945, he was transferred to the London MIRS office.[9]

Dieter Kober was in his junior year in college at the University of Nebraska and enjoying the music program there. When the Japanese attacked Pearl Harbor, he heard the news while practicing in the music department. Like many in his generation, not only did he remember where he was, but he also remembered his feelings. "Well, my feeling was, well, I was happy," he said. "Because at least this guy's [Hitler's] going to get it." Soon after, he was drafted and sent to Camp Kearns in Nebraska for basic training. Before long the army realized he was smart and a German Jew and sent him to Camp Ritchie for intelligence training. He arrived at Fort Hunt in July 1943. While there, he spent some of his time at the Pentagon processing German field-unit files. He also was an expert on German youth and the German air force.[10]

After Paul Fairbrook and his family arrived in the United States, they settled in New York City. Paul's father was able to parlay his stamp collection into a business as a stamp dealer. Paul worked in an antique shop and a tailor shop and attended high school. In the summer, he was hired as a busboy at the exclusive Greenbrier Hotel in White Sulphur Springs, West Virginia. He said that if the management knew he was a Jew, he would have never landed the job, nor would he have been allowed to stay at the hotel as a guest. He worked at hotels in Washington, DC and New York, working his way up through the hospitality industry until he was a room clerk at the Park Central Hotel in New York.

Paul was working at the Park Central Hotel when the Japanese attacked Pearl Harbor. He tried to join the Marines—no luck. He tried to join the navy—no luck. He tried to also join the army, again, no luck, but he was told that he was listed as an enemy alien, since he was still considered a citizen of Germany. However, with the army, he was told that before long he might well be drafted, which happened in January 1943. He was sent to Camp Upton in New York State, then Fort McClellan in Alabama for basic training. But as soon as the army heard his accent and recognized that he was fluent in German, he was sent to Camp Ritchie for intelligence training. He finished his training at Camp Ritchie and was transferred to MIRS section at PO Box 1142. Fairbrook and his colleagues noted that they spent much of their time at the Pentagon. In fact, several spent more time there than at Fort Hunt. Because of that, they knew the building quite well. They also knew they needed more desks and other furniture for their operation at PO Box 1142. On D-day, he and his co-conspirators secured the use of a truck, went to the Pentagon, and while everyone there was focused on the D-day invasion, they confiscated the furniture they needed and hauled it to Fort Hunt.

Most of the documents received at PO Box 1142 had already gone through one level of processing in the London office. The material would arrive at Fort Hunt in big sacks. From there, Sergeant Kober described what happened next. "Sergeant [Walter L.] Schmidt went through that big sack that came from overseas and then he would say: 'Okay, divisional units—that goes to Sergeant Kober. Here's something about howitzers—that goes to Sergeant so-and-so.'" Kober continued, "If the guy who got [documents] for the howitzer saw something that would be good for another department, he would transfer it. We had first-class people working there that weren't just doing a job. They were really thinking it." Kober specialized in divisional units. Earlier, he had reviewed materials on youth groups. Paul Fairbrook focused on the German High Command as well as the types of units. He and his MIRS colleagues documented the German military down to the divisional level, and by the end of the war, they knew where each division was located, who the commander was, and when divisions were consolidated, as attrition decimated the ranks. Another man dealt with the replacement army. Still another analyzed everything concerning installations in Germany while someone else concentrated on German military bases in conquered lands. The *Schutzstaffel*, German for "protective echelon," or more commonly known as the SS or Waffen-SS was so important, one man specialized on these forces.[11]

Within each general area, there were subspecialties, such as someone who knew about German houses of prostitution. During the war, the Germans established some 500 brothels in Germany and occupied territories. The female sex workers were generally prisoners forced to work in these establishments. Each soldier and sailor was given a card after they had visited the brothel with the name of the woman he had visited. These cards became valuable tools for the men at MIRS. They showed where the soldiers/sailors had been, which was a mechanism to track the locations of various units. The information could also be passed along to interrogators, which could serve several purposes. If an interrogator could ask an unsuspecting German if a particular woman was still at a particular bordello (Chapter 5), that might throw him off-guard, wondering where the questioner obtained the information. In other cases, perhaps the prisoner felt guilty about his encounter—maybe he was married, or religious, or had some other reason for feeling guilty—which might make him worry about which other revelations about his private life his interrogator might know.[12]

When the MIRS program became operational in 1943, the men had no idea which documents would prove most useful. Would official correspondence have the highest level of importance? How about newspapers? Or maybe personal letters would provide the most value. It did not take long, however, to learn that the German soldier *Soldbuch* (passbook) was an unexpected treasure trove of information. These were like individual passports, that, like the cards from German brothels, contained valuable information. Dieter Kober explained "that each German soldier had a so-called [passbook], sort of a type of passport. It included all his pay records as well as where he served. And these things were a gold mine to find out ... what the experience of those units was. It really did not matter where they came from, everything was assumed to have value." Paul Fairbrook joked that whenever a German soldier sneezed, it was documented in his passbook. Paul went on to describe a specific stamp he observed in several passbooks. "After I saw Pa/252/j two or three times with the signature of that 'Pa,' we would know that that was the office in the military headquarters which gave out orders, gave out ribbons and stuff." The "Pa" meant an award, the number was the unit number, the letter was the type of unit, and so forth. "If I got several pay books like that with the same rubber stamp," Fairbrook said, "then I would read in the German military newspaper that Colonel so-and-so got that order, by order of [military headquarters]." From the "'Pa/252' [for example] I would be able to interpolate what each unit did." As Fairbrook said, cross-referencing to German military newspapers was a valuable tool.[13]

German military or civilian newspapers, by themselves, had value for intelligence gathering as well. One man's responsibility was to cull through newspapers, looking for useful articles, but mostly concentrating on death notices. Dieter Kober later explained that "at the beginning of the war, [it] was still possible to deduce locations of [German] units [by reading death notices]." The notices would read: "'Oh, son Lewis, Lieutenant so-and-so died at the Central Front in Russia with the regiment so and-so.' That's exactly what we were waiting for." The death of "son Lewis" was not important, but the name and location of his regiment when he was killed was significant. From the wealth of captured documents, Kober observed that the Germans made tracking the military easy, because "the Germans were quite systematic" in the way they managed their military branches. "But," Kober recalled, "I think we were more systematic in discovering that system."[14]

Whereas the London office was mostly responsible for quickly sending relevant information from captured documents to SHAEF, the men in MIRS at PO Box 1142, as noted earlier, spent much of their time compiling versions of the Red Book. The first order of battle book was produced pre-MIRS by the Pentagon Military Intelligence office, with a pink cover and thus called the "pink book." Using a variety of sources, many anecdotal, it identified

384 German combat divisions in Europe. The British, on the other hand, had produced order of battle books—one yellow and the other brown—that had identified 234 German divisions. It was critical for the Allied forces to know how many combat divisions they were facing, so American and British intelligence understood the need to combine their efforts to give their fighting forces the most accurate information possible. The solution was to create one "Order of Battle of the German Army" book that could be used by both allies. Thus, the birth of the Red Book.

So, what exactly was the Red Book? Lieutenant Charles Winick said, "it was continually updated, and was the document used in the field that contained the most current information on the forces themselves, the units, and their leadership, and the degree of the quality of the leadership." He went on to say that the goal for each iteration of the Red Book was "to provide optimum information in terms of quality and quantity about what was known about [a particular] colonel: how many years had he been there, what was his training, and what decorations had he received, as much information as possible."[15]

Captain Kluge offered his take on the Red Book. He said it was updated every day with new information gleaned from captured documents. With a critical mass of new information, his staff translated and drafted their reports, which were packaged and sent to the Pentagon where a separate staff revised the book. When Kluge was asked who used the Red Book, he said, "The general who would be leading a division [as well as] General Eisenhower [and] General Marshall [who] would see it also. It was the latest intelligence for the commanders in the field. So they knew what they were up against." Kluge added that his staff constantly updated what was happening "in the European theater where the fighting was most intense." Any new information they could uncover on Hermann Göring or Adolf Hitler and their staffs was crucial as well.[16]

Dieter Kober said that "when we first came [to PO Box 1142], let's say in the beginning stages ... we lived together, we ate together, we worked together. One thing we knew immediately, what our objective was, to produce what was called a Red Book." Kober elaborated further, saying that he and his colleagues were proud of their accomplishments. One of his jobs was to track German divisions for the Red Book, and, years later, he remained confident that his research produced accurate results. Exactly how accurate became clear some 65 years later when he was sharing stories with a friend who had been in the German army. Kober was living between Chicago and Dresden, Germany, and he invited his friend over to help him celebrate his 88th birthday in Dresden in 2008. His friend described the Battle of Kursk

(1943) and how he was severely injured as a member of the 255th Infantry Regiment. Kober told him to hold that thought for a moment, then went upstairs, retrieved his old Red Book, copied the section on the 255th Infantry Regiment, and said: "Look here, your division was formed in Dresden [and trained in the Protectorate of Bohemia and Moravia]. That's where you were trained, is that right?" His friend answered: "Yes." Kober went on to describe the history of the division, how its mission changed over time, and where it was located during the war. His friend said that everything he described was "absolutely true." Kober said that "after all these years, this one little incident showed that we were really doing fairly accurate work."[17]

The Red Book was published in three editions, the first in April 1943, the second in February 1944, and the final in March 1945. Each edition was thicker than the previous one, with the third a colossal 670 pages. Producing the Red Book was a nearly around-the-clock effort as it neared completion. Four teams worked in 12- to 16-hour shifts to pull the information together. Professor Tucker did the final edit, and it showed, because the prose was clear and usually non-technical.

The 1944 edition was the most important, because in many ways it provided a blueprint for the invasion of Normandy on D-day. It had other value as well. By identifying commanders, troop strength, divisions and their sub-groupings, and current and previous geographical locations, it was often valuable for interrogating prisoners. As noted earlier (Chapter 4), trainees at Camp Ritchie complained about the time they were forced to spend studying and memorizing portions of the Red Book, but in their assignments, they quickly understood the value of the effort.[18]

To make it abundantly clear that the Red Book was not for general or casual consumption, the title page read: "This document must not fall into enemy hands." The foreword for the 1944 edition noted that the format was similar to the 1943 edition so that anyone familiar with the earlier version could easily follow the new one. It also noted that it was "more accurate, more complete, and easier to use." It also included a new section on the replacement training program and "a much more exhaustive catalog of the types of small units in the German army." The cross-referencing system for divisions was user-friendly, and, finally, there were "complete indices of German names and of German terms and designations used in the book." If users had comments or corrections, they could submit them to an address in the War Department.[19]

Some sections were nuanced for obvious reasons. So, for example, the preparers went into great detail to identify and describe the strength of the German military—primarily in France and Belgium—that the Allies might be facing soon when they invaded Normandy. Thus, in France, German presence was divided into six regional areas, and within those regions, German forces occupied some 40 cities and towns. The Germans also maintained military headquarters in at least 30 Belgian towns and cities. The MIRS staff devoted three pages to France and Belgium in its "Army Administration in Occupied Countries" section, whereas Italy, in which the Allies were heavily engaged at the time, received only a one-paragraph description.

The 1944 edition devoted attention to and also honed in on the German SS. The MIRS researchers were learning more and more about this branch and the purpose for the Red Book was to explain *what* it was and how it functioned. The SS was the political arm of the Wehrmacht, directly under the Nazi Party and Hitler. It functioned with both military and police units. The military side was designated as the Waffen-SS; before the war, the Waffen-SS reported directly to Hitler for whatever purposes he deemed important. With the invasion of Poland, the function shifted to a military function, with *Panzer* (tank) divisions, motorized divisions, and mountain divisions—18 in all. At the time of the 1944 Red Book publication, it was estimated that about half of the divisions were actively engaged in combat, functioning in support with non-SS forces in some cases, acting independently, or, in some cases, taking the lead, bringing in non-SS forces for support.

The SS police function was divided into several parts. By 1944, virtually all police functions in Germany were under the strict control of the SS. They were the local municipal beat cops, the fire fighters, the river patrol force, and the guards who directed citizens to bomb shelters during Allied attacks. The Gestapo was the most notorious of the SS units, operating without civil restraints. It could arrest and/or detain anyone and was not subject to judicial appeal. Further, it had "as its special task, the prevention and liquidation of all activity hostile to the [Nazi] regime." The uniformed Gestapo SS-TV units guarded prisoners in concentration camps. The SS Security Service functioned as the major intelligence arm of the German government, spying on foreign and domestic targets, often cooperating with other intelligence arms of the military. Security police, whose primary function was to conduct criminal investigations, was another arm of the SS police force.[20]

In addition to describing the various functions of the SS, the Red Book authors believed it was important for Americans to be able to recognize who they were up against. To that end, they described the uniforms of the SS branches, including a description and image of the distinctive runic ⚡⚡ symbol on their collars. While the staff of MIRS provided the necessary details for the who and what of the German SS forces, they learned about the dark side of the SS. For example, their research uncovered the notorious *Bataillon der Waffen-SS z.b.V.* (the abbreviation for *zur besonderen Verwendun,* which meant its purpose was for special deployment or special duties) and its *Einsatzkommandos* sub-group of z.b.V., usually composed of 500–1,000 men, whose primary purpose was to exterminate Jews, Polish intellectuals, Romani (gypsies), and communists in the captured territories behind the advancing German fronts. They were also responsible for stealing an estimated 300,000 art treasures from the Eastern war theater, including everything in the Amber Room of the Catherine Palace in Leningrad (St. Petersburg). At the height of their activity in 1942, they were sending an estimated 40–50 railroad cars of loot to Berlin.[21]

The 1945 Red Book volume was larger and more comprehensive than the previous editions. Yet, because the war with Germany was virtually over when it was published in March 1945, the foreword said the book "endeavors to give as complete as possible an analysis of the German order of battle in all its aspects, including historical development and the geographical and other affiliations of units." Later, the introduction section noted that the volume would be useful for ending the war, and it would help to demobilize the German army and demilitarize Germany.

Within, the 1945 Red Book continued to update the earlier versions. For example, the authors continued to believe the SS units were important, but it took a slightly different approach in its description. It opened with the hierarchy of the High Command, followed by SS armies and corps. Next, the division structures were described in more detail. At the time of publication, the MIRS staff had identified 31 SS divisions, but it also believed one or two were under development. The types of divisions conformed to divisions in the regular army, with one important exception, which was that the SS divisions were "long believed to have special privileges in their strength and equipment." At that time (1945), however, the current belief was that those distinctions applied to only a few "crack divisions."' In part, SS divisions held their vaunted image because many were made up of German or ethnic Germanic volunteers, which could be Scandinavians, Dutch, and others. Increasingly, though, non-Germans—mostly East European soldiers—made up more and more of the SS units.

The 1945 edition, as well as earlier versions, provided the most up-to-date detailed analyses of individual military units. For example, for each German corps, the book listed the commander, the chief of staff, if known, the city or region of origin, and its history. In 1944, the commander of the XXV Infantry Corps in 1944 was General Fahrmbacher, his chief of staff was unknown, and its place of origin was Baden-Baden. It had been part of the peacetime standing army, had served in the Western theater, and was currently stationed in France. In 1945, the XXV commanding officer was still General Fahrmbacher and his chief of staff was Colonel I. G. Bader. Since August 1944, the XXV corps was isolated in Brittany. In 1944, another corps, the XXIII, was commanded by General Karl Hilpert, the chief of staff was unknown, the corps' origin city was Bonn, and it had fought in the East and the West. By 1945, the XXIII corps was in the thick of battle in the East, and MIRS no longer had information on the commander nor his chief of staff. The staff had no way of knowing that shortly after publication of the Red Book, General Hilpert and his corps surrendered to the Soviet Red Army on May 7, 1945. He was executed by the Russians two years later.[22]

MIRS staff frequently referred to the Red Book, and clearly it was their pride and joy. But it was not the only publication. There was a Gray Book, whose official title was "Military Headquarters and Installations in Germany." It was issued in March 1944 and tabulated over 10,000 items. Information changed so often that frequent amendments and updates supplemented this volume. A postwar report on the MIRS program lamented that this volume should have gone through updated editions, but it was published in London, and that office was not able to keep up with changes as they occurred.

The Yellow Book was a detailed analysis of the replacement German army. In retrospect, this volume was considered one of the most valuable contributions of the Washington MIRS. It focused on replacement and training units, overall education systems, and where each was located. The Yellow Book spelled out—as far as possible—how replacement units were integrated into field units in their numbering, composition, and functions. MIRS staff were able to predict developments in the field army from changes in the replacement army. By following the replacement army, the MIRS staff could observe the sources of reinforcements, including areas built up and drawn down. The Yellow Book also pointed out that many of the new German soldiers were conscripts from conquered lands, who for obvious reasons would have much preferred to be anywhere else rather than in the German Wehrmacht. Further, as the war was winding down, the information on the non-German soldiers was useful, as the Allies screened surrendering units before they were disbanded.[23]

There was a Green Book too, along with a fascinating story to go along with its origins. Walter Schueman (in the official roster for MIRS his name was spelled Schoeman) had been stationed at Fort Hunt since September 1943, and his major responsibility was analyzing German field units and personalities. Like his colleagues, he was directly involved with pulling together the Red

Book publication. Toward the end of 1944, he was transferred to the London MIRS office. While there, his commanding officer, Major Andrew Choos, came to him and said the American military was going to need "to retrain people to go to the Far East." Choos continued, "We need somebody to organize the school for them. You did very well organizing the school here ... I would like you to do this, but we need a text." To which Schueman replied that the military would "need an [new] order of battle book. That's when I ... created a Japanese Order of Battle book, based on the Red Book." He later joked that "they didn't have any victims, so they picked me [to compile the book]." He continued: "The first thing I told them is I don't know Japanese. The second thing I told them is that I don't intend to learn Japanese. The third was, why pick me?" He took the information provided—all in English—and assembled the Japanese "Order of Battle." He "asked for some Nisei to come over to help," and "when they came over, they couldn't find any fault with my book." As he was compiling the book, in the back of his mind, he wondered how much value it would have. He heard that General Douglas MacArthur had little use for military intelligence and therefore assumed that the Green Book would be a waste of time. He later learned that his work was not wasted, and he received a commendation for his effort.[24]

In addition to the "color" books, MIRS produced other publications as well, over 65 in all. Using the handy mimeograph machine, the staff produced dozens of handbooks that focused on many specific topics of the German army. These were widely disseminated and useful. Another important publication was "The Exploitation of German Documents." It included 23 facsimile documents, plus descriptions of 100 types of documents. Perhaps the most valuable tool was how to understand and analyze the German soldier passbook, along with the German terms used in these books. The 53-page-long documents volume was valuable, but it very well could have been expanded with even more useful information. The problem was that Sergeant Alfred T. Newton, who was in charge of this project, was transferred to London before he was able to complete the book.[25]

In certain instances, a particular topic or discovery would warrant an in-depth analysis. Such as the case with an essay entitled "Political Indoctrination and Morale-Building in the German Army," written by Paul Fairbrook in December 1944. Paul routinely analyzed captured German High Command organizational charts. They remained relatively static, with Hitler in a box at the top, with subordinate positions arranged in the boxes below. One day, sometime shortly after July 20, 1944, Fairbrook was stunned to notice a new position in a box with a line connecting to and thus reporting

Postcard of Fort Hunt as a Coast Artillery fort, c. 1910. (George Washington Memorial Parkway)

Firing of a Coast Artillery 10-inch rifle on disappearing carriage (Fort Hunt had 8-inch rifles on disappearing carriages). From Fort Stevens State Park, Hammond Oregon. (Courtesy of Friends of Old Fort Stevens)

The Bonus Expeditionary Army marching on Washington, DC in 1932. (The National Parks and Conservation Association)

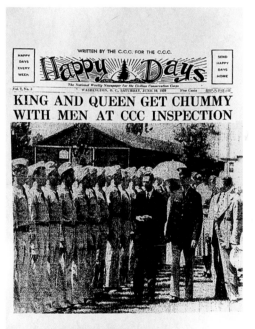

Adolf Hitler addressing the *Reichstag*, March 23, 1933. (https://commons.wikimedia.org/wiki/File:Bundesarchiv_Bild_102-14439, licensed under CC-BY-SA 3.0)

Fort Hunt Civilian Conservation Corps newspaper *Happy Days* (June 10, 1939), featuring the visit from King George VI and Queen Elizabeth, along with Eleanor Roosevelt, to the CCC camp. (George Washington Memorial Parkway)

In January 1939, Gilbert and Eleanor Kraus, a wealthy Jewish American couple, rescued 50 Jewish children from Vienna, Austria, by bringing them to the United States. With the help of others, including members of the Independent Order Brith Sholom (a Jewish fraternal organization based in Philadelphia), and Jews in Berlin and Vienna, the Krauses worked within U.S. immigration law to rescue these children. The 50 children were transported to the United States on board the USS *President Harding*. Here they are waving to the Statue of Liberty in New York Harbor upon arrival on June 7, 1939. (Alamy Images)

Rudolf (Rudy) Pins (right) with his mother and brother Jacob, c. 1930. (Jacob Pins Forum)

"Enclosure A" Fort Hunt Interrogation Center, PO Box 1142. (National Archives and Records Administration)

Main administration building (interior), Fort Hunt Interrogation Center, PO Box 1142. (National Archives and Records Administration)

"Enclosure B" Fort Hunt Interrogation Center, PO Box 1142. (National Archives and Records Administration)

Transport bus for prisoners with blacked-out windows, Fort Hunt Interrogation Center, PO Box 1142. (National Archives and Records Administration)

Prisoner quarters, Fort Hunt Interrogation Center, PO Box 1142. (National Archives and Records Administration)

American soldiers dressed as "German" soldiers transported to assignments in a German "half-track" transport vehicle, Camp Ritchie, Military Intelligence Training Center. (National Archives and Records Adminstration)

Artist rendering by Mark Churms of soldiers near the entrance of Fort Hunt, with transport bus in background. (National Park Service)

Ernest Rosenthal's certificate for completing training at Camp Ritchie. (Courtesy of Stephen and Roberta Rosenthal)

American soldier impersonating *"Der Führer"* with American soldiers dressed as Germans, stirring up the audience, Camp Ritchie, Military Intelligence Training Center. (National Archives and Records Adminstration)

Army trainee interrogating American soldier posing as a German prisoner, Camp Ritchie, Military Intelligence Training Center. (National Archives and Records Adminstration)

German prisoners of war at Fort Hunt Interrogation Center, PO Box 1142. (National Archives and Records Administration)

Werner Henke, the only German prisoner shot and killed while trying to escape from Fort Hunt. (Bundesarchiv-Bild-146-1980-115-23a)

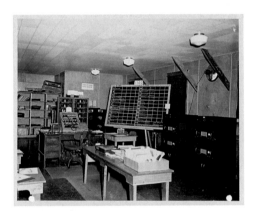

Chief monitor control room and control board, "Enclosure A" Fort Hunt Interrogation Center, PO Box 1142. (National Archives and Records Administration)

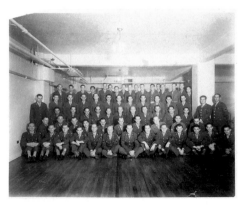

Fort Hunt interrogators, Fort Hunt Interrogation Center, PO Box 1142. (National Archives and Records Administration)

Editing and evaluation room, Fort Hunt Interrogation Center, PO Box 1142. (National Archives and Records Administration)

Surrender of *U-234* to the USS *Sutton*, May 15, 1945. (National Archives and Records Administration)

Lieutenant General Ulrich Kessler's basic personnel record photo after he was captured and sent to Fort Hunt following the surrender of *U-234*. (National Archives and Records Administration)

U-234 escorted into Portsmouth, New Hampshire Harbor. (Courtesy of *CJ Foster's Daily Democrat,* May 28, 2008)

In 1951 or 1952, Rudy Pins drove Gustav Hilger and his wife, Maria, to Fort Hunt. The hut in which Hilger stayed while at the fort (shown here) was converted into a restroom. (Photo donated by Rudy Pins. George Washington Memorial Parkway.)

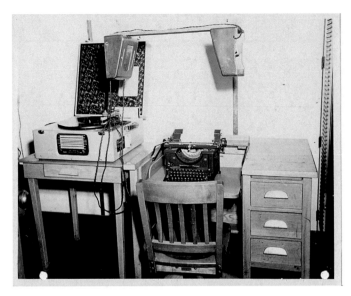

Monitor listening station with a Memovox reproducing machine used to monitor prisoner conversations, Fort Hunt Interrogation Center, PO Box 1142. (National Archives and Records Administration)

Hidden eavesdropping microphone in prisoner quarters, Fort Hunt Interrogation Center, PO Box 1142. (National Archives and Records Administration)

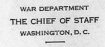

WAR DEPARTMENT

THE CHIEF OF STAFF

WASHINGTON, D. C.

OFFICIAL BUSINESS

WASHINGTON D. C.
MAR 15
12-PM
1946

Staff Sgt. A.L.Willson,Jr.,
Sgt. Arno J. Mayer,
260 Fort Washington Avenue,
New York 32,
New York.

WAR DEPARTMENT

THE CHIEF OF STAFF

WASHINGTON

15 March 1946

Dear Sergeants Willson and Mayer:

Mrs. Eisenhower has been intermittently ill and always very busy. Consequently she asked me whether I could find the time to answer your very nice note written on the 11th of March. It is so unusual for anyone to take the trouble, later, to repeat their thanks for a casual ride that she was quite touched by your courtesy and wanted to make sure that your note was acknowledged. Both she and I look for opportunities to pick up smart looking soldiers - not only because we like them but because we invariably learn something from them.

Sincerely,

Dwight D. Eisenhower

Staff Sgt. A.L.Willson,Jr.,
Sgt. Arno J. Mayer,
260 Fort Washington Avenue,
New York 32,
New York.

Envelope and letter from General Dwight D. Eisenhower to Leslie Willson and Arno Mayer thanking them for thanking Mamie Eisenhower for giving them a ride. (Donated by Leslie Willson and Arno Mayer, George Washington Memorial Parkway)

Artist rendering by Mark Churms of the Military Intelligence Research Service (MIRS) office based on a description by Paul Fairbrook. He actually identified several of the men in the image. (National Park Service)

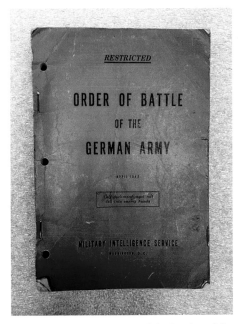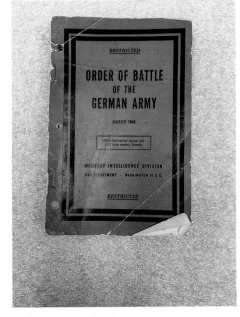

The 1943 and 1945 editions of the "Red Book," and the "Order of Battle of the German Army," MIRS Publication. (George Washington Memorial Parkway Collection)

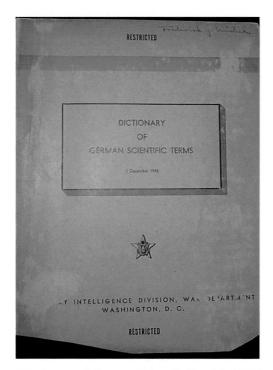

"Dictionary of German Scientific Terms," MIRS publication. (George Washington Memorial Parkway)

"Handbook on German Army Identification," MIRS Publication (George Washington Memorial Parkway)

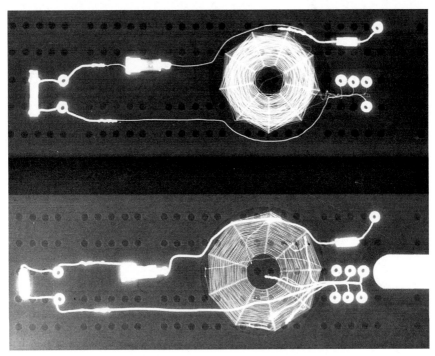

X-ray image of a radio transmitter hidden inside a cribbage board. This would be included in a "care" package sent to American POWs. (George Washington Memorial Parkway)

European theater barter kit (left) and Pacific theater barter kit (right) carried by U.S. Airmen to use to "barter" for better treatment if shot down. Image courtesy of J.M. Caiella/U.S. Naval Institute

Dr. Heinz Schlicke. (Wikimedia Commons)

Dr. Wernher von Braun. (National Aeronautics and Space Administration)

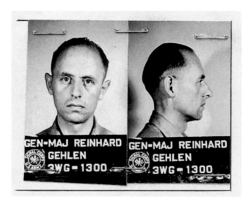

Major General Reinhard Gehlen basic personnel record photo. (National Archives and Records Administration)

Julius Streicher at Nuremberg. He was convicted of crimes against humanity on October 1, 1946 and hanged on October 16, 1946. (Wikimedia Commons in the public domain)

Japanese General Hiroshi Oshima meeting with Adolph Hitler (1942). Image taken by anonymous German photographer. (Wikimedia Commons)

Hermann Göring with Paul Kubala the day after he surrendered to the Americans, May 7, 1945. He died by suicide, October 15, 1946. (Alamy Images)

American soldiers at Fort Hunt. Image provided by Rudy Pins, who is in the back row, far right. (George Washington Memorial Parkway)

Fort Hunt veterans at the Fort Hunt Reunion 2007. (National Park Service)

USS *Oklahoma* memorial, Pearl Harbor, Hawaii. (National Park Service)

Vincent Santucci and Brandon Bies at the monument commemorating the service of the soldiers at PO Box 1142 at Fort Hunt Park. (National Park Service)

directly to the *Führer*. The new position was the National Socialist Propaganda Affairs Officer, and Fairbrook understood that the position was created in direct response to the assassination attempt on Hitler's life on July 20. Paul knew it had important ramifications for the German political and military hierarchy, and he spent several weeks learning as much as he could about this new development. He shared his findings in a report.

Paul understood that for a very long time, the Germans believed that morale and inner cohesion were critical components for an effective fighting force. Under Hitler, these beliefs grew even stronger, which led to integrating political indoctrination with military morale building. Fairbrook observed that in the previous two years, military reverses had seriously dampened troop morale, which was normal for any war, but of equal concern, the Nazi hierarchy feared that "the political reliability of the entire army was in question." As a result, Hitler and his inner circle devised a plan to "instill in the German solider not only a sense of loyalty to his military superiors but also to the National Socialist Party and government and to insure political control at all levels."

Toward the end of 1943, Hitler was growing increasingly dissatisfied with the existing system and started to revamp the political indoctrination and morale building program, so Fairbrook observed that the political side was becoming an obsession for him. In November, the positions of National Socialist guidance officers came into being, followed in December with the creation of the National Socialist Guidance Staff as part of the Armed Forces High Command, reporting directly to Hitler for direction. Then, in February 1944, Field Marshall Wilhelm Keitel—on direct orders from Hitler—established National Socialist Guidance Staff officers in each branch of the German military, who would report directly to Hitler. All of this seemed a good idea until July 20, 1944, when General Claus von Stauffenberg and his accomplices unsuccessfully attempted to assassinate Hitler. Following the attempt on Hitler's life, not surprisingly, Fairbrook observed that "the National Socialist guidance program has been enormously intensified and great efforts have been made to assure the political reliability of the general staff." On July 29, Chief of the General Army Staff, General Heinz Guderian required every member of the General Staff Corps to publicly declare that they were or had become dedicated members of the Nazi Party. If any could not do so, they were required to resign.

From that point until Fairbrook prepared his report (December 21, 1944), the Nazi indoctrination and morale reorganization moved quickly. National Socialist guidance officers became the norm at every level, from army groups, through armies, corps, and divisions. Regiments and battalions on down did not have permanent guidance officers, but each had designated officers to fulfill those responsibilities. They were appointed by senior officers in the next highest level (for example, division commanders would appoint regimental guidance officers). Finally, all political, indoctrination, and morale-building speeches, publications, films, and everything else were produced from or approved by central headquarters. Everything became much more doctrinaire, adhering closely to the Nazi Party line. Clearly, after the assassination attempt on Hitler, he was growing more paranoid and was devoting much more attention to the political side of the Third Reich.[26]

Another specialized report was on the "Organization of the High Command of the German Army (Fall 1944)," also produced by Paul Fairbrook. He traced the evolution of the Nazi military hierarchy from Hitler's rise to power too late in 1944. Early on, Hitler recognized that to achieve cohesion between the political and military arms of Germany, he would need to take control of both, but for overall day-to-day management of the three branches of the military—army, navy, and air force—he would need a High Command staff of very senior officers. This replaced the single overall leader of the previous office of the German War Ministry. Early on, the High Command structure worked relatively well, but when the military started fighting on multiple fronts, especially during the last two years of the war, the system did not function well. The High Command system required adaptations, recognizing the different challenges of each front, which it did not make. Further, as the war progressed, and as military reverses became the norm rather than the exception, Hitler grew more distrustful of his commanders, continuously interfering in operations to such a degree that the German general staff was reduced to "theater command staff, which did not even have complete independence in the conduct of operations in its own theater of war."[27]

Dieter Kober, like his colleagues, spent much of his time at Fort Hunt working on the Red Book. He also became the MIRS expert on Hitler Youth. Every document relating to this program was directed to him, and before long he realized that there was great value in the collective pieces associated with understanding this program. Early on, nearly every German soldier had been in the Hitler Youth program and many still carried the membership cards with them. These cards showed where the soldiers were from and demonstrated to Dieter that German soldiers valued their involvement in the youth program in their development as soldiers. Kober also found much useful information about the youth program by pouring through newspapers. Over a three-month period, he assembled everything he had gathered and published a booklet on the Hitler Youth program.[28]

On occasion, MIRS staff would uncover a nugget of information that they believed needed to be brought to the immediate attention of the Pentagon staff. Captain John Kluge described how the system worked in one case. The soldier assigned to German generals had been studying one German general—who was not named—and concluded that some of his action exhibited erratic behavior. Kluge called him a "nut job," who likely would not use good judgment as a commander. The German general expert learned that the "nut job" general was being transferred from division x to division y. He passed that information along to the specialist on German military units. Although not trained in psychology, the men in MIRS often could spot something or someone like this general that seemed significant.

Sometimes, Kluge and his men would be fascinated by something out of the ordinary, which they would try to track down. "We could never understand why the Russians were able to move so fast," he said. What he and his staff discovered was that the Russians "would [carry large liquid containing] tanks on railroad cars. And whatever they saw in the countryside ... cabbage, rhubarb, anything would go in this tank [to make their] soup. ... [They were on the constant] move toward Berlin. And if you asked a Russian soldier where he was going, he was going to Berlin to kill Germans." [29]

As often happens in times of war, whether in foxholes or offices, colleagues working closely together, who may have not known each other before, become good friends. This was the case with Dieter Kober and Paul Fairbrook. They met and became friends at Fort Hunt. After D-day, the volume of captured documents arriving in the London MIRS was so overwhelming, both men and several colleagues were transferred to London to help with the influx. American military intelligence quickly recognized that their expertise was more desperately needed in the analysis program, and after six weeks, they were sent back to PO Box 1142, where they stayed for the remainder of the war.

Paul Fairbrook and his colleagues at Fort Hunt took tremendous pride in their work. "We were very, very knowledgeable at MIRS about the German situation," Fairbrook later recalled. He went on to say that "some of us, I think, probably knew more about the conduct of the war than a lot of other people in the army. ... We knew about the disaster of our paratroopers in Nijmegen in Holland, where the Germans had been tipped off and killed so many of our troops. ... We knew an awful lot whether we did it from our documents or because we were so close to the Pentagon—but we really knew what was going on." Fairbrook also noted that his understanding of German organizations, which were well-defined and a major part of his responsibility at Fort Hunt, was enormously helpful in his later career. He ran a food service program at several universities, and by translating the organizational structures that were engrained in his psyche from Fort Hunt, he understood the university politics of who was in charge of which programs, who reported to whom, who he needed to keep happy, and who he needed to ensure was never unhappy.[30]

Fort Hunt and MIRS helped Dieter Kober in his later career as well, but in a very different way. Kober became a famous musician and music conductor after the war. With his assignments at PO Box 1142 and the Pentagon, he had spare time to watch the National Symphony Orchestra and chamber music in Washington, DC. He was allowed to travel as well, and saw the Philadelphia Orchestra, the Boston Symphony, and other groups on the East Coast. He even snuck in to watch Arturo Toscanini conducting the NBC Symphony Orchestra and thought he also might have been the only person caught and escorted out of the studio where it performed. In addition to seeing these notable ensembles, he also brought his cello to his assignments. He was not able to practice as much as he would have liked, but he practiced when he could and joined others in amateur chamber groups. Also, in the Fort Hunt barracks, Dieter would stand on the footlocker at the base of his bed and practice conducting, as if he led a major orchestra under his baton.[31]

John Kluge used his Fort Hunt experience in his later business ventures. While at PO Box 1142, he learned that with just a small sliver of information, he could fool German officers that he possessed far more knowledge about certain things, than he really knew (Chapter 5). He used similar techniques later in his media business. He was interested in acquiring a particular program for his television station. He planted a story that he knew other stations would pick up. He would make sure that they thought he was willing to pay a great deal of money to purchase a particular program. In reality, he had no interest in that show, but he really wanted to buy another program. His competitors would go to great lengths to bid on the show they thought he wanted, thus depleting their resources. He would then swoop in and buy the program he really wanted for a much more reasonable price.[32]

The MIRS program was a remarkable success in many ways. The men recruited for the assignment had no background or prior training in military intelligence, but their lack of previous experience was offset by with their intelligence and their desire to defeat the Nazis. Most had their own axes to grind. Some lost family in the Holocaust; others were forced to leave everything behind when they and their families left Germany. Most would look back on their work with satisfaction, and the hierarchy in the War Department agreed. Several months after the war with Germany had ended, the U.S. Army did an after-action assessment of the MIRS program. The report concluded, saying that "MIRS performed a vitally necessary function with a degree of success which was universally acknowledged by intelligence personnel of the British and United States Armies." The report went on to say that "more important for the future, perhaps, the two branches of MIRS [London and Fort Hunt] finally evolved the most efficient and scientific techniques for the reception and cataloging of enemy documents, their circulation to all interested agencies, and their exploitation for intelligence purposes." The analysis concluded with the statement that the World War II MIRS program "pioneered in a field of strategic intelligence which may take on added importance in times to come."[33]

CHAPTER 8

The Creamery That Did Not Know How to Make Cream

"Writers had to know how to write badly, and it was a requirement. They couldn't write well."

SILVIO BEDINI

In the fall of 1966, the CBS television network launched a new comedy series, *Hogan's Heroes*, set in a World War II German POW camp—*Stalag 13*. The show continued for five seasons, and in its first year, it was one of television's ten most-watched series. While it was popular with the general audience, some Americans, particularly World War II veterans, thought it was inappropriate to suggest that there was anything funny about the Nazis. What few television viewers knew, however, was that the three major German actors—Sergeant Schultz (John Banner), Colonel Klink (Werner Klemperer, son of the famous classical musical conductor Otto Klemperer), and General Albert Burkhalter (Leon Aschkenasy who went by Leon Askin) —were Jews in real life who had fled Germany and Austria when Hitler came to power. Askin had a particularly compelling story. He fled to the United States from Austria in 1940, after receiving beatings from the Nazi storm troopers and SS. His parents were murdered in the Treblinka death camp. On the Allied (POW) side, Corporal Louis LeBeau (Robert Clary) was Jewish, born in France, and imprisoned in a Nazi concentration camp.

At least one Fort Hunt veteran loved the show. Silvio Bedini watched episode after episode with his family and especially enjoyed watching Colonel Hogan and his men when they hid radios in coffee pots. "You know," he would tell his family, "that's not too far off from what really happened." Years later, when Bedini learned that he could describe his experiences in detail, he elaborated on the comment to his family. He said *Hogan's Heroes* was so true to real life, he was convinced that someone who had worked in Military Intelligence Service-X (MIS-X) during the war, must have been the writer for the show.

Silvio Bedini was born in Connecticut in 1917. When he was nine, he had surgery and was bedridden for several weeks in recuperation. He was already an avid reader, and one day he read a magazine article that described something called cryptography. He wanted to find out more about this word and what it meant. He learned that cryptography was a process in which plain transmitted text is converted into unintelligible text such that only the intended receiver could decode and read it. It could also be used to authenticate a person's identity. Before long, cryptography became Silvio's obsession, something that stayed with him for the rest of his life. At this tender age, he had no idea that, later on, he would become the expert who developed a cryptographic system that would allow American POWs to communicate with him and others at Fort Hunt.

In the intervening period, he attended and graduated from Columbia University. After the Japanese attack on Pearl Harbor, he knew he wanted to do his part in military service, and, if at all possible, he wanted to do something in cryptography. He joined the army, and his first assignment was in Chicopee Falls, New York. He took and passed a correspondence course in cryptography and hoped that would be his ticket to an assignment in the field. One day, out of the blue, his commanding officer called him into his office and told him to pack his belongings because he was going to be reassigned to Washington, DC. Later, he discovered that one of his professors from Columbia had intervened on his behalf and contacted several friends in the army to vouch for what a wonderful asset Bedini would be in military intelligence.

He was assigned to PO Box 1142 but not as a cryptographer at first. When he arrived in 1942, the MIS-Y program (interrogation and monitoring) was underway, but he knew that it was not for him. He joked that his understanding of German was as strong as his understanding of Yugoslavian—none at all. He struggled for three months in the MIS-Y program, but then he was assigned to a new building called the "Creamery," in which he became the first cryptographer in the U.S. Army. He was placed in charge of creating a coding system to communicate with American POWs held in German camps, which became a critical part of the MIS-X program.

Like much of World War II military intelligence, the Americans borrowed from the British cryptography system, which had served them well. Bedini studied that system and quickly decided that it was more complicated than what he needed. The British system used sophisticated mathematical equations, which was a problem for Silvio because he recalled that "I flunked every course in arithmetic and mathematics through school." Bedini said, "I never passed one. I had to take them all over. ... So, consequently, I have no mathematical skill at all." Bedini used what he found useful from the British cryptology system and created a system that worked amazingly well.

Enlisted men assigned to Fort Hunt, whose grammar and handwriting skills were marginal, wrote coded letters to American POWs. "Writers had to know how to write badly, and it was a requirement. They couldn't write well," Bedini said. "This is one of the things that we were very careful about. ... It's easier to write better, than to write poorly. When you try to write poorly, it never comes out right." The purpose was simple: he did not want the Germans to suspect that intelligence officers, using multi-syllable words, were the ones writing the letters using hidden meanings. In fact, the letters that appeared to come from family or friends, did indeed contain hidden messages alerting POWs that special care packages were on the way. POWs wrote back to say they received the messages; they used the same coding system to report on any intelligence they had picked up in the camps. One of the most difficult aspects of Bedini's program was keeping track of who wrote letters to whom, which kind of stationery was used (whether it was perfumed or not), along with any other distinguishing elements that might be detected by the Germans if not included in the letters.

Another soldier stationed to Fort Hunt, Augustus W. Soule, Jr., provided more detail as to how the cryptography system worked. He said there were about 30 letter writers who worked separately from the other functions in the Creamery. For his work, he said he had complete freedom in what was included in the letters, except for the embedded codes, which told prisoners that a package was coming, and where to check in the package for whatever was smuggled in. He did not recall receiving letters back from American prisoners, but he recognized that several letters he wrote went to a school friend he knew from before the war. When the war was over, and he was able to reunite with his buddy, he learned that yes, indeed, his friend had received his letters.[1]

Later in the war, as more Americans were held in POW camps, and as the volume of incoming and outgoing mail grew, the cryptology section started working with the families of some of the POWs to prepare the returning letters. Daniel Buck, one of the men assigned to Bedini's section, reported that he and his colleagues would decode the information, then send the letters to the families; but, when the families would write a response, they would include the coded message prepared by MIS-X. Thus, the continuity of language, penmanship, and stationery would remain constant.

Silvio Bedini created the cryptography system, but the big question was: would it work? Silvio sent the first message from Fort Hunt to Colonel Albert P. (Bud) Clark, an airman held at *Stalag Luft III,* in Sagan, Germany (later part of Poland). The camp was famous as the site of the escape attempt known as the "Great Escape." Colonel Clark not only received the coded message; he sent a return message that was short, reading simply that he was "with 87 officers, period." Then he asked MIS-X to "send instructions, period." Thus, the coding system and the transmission mechanism both worked.

Once Bedini and the men in *Stalag Luft III* recognized that the system worked, they began communicating back and forth. On one occasion, the code correspondent in the camp wrote that the Army Air Corps needed to repair the forward hatch on the B-17, because it often stuck, which was dangerous in case of emergencies. Mentioning the B-17 would, of course, be a tip-off to the Germans if they intercepted the message, so the code for the airplane was a "fort." Another message from the camp passed along the warning to anyone who was trying to evade capture to avoid Tours, France, because it was heavily patrolled.[2]

Bedini was instrumental in establishing a training program to teach Americans the coding system. By the end of the war, some 250 officers were trained as trainers, who in turn trained 352,000 airmen to use Bedini's cryptographic system. By the end of the war, 95,532 American servicemen fell into enemy hands, and nearly all were held in POW camps. Through the cryptology program, at least one officer in each camp was designated as the correspondent with MIS-X. As noted above, they would provide useful information about anything they could observe—such as troop movements, enemy morale, and so forth—plus they would receive valuable information from the United States, critical for their morale. Some 737 American prisoners successfully escaped from POW camps, and in most cases, they used assistance provided by MIS-X.[3]

In reality, the cryptographic communication system worked better than Bedini could have imagined. Some 60 years later, Lawrence Dennis recalled how well the system worked. His plane was shot down over Norway in 1943; he was captured by the Germans and sent to a POW camp in Germany. When he arrived in the camp, a fellow prisoner taught him how to read and send the coded messages, a skill he picked up very quickly. He did not recall all of the messages he sent or received, but one stood out in his memory. The letter was from a girl by the name of Erma Watkins, who was supposed to be a friend from his high school. He did not know anyone by that name but was amazed at how much she knew about him, his hometown, and his high school. In one message from his "girlfriend, Erma," there was a coded message that read: "General Eisenhower [is] planning for your welfare and safety. Sit tight and await orders."

The accuracy of the details in letters was important, but, in addition to the morale boosts from General Eisenhower, letters would also announce that a particular package would arrive soon, containing a cribbage board. A radio would be embedded in that board. In many ways, these radios were crucial for prisoners' mental states. As Dennis recalled, he and his fellow POWs "knew how the war was going from the various radios [that had been smuggled into camp] and so we knew it was going to last about so long and that was it. When the Battle of the Bulge took place, we heard about that. Boy, were we downhearted for a while until Patton [came to the rescue]." In addition to the general news, Dennis learned to monitor the BBC broadcasts, because often embedded messages were tucked into the programing.

Much of what Dennis recalled was his life in the prison camp. He said the duress and depression were often nearly overwhelming. One man committed suicide by running to the outer fence where the German guards shot him. "From that point on, anybody we thought was distressed and thinking about committing suicide, we looked after him. If we noticed that he might be thinking about that, we tried to take him into our comradeship and keep him from doing that." In addition to the radios smuggled into camp, Dennis was able to rig a shortwave radio as well. He remained in the camp until the war was over. When he and his fellow soldiers were liberated, he was sent directly to Fort Hunt for debriefing. He was asked how the encoding system had worked and was shown the letters he had written, for the purpose of determining whether he or someone else, like a German eavesdropper, was the author. He was also asked about the interrogation he had received from the Germans when he was captured.[4]

Spencer Gulick was another airman who benefited from the MIS-X code system. Gulick left Columbia University after three years to join the Army Air Corps. He was piloting an A-20 bomber over North Africa when he was shot down and taken prisoner by the Germans. He was transferred to *Stalag Luft III*. The Germans selected this site because it was far from the war zones and because of its sandy soil, thinking it would be virtually impossible for prisoners to tunnel under the camp and escape. Clearly, they neither understood the intelligence nor the ingenuity of their captives. In 1943, three men successfully escaped through a tunnel whose entrance was covered by a wooden horse that was ostensibly used for exercise, but, in reality, it was used to cover the tunnel. Spencer Gulick described the second escape, which became legendary, known as the "Great Escape." At 28-feet deep and over 335-feet long, this tunnel was a major undertaking. In March 1943, 78 prisoners crawled through the tunnel, but unlike the earlier effort, all but three were captured. More than half were summarily executed.

Gulick was present during the Great Escape but did not participate. He took part in the cultural activities of prisoners, however, including singing in the performance of Handel's *Messiah* in December 1944. His connection to MIS-X was tangential. He knew about the code system, participated in the program, but was not the principal code communicator in the camp. He remained in the camp until it was liberated in 1945. He was sent to Fort Hunt, where he talked about using the code system, as well as the interrogation techniques used on Allied pilots by the Germans.[5]

Like Leonard Gulick, David Jones and Thomas Griffin spent some of their wartime experience in *Stalag Luft III*. Jones's plane was shot down in North Africa in December 1942, and Griffin's plane was shot down over Sicily on July 4, 1943. They both ended up in the same prison camp. Griffin joked that he followed Jones anywhere he went, and, indeed, their careers to that point, were in tandem. Early in the war, both men were participants and survivors in one of the most daring and celebrated events for American airmen—the Doolittle Raid on Tokyo on April 18, 1942. Jones was a pilot on one plane and Griffin was the navigator on another. With their experiences with the Doolittle Raiders and their incarceration at *Stalag Luft III,* they became lifelong friends, so that 60 years after the war they could still have fun teasing each other. Here, they debated whether American airmen were required to attempt to escape or not:

Thomas Griffin: "I think we were told it was your duty to try to escape."

David Jones: "No. No. It was not."

Griffin: "Didn't they say that?"

Jones: "With the British, it's a requirement. With us, no, there was [never a requirement to try to escape]."

Griffin: "I never realized that. We were right with them doing what they were doing."

Jones: "But you can. That's what we did, what everybody did. But no, it was not—it was not a written [requirement]."

What they were referring to was their planning for and participation with the British POWs in the "Great Escape." Jones described participating with a group of two other Americans working their shifts digging the tunnel with spoons. By the time the tunnel was finished, the Germans had separated the American and British POWs, such that Jones and Griffin were not candidates for the escape group. Both expressed relief years later that they were not included, since 50 of the 78 escapees were executed.

Neither Jones nor Griffin were directly tied into the coding system connected to Fort Hunt, but both were well aware of the program. They provided valuable perspectives on how the system worked for the majority of prisoners who were involved in its operation. For example, they knew that three or four of their fellow POWs were sending and receiving coded messages. One colleague was specially assigned to monitoring the BBC for its coded messages; the others were tied directly to MIS-X. Griffin understood that the American military calculated that a percentage of airmen would be captured, and based on that arithmetic, "a certain number of people got these [coded messages]." When the men in the barracks heard that there was a letter from "Aunt Tilly in Springfield, it was a coded message." Griffin and Jones were also aware of when "care" packages arrived with decks of cards, Monopoly sets, baseballs with transmitters, and so forth. The men tied into PO Box 1142 knew what to look for when a package was due to arrive. Others would ensure that upon the arrival of packages, the German guards would have no chance to inspect the contents. Several prisoners cobbled together parts from the "care" packages or from German guards to build and maintain radios.

Griffin recalled that "he got the job of securing these illegal things—maps and civilian clothes, or clothes that had been made to look like civilian clothes, and escape equipment—that came into the camp that had to be hidden. And that became my job, to put them up in attics, or down under the floor, between the wallboards, or someplace, so that we could get them when we needed them, and so that it would be difficult for the Germans to find them." He "thought we had a real wonderful [hiding] place, but they found it." He had to spend several weeks in the "cooler"—solitary confinement.

Jones and Griffin also provided information about their German guards. The prisoners constantly called the Germans "goons," which, of course, in vernacular American English was extremely derogatory. When the guards asked for the origin of the word goon, they were told it was short for "German Officer or Non-Com." The POWs were aware that the Germans had plants that they would place in certain barracks to snoop. These men were referred to as "ferrets." The Americans developed an elaborate system to determine if a new prisoner was a ferret. They would quiz them on history, baseball, geography, and other topics; if they determined that they were ferrets, they would feed them false information that they knew would be passed along to the camp commander. Griffin and Jones were certain that the Germans did not eavesdrop on the barracks with listening devices. Instead, they were obsessed that the British and Americans were building tunnels, and their surveillance efforts were devoted to trying to sniff out the diggers.[6]

The men confined to *Stalag Luft III*, or other prison camps with *"luft"*, were treated much better than most POWs. The *luft* was the designation of airmen, and Hermann Göring, who was the commander of the *Luftwaffe*, convinced Hitler that airmen, no matter which country they flew for, were special, and thus should receive special treatment. When Griffin was caught hiding contraband in his barracks, his punishment was time in the cooler. In other prison camps, the punishment likely would have been much more severe. When the prisoners who participated in the Great Escape were captured, Hitler wanted to summarily execute all escapees. Göring made the case that German pilots held in Allied prison camps likely would face the same fate if the executions took place. Göring partially prevailed in that not all were shot, but Hitler insisted on carrying out the executions of two-thirds of the escapees.[7]

David Jones and Thomas Griffin did not remember and were fairly certain that they did not have kits to assist them in avoiding capture if their planes went down. The escape and evasion men at Fort Hunt recognized this deficiency and went to work preparing survival kits. The reason was obvious. Avoiding capture altogether was the highest priority. Developed primarily for airmen, the escape and evasion package included heavy shoes, understanding that someone might need to walk long distances. They also carried two passport photos in waterproof casings, a tiny compass, thin tissue maps of areas where they might need to travel, and a thin, serrated wire, known as a Gigli surgical saw, that could cut through steel. In their kits, they also carried a signaling mirror, fishhooks and line, bandages, iodine, gold coins, and halazone tablets to purify water. They did not carry anything that might indicate their unit or their unit's location.

The army understood the importance of providing not only survival equipment but also training on how to use the kits and general survival techniques. To that end, they brought in Henry J. Staudigl, a former Hollywood screenwriter, and Robert Kloss, trained in army intelligence, to produce a manual for the program. Kloss later recalled, "one of my jobs was to open the safe each morning, take out the reading material consisting of different manuals, and put them on the tables to read." From these materials, "we produced a three-inch-thick, eight-and-a-half by 13 hardbound manual entitled 'Evasion and Escape.'" Kloss worked in a building referred to as "the Schoolhouse," and MIS-X would bring in "groups of intelligence officers, all from the [Army] Air Corps, and after training they'd go back to their air bases to relate their instructions to air force personnel." Additionally, about 100 "Air Corps personnel that were shot down and evaded capture with the help of the

French Underground, ... came to Fort Hunt and related their experiences in classes, which provided helpful information for intelligence officers."[8]

James Ahrens was one of the intelligence officers brought to Fort Hunt for training as an instructor in the escape and evasion program in 1943. After he completed his three-month course, he was sent to East Coast and southern airfields primarily to train B-17 pilots. First he would "give a brief lecture about methods of escaping and avoiding capture. And then we would show a film which had been prepared by the army, regarding the kind of interrogations that the Germans or people who captured them were given." Then "an individual officer or enlisted man who had been shot down ... over Europe and who had successfully escaped and come back to the States or escaped to England," would share his experiences. "Most of them managed to escape capture and a good many of them had been shot down over France, some of them over Germany." Pilots were told that the French Maquis (underground resistance fighters) "were very active and they were prepared to help anybody to escape the German occupation." Finally, if they were not able to connect with the French Underground, pilots were instructed to head south/southwest toward Spain, using the compass in their escape kits. If they could somehow get through the Pyrenees Mountains, then beat many odds and make their way across Spain to Gibraltar, which was British and remained under Allied control, they would be safe. Even if they could just get to Spain, which was neutral, their options were much better than remaining in France.[9]

Ralph Patton was one of the lucky airmen who was shot down but evaded capture. He piloted a B-17 for eight successful missions, and on the ninth, he and his crew were shot down. They parachuted into the interior of Brittany and were fortunate to connect with the French Underground. Patton did have an escape kit, and he said the water purification tablets and the other items were useful, but the silk map was virtually useless, because it covered too large an area. When he was asked whether he had attended the briefings on escaping and avoiding capture, Patton said he was "not sure that the intelligence briefing on how to evade capture was of much value because 90 percent of it was luck. You had to be where the Germans weren't." The French Underground hid him and his crew for 63 days, then "with the help of British Intelligence Service MI9 and the British Royal Navy, the 15th Motor Gunboat Flotilla, a PT-type boat came into the shore on the northern coast of France and took 25 of us back to jolly old England."[10]

Another pilot, David Childs said that before each flight, pilots in his P-47 Thunderbolt squadron would exchange their billfolds for their escape kits. He said they were "about six-inches square and little more than an inch thick. They fit in the patch pocket of our flying suits. They are fully packed with survival and escape gear: cloth map, compass, chocolate power bar, water purifying tablets, and more." He also thought the escape and evasion training was helpful. Or more accurately, the kit and the training would have been helpful, except that David Childs was not as fortunate as others described above.

On November 17, 1944, his P-47 was hit while he was attacking two German locomotives. The cockpit caught on fire. He was lucky to bail out, but when he hit the ground, in addition to the severe burns he received, he found that his escape kit had been ripped away from his flight suit. Many thoughts were passing through his mind as he tried to deal with his predicament. He knew he was in Germany, and one thing came to his vague memory from the escape and evasion course: "Avoid civilians. In Germany, your chances are better with the military." He heard voices, and tried to find cover, but he could barely move. The voices came closer, and finally he heard the accented command: "Hands up!" The next thing he heard from the same man was, "For you, the war is over. Will you have a cigarette?" He had been captured by a German patrol. Childs was transported to a German hospital in *Stalag IV-B*, then to three other POW camps for six months. During this time, his bride and family did not know whether he was alive or dead, because he was listed as Missing in Action. After a very long recuperation, he returned to his family farm in Eastern Oregon.[11]

In addition to the cryptology, and escape and evasion programs, the "Warehouse" building at PO Box 1142 housed the technical section of the MIS-X program. Beginning in early 1943, officers and technicians started arriving to staff what would become the best kept secret program at Fort Hunt. Years later, when National Park Service staff started its oral history program with veterans that had been stationed at Fort Hunt, men in the MIS-Y or MIRS programs admitted that during the war, they were completely clueless as to what was happening in the Warehouse. Men knew something about the MIS-Y program, in that they frequently saw German soldiers in Fort Hunt, wandering the grounds or participating in sports activities. But it is probably safe to say that the only ones who knew what was going on in MIS-X were its participants. Some of the men in other programs, like Walter Cini, who was in MIS-Y, recalled some 60 years later that the men from MIS-X "were buddies [that we] spent many hours doing all sorts of things. ... But I never heard anything about what they were doing."[12]

The specialists in the Warehouse were developing escape and communication devices for the American soldiers held in POW camps. Borrowing from the success of the British MI9 POW model, which had a two-and-a-half-year head start, Captain Robley Winfrey gave his men spending cash and sent them into town to buy shoe brushes, shaving brushes, ping-pong sets, cribbage boards, Monopoly boards, checker boards, smoking pipes, baseballs, talcum powder in wax tubes, and just about anything they thought might be useful for hiding radios, maps, compasses, money, fake passports, and other escape tools. One of the men inside the Warehouse was Lloyd Shoemaker. Years later, he described the inner workings of MIS-X in his *The Escape Factory* (1990). His main job was finding and purchasing items that could hide useful items. He helped develop the scheme to sneak these items through the Germans to American POWs, but he also had intimate knowledge of the workings of MIS-X.

Through trial and error, the team discovered some items worked, others did not. American game boards—like chess boards—made from cardboard had limited use. On the other hand, chess pieces were perfect to hide things in. Eventually, they discovered that cribbage boards and baseballs were great for concealing radios. Cribbage boards were perfect for many uses and could even conceal small guns! A deck of cards was perfect to hide pieces of maps. Ping-pong paddles were ideal to hide documents, maps, and money. POWs were instructed to peal the cards or paddles apart and inside they would find pieces that, when put together, would provide a detailed map of the area around their POW camp. Smoking pipes and pens could conceal compasses. Pieces for printing presses could be smuggled into camps, and toothbrushes were just right for applying ink. With this crude system, prisoners could produce passports, counterfeit money, and other documents. By the end of the war, the 20 men assigned to the escape and evasion unit became more and more creative and brazen in creating their package preparation. Lawrence Soule, who worked in the cryptography section but was allowed to observe the package preparation process, said that he saw his colleagues put a pistol in a chess set, bombs in other packages, and money and maps in almost every package.

Sending contraband products through the mail required creativity. The British had established dummy charitable organizations from which to send escape and communication tools to their people. So, the Americans copied their model. The War Prisoner's Benefit Foundation, Servicemen's Relief, and other organizations with similar names became the primary vehicles for sending materials. The contacts in POW camps knew that when something arrived from these organizations it was a care package from MIS-X. Lloyd Shoemaker described one such shipment to *Stalag Luft III.* A cribbage board concealed a crystal radio; 20 compasses were hidden in chess pieces; counterfeit German work permits, real German Reichsmarks, and travel passes were concealed in the chess board. Checkers game boards held German ration cards that could be used in restaurants; and ping-pong paddles held extensive maps of the area around the camp. Everything was carefully packed, and the return addresses and names were from the bogus benevolent organizations. To further conceal where the packages originated, they were driven to and mailed from a post office in Baltimore. MIS-X sent a coded message to the camp to say these items were coming; they arrived about two months later.[13]

Veterans reported using the tools they received from MIS-X to escape. William Cory who had been imprisoned for two years, along with three colleagues, dug a tunnel and escaped from *Oflag 64* in Poland in January 1945, using an MIS-X map. They made their way out of Europe and back to the United States in February.[14]

Kenneth Kurtenbach was imprisoned in 1942 and held in *Stalag Luft 17-b* for over two years. His fellow prisoners elected him as their leader, and he became the conduit between MIS-X and his colleagues. He would pass along the parcels to others in the camp to help them escape, but as Kurtenbach said, "Whenever we received supplies ... it reaffirmed our ability to remember where we were and where we wanted to be. ... When a would-be escaper received supplies, it was well worth it."[15]

There is no greater evidence of the lengths MIS-X went to maintain its secrecy than Kurtenbach's experience. He regularly corresponded with PO Box 1142, but it would be nearly 50 years later that Kurtenbach finally learned how the MIS-X system, that he was such an integral part of, actually functioned. He learned about MIS-X from Lloyd Shoemaker's book!

CHAPTER 9

Both Ends of the Postwar Nazi Spectrum

"I learned something from this thing. You work with those who disagree with you in order to find a way of learning from them,"

JOHN GUNTHER DEAN

Toward the end, and at the conclusion of World War II, many German Jewish-American soldiers continued their military intelligence work. Some stayed on at Fort Hunt or other military installations participating in the top-secret American program called Operation *Paperclip*. Others analyzed, translated, and filed the thousands upon thousands of documents gathered at the end of the war. Many were sent to Europe to interrogate captured Germans. Still others went to Nuremberg as interrogators or interpreters for Nazis charged with war crimes.

On the other side, many Germans involved in various levels of the Nazi war machine faced uncertain futures. If they had special scientific or engineering expertise, would they be able to continue in their professions? If so, where and with whom? If they were in the upper echelons of the Nazi war or political hierarchy, they knew that if they did not find safe havens, and quickly, they did not have many positive prospects. Rank-and-file German soldiers, sailors, and airmen faced uncertain futures as well. What would life be like for them and their families after the war?

For some German scientists, their options became clear shortly after the conclusion of the war. Dr. Heinz Schlicke, the scientist on board *U-234*, had an offer that seemed ideal. He could remain in the United States, share what he knew about microwave technology and radars, and have a very good life. While Schlicke was in the interrogation phase of his time at Fort Hunt, the army assigned John Gunther Dean as the morale officer to soften the potentially rough edges that came with his interrogation. Dean later said that Schlicke "was young, sports-oriented, and we wanted to be nice to him. Somebody had to go and do things with him; so I did. ... My job was to see what he could do for the United States. And I was told to do this." Dean also said that "it took quite some time before he was willing to cooperate," adding that "the war had ended in Europe, and he said he was willing to help us, but his wife was—at that point—in the Russian zone." Dean passed that knowledge along to his superiors, and he was selected as the person to go to Europe and retrieve Schlicke's family.

"Everything was worked out," Dean later recalled. "I was being passed from one guy to another guy who were agents of the U.S. and everything else, and then I had to go into and get the wife and the two kids, [then] get over the border." He was in civilian clothes, rather than his military uniform. If he was stopped and questioned and was identified as an American soldier out of uniform, he could have been considered a spy by the Russians, which would have meant big trouble for him and the Schlicke family. When he reached the United States, he said "the husband and wife hadn't seen each other [in a very long time]. I fixed up in the place where I was told to go, and it was in a barn, and I made a lot of hay for them, and I took the two kids." Dr. Schlicke was happy to be with his family, the United States was happy to have him and his expertise, and John Gunther Dean was happy he had played a role in the reunion. Dean had also learned an important life lesson: he knew Schlicke was a Nazi, but "I learned something from this thing. You work with those who disagree with you in order to find a way of learning from them."[1]

The American government's assessment that Dr. Schlicke would be a valuable asset as an electrical engineer, as well as in the development of technology in the Cold War was well founded. After he completed his obligation to the government to document his knowledge of microwave technology, he became a chief scientist at Allen-Bradley in Milwaukee, Wisconsin. He was a life fellow and twice president of the EMC (Electromagnetic Compatibility) Society of the Institute of Electrical Engineers, as well as a Life Fellow of the American Association for the Advancement of Science. He was a United States delegate for a scientific and cultural exchange with the former Union of Soviet Socialist Republics. He lectured widely to industry and universities and was the author of five books and co-author of four others, as well as author of 60 professional articles. He also held 20 patents.[2]

Dr. Heinz Schlicke was one of the first of a group of some 1800 German scientists recruited in the top-secret program codenamed Operation *Paperclip*. The main purpose was to recruit talented German specialists and tap into their expertise, first to speed the end of the war with Japan, and second to give the United States a leg up as the Cold War with the Soviet Union started to heat up. Unlike the Russians, who essentially kidnapped some 2,200 German scientists almost overnight in October 1946, the Americans relied on their best persuasive pitches to German scientists and engineers, who were experts in fields in which Germany had advanced beyond other countries.

Just because the United States government was anxious to recruit the best and brightest German experts, did not mean that it ignored potential loyalty or security concerns. Thus, soldiers like John Gunther Dean and his colleagues assumed new postwar roles. Some remained at Fort Hunt, others were assigned to Fort Strong in Boston Harbor, and still others were assigned to both locations. Included in their duties, they continued with interrogations, eavesdropping on conversations, and engaging in conversations. They also reviewed and censored incoming and outgoing mail. The purpose now, however, was to determine if the Germans would be loyal to the United States.

Peter Weiss monitored conversations, but he believed he learned more from conversations with the Germans around the fort on multiple topics. He said he "would ask them whether they were members of the [Nazi] Party, how they became members of the Party, and what they thought when they became members of the party. ... In cases where I was inclined to give them some credibility during the day, I used to torture myself at night" wondering, "have I been had by this guy?"

Peter said that monitoring seldom produced much beyond the weather, families, and other similar topics, but on one occasion, eavesdropping uncovered a conversation that could have had a tragic ending. The Americans placed a German (number 1) who had been assigned to the German Embassy in Madrid with another German (number 2) who had also spent time on a temporary posting in Madrid. German number 2 started telling German number 1 "about the woman that he had picked up ... while he was in Madrid, [and] about this fabulous brief affair that he had; it turned out to be [German number 1's wife]." Peter continued, "At one point, they stopped talking. We just heard screams. We had to send somebody in because they were about to kill each other." Weiss said that he and his colleagues felt guilty about censoring outgoing mail. Nothing really needed to be censored, but more than that, Weiss and his colleagues shared some intimate details in the letters, for which they later felt guilty.[3]

Once the American government determined that a German expert could contribute to the buildup for the Cold War, the contact with American soldiers shifted from interrogation to orientation to the United States. Among the new German recruits, nearly 500 were experts in air-based technology, with specialties such as jet propulsion and jet aircraft design, helicopters, solid fuel, general aerodynamics, autopilot technology, aeronautical medicine, and wind tunnels. Of that number, more than 200 had advanced expertise in rockets and missile technology. Engineers who had designed submarines, underwater explosions, torpedoes, and ships in all shapes and sizes, rounded out the marine group. Then, experts in diverse fields such as optics, nuclear physics, chemistry, thermodynamics, ceramics, light and heavy diesel engines, and radar were recruited as well. Several of the *Paperclip* scientists—some well-known, others not—became leaders both in the United States and abroad in their fields.[4]

The Americans had a particular interest in the German advancements in jet aircraft and guided missiles. The Messerschmitt Me 262 jet was a lethal German weapon, which was far more advanced than any Allied aircraft. The United States military was anxious to learn as much as possible about the Me 262.

The American military establishment was also anxious to pick the German scientists' brains concerning the rocket systems, German rockets were introduced late in the war, and while they did not impact the outcome of the war, they were deadly and unstoppable. The V-2 rocket could travel 200 miles at an altitude of over 50 miles, at a speed of over 3,500mph, and with its gyroscope guidance system, the rocket could be aimed close enough to its intended target to cause serious damage. German rockets had killed thousands of civilians and military personnel mostly in England and Belgium and caused many millions of dollars of property damage. In time, the Americans also learned that some 20,000 concentration camp slaves died as well, literally worked to death, performing the dirty work related to the rocket program. Thus, there was a moral issue with the rocket program: should the United States accept, and, indeed, welcome the scientists, who had created so much pain and suffering to the Allies and prisoners during the war, to American shores?

German scientists had built upon the early rocket developments of the American pioneer, Robert H. Goddard, taking the technology to new levels. The German rocket program was one of Hitler's pet projects; the leader of the program's development and implementation was Dr. Wernher von Braun. As the "von" in Braun's surname suggests, he was born into an ancient noble German family, so he could have held the title of Baron. At an early age he was fascinated with astronomy, any vehicle that went fast, and classical music. In the last area he was an accomplished piano and cello player and considered a career as a composer, having studied with noted classical composer Paul Hindemith. He was privileged and attended some of the finest schools in Germany, eventually completing a doctorate in physics at the Friedrich Wilhelm University of Berlin in 1934.

Braun, like many of his fellow Germans at the time, believed that his home country had been treated poorly at the conclusion of World War I, but his relationship with the evolving Nazi regime was complicated. He joined the Nazi Party in 1937, later claiming that he understood that if he wanted to pursue his passion for developing rockets, he needed to join the Nazi Party. He also became an SS officer in the army. Like many German elite, he claimed to not care for Hitler. He would later say that "to us, Hitler was only a pompous fool with a Charlie Chaplin mustache ... wholly without scruples, a godless man who thought himself the only god." But his feelings for Hitler aside, he also admitted that he "fared relatively rather well under totalitarianism;" and indeed he did.

Braun's doctoral thesis focused on liquid rocket fuel, and he and his fellow students started experimenting with building and testing rockets in 1934. Walter Dornberger, who would later become the overall commander of the Nazi rocket program, first noticed Braun at the university in Berlin. Dornberger recognized the young man's potential and placed him in charge of technical development of the rocket program at Peenemünde, on a remote island near the northeastern corner of Germany. Peenemünde was an ideal location for rocket testing. Braun and his staff could perfect their rocket designs—eventually creating the *Vergeltungswaffe-Zwei* (translated as the Vengeance Weapon 2 or V-2 rockets)—which they would test fire into the Baltic.

The real work on the V-2 rockets, however, took place near Nordhausen, in central Germany. Prisoners were transported from the Buchenwald concentration camp to the Dora-Mittelbau concentration camp. From there they were forced to work underground in brutal 12–14 hour shifts with little food, no sanitation facilities, and without the ability to see daylight for days on end. The purpose was to enlarge several existing tunnels, and then to construct and test the V-2 rockets. The work was so horrendous and an estimated 20,000 of the 60,000 workers died or were executed in the tunnels. Nazi concentration camps were among the most brutal examples of what pain and suffering humans can inflict on other humans, but the conditions in the tunnels near Nordhausen might very well have been the worst of this already horrific system. Braun knew of and visited the tunnels and was well aware of the slave labor and of the horrendous working conditions, but he later claimed that he felt powerless to do anything about them.

In March 1944, Braun had a little too much to drink and reportedly started musing that Germany would probably lose the war, which was fine with him, since he really preferred building spaceships rather than war rockets. For his remarks, he was arrested and detained for two weeks. His long association with General Dornberger worked to his benefit, however, and he was released to continue his work on the V-2 rockets. While he should not have said anything about his feelings concerning the disposition of the war, Braun and his staff knew that the Russians were closing in from the East, and the British and Americans were coming from the West, and it was just a matter of time before the war would be over. Finally, when Braun and his fellow rocket scientists learned that Hitler had committed suicide, he decided that he wanted to surrender to and build rockets for the United States. Hiding with his fellow rocket engineers in Bavaria at the time, Braun asked his younger brother, Magnus, to go, find and surrender to American soldiers. A day later, Wernher had surrendered to American soldiers as well, and within months, he and many of his men were on their way to the United States.[5]

When Wernher von Braun came to the United States, he was considered such a valuable future asset, the military immediately assigned a morale officer to him and his colleagues in the person of Arno Mayer. Mayer delivered newspapers and other reading materials to the men every day. As the Christmas season approached, Braun asked Arno if he could arrange for a Christian minister to hold a service for them. Arno secured a room and arranged for a minister to conduct a service. Arno Mayer then had to translate the entire service from English into German, which was a challenge, since Arno was Jewish and unfamiliar with the Christian liturgy.[6]

After spending time in the east, Wernher von Braun and his associates were sent on to Fort Bliss near El Paso, Texas, where they continued their work on the American rocket program. In 1950, they were transferred to Huntsville, Alabama, to work on the space program. Von Braun's experience on his entry to the United States was different from most. He was treated almost like royalty, having Arno Mayer close by to help him and his colleagues assimilate into American society and culture. More typical was what greeted one of Braun's colleagues who came later—Dieter Grau. He spent several weeks at Fort Hunt and his interrogation included questions about his political affiliations and his responsibilities in the rocket program. In addition, he was given an orientation to life in the United States, where he learned about United States customs, currency, and other aspects of his new home. After his time at Fort Hunt, he was transferred to Fort Bliss, like most of his colleagues. Grau understood that he would be staying in the country for six months, after which time he would be sent back to Germany, and, to ease his transition, he was allowed to bring his wife and family to live with him in Texas. His six-month stay was extended to the remainder of his life in the United States.

Years later, Dieter Grau described his responsibilities in Germany and filled in many details about the last several months he and his fellow scientists spent in Germany. Before the war, Grau received a degree as an electrical engineer and went to work for the Siemens Company. He was drafted into the German army in 1939 and assigned to the Eastern Front as a tank maintenance engineer. A short time later, he was transferred back to his position at Siemens and assigned to maintain the power grid for Peenemünde. He was again sent to the Russian front, then recalled to Peenemünde in July 1943. On his second tour at the rocket site, he was assigned to check for any failures or errors in the V-2 before a test flight. In this new role, he became one of Braun's close confidants, who expanded his role to travel to factories to check on the quality of manufactured rocket parts.

As the war was drawing to a close, Grau described what it was like to be part of the rocket program. As the Red Army was rapidly moving toward Peenemünde, the operation was moved to Bavaria. Grau said that he was fearful that the Russians would kill him, but he also had the legitimate concern that his own country would kill him and his colleagues rather than taking a chance that they might fall into enemy hands if the Russians would have overrun Peenemünde. Eventually, after the war was over, Dieter Grau learned that Braun had emigrated to the United States, and in February 1946, he joined his former boss in America.[7]

Another engineer, Hans Fichtner, recalled that he went to see Braun when he arrived at Peenemünde, and asked what he would be doing. Braun assigned him to a small team designing the rocket guidance system. It was the perfect job for Fichtner in Germany and became a highly desirable skill when he joined Braun at Fort Bliss and Huntsville.

Oscar Holderer quickly found his niche as a mechanical engineer with the rocket program. He solved a problem as the Germans were test firing V-2 rockets. They would launch them into the Baltic, but the rockets sank on impact. Holderer designed flaps that would slow the rocket descent enough so parachutes could be deployed, allowing for recovery. The Germans continued to hone their skills in the States and were major contributors to the success of America's space program.[8]

For good reason, Wernher von Braun is considered by many as the father of the American space program. Among his many accomplishments, he oversaw the development of the Saturn V super heavy-lift launch vehicle that propelled the Apollo spacecraft to the Moon. But he was not the only *Paperclip* scientist to make major contributions. Fellow German physicist Krafft Ehricke designed the Atlas rocket; Kurt Debus was the director of the Kennedy Space Center; Hans von Ohain developed the gas turbine engine; Herbert A. Wagner was a pioneer in sea-to-air missiles; and Hubertus Strughold was the father of space medicine.[9]

Percolating just below the surface, however, was the fact that Braun and others in the Operation *Paperclip* program had unsavory pasts in the Nazi regime. The United States government knew and successfully kept under wraps that Braun was a member of the Nazi Party, and an officer in the SS, so successfully that when he died in 1977 from pancreatic cancer, most Americans knew of him only as the rocket scientist responsible for many of the major projects in the space program. Seven years after his death, however, Americans began to learn of his dark past. The East German government had been trying to feed details of his Nazi and SS connections—without success—to the American press since the 1960s. The revelation of the fact that he had been a card-carrying member of the Nazi Party, in addition to his connection to the secret underground rocket facility, where slaves from the Dora-Mittelbau camp worked and died, came to light when one of his closest associates, Arthur Louis Hugo Rudolph, renounced his American citizenship and voluntarily returned to Germany in 1984.

In 1979, the United States Office of Special Investigations learned that Rudolph had managed the underground facility and thus was potentially guilty of war crimes. Rather than face a possible trial or contest a denaturalization hearing, Rudolph volunteered to leave the United States. Americans soon learned the sordid details of Braun's and Rudolph's Nazi connection, as well as the details of the V-2 underground factory.[10]

We recently have learned even more about the Germans brought to the United States under the Operation *Paperclip* program from the excellent book on the program by Annie Jacobsen. She is quite critical of the dark side of the program, pointing out that, in addition to Rudolph and Braun, several of the Germans had worked side by side with Adolf Hitler; others were dedicated Nazi Party members, and several had stood trial at Nuremburg. One was convicted of murder and slavery but still allowed to come to the United States. Leaders in the Pentagon and the CIA justified these recruits because they feared the Russians would recruit them if they did not.[11]

German scientists had potential value for the United States as it competed with the Soviet Union on multiple fronts during the Cold War. But what about German military leaders? One of the first German generals the United States needed to deal with was Ulrich Kessler, who was one of the passengers on the *U-234* headed for Japan at the end of the war. Once Kessler recognized that his arrogance was not going to get him anywhere, he provided useful information to help the United States end the war with Japan.

In addition to the help the Americans obtained from Kessler to continue the fight against Japan, they were hoping to gain information from the Japanese ambassador to Germany, whom they arrested at the conclusion of the war with Germany. General Hiroshi Oshima was a close confidant to Hitler and was in the inner Nazi circle for many important decisions. In one of the great ironies of the war, Oshima sent detailed cables of Nazi actions to his home government in Japan. What he, the Nazis, and his Japanese colleagues did not know was that the Americans had broken the code under which he sent his messages, and in many instances had read the messages before his colleagues in Japan. American General George C. Marshall said that Oshima was "our main basis of information regarding Hitler's intentions in Europe." The Americans were hoping to learn more while Oshima was in custody at Fort Hunt.

Rudy Pins said that Oshima, as a diplomat and a high-value prisoner, was allowed to live in a small hut within the fort. According to Peter Weiss, Oshima "spoke fairly good English and loved bourbon, American bourbon." One evening, the top officers at PO Box 1142 decided they would try to learn as much as they could from Oshima. They arranged for him to join them in the officers' mess and arranged to have the conversation recorded. Three or four American officers came into the room and one asked Oshima: "'So would you like some bourbon?' And he said, 'Yes, please.' And so, they poured the bourbon. They started making small talk. And it could be 15 minutes or so, and so 'Would you like some more bourbon?' And he said 'Yes, please' and always in the same tone of voice." Peter continued, "He never lost his cool. But they [the American officers] did. After the fifth or sixth round ... their tongues got a little thick, and they started telling him stuff that he wasn't supposed to know. So, we had to go and break that up." The American asked Oshima: "Do you know what we do here?" And he said, "No. But I do know it now."[12]

At the conclusion of the war, United Kingdom and United States leaders agreed that they would best be served if German commanders were brought to one place to begin the interrogation process. To that end, Fort Hunt became the first stop for many German generals. Whereas the scientists could help with the technological issues in competition with the Russians, German military leaders had the potential to help the Allies with the knowledge they had gained fighting the Red Army. Walter Vierow was one of the first German generals brought to Fort Hunt after the war. He was captured by the Americans and brought to the United States because of his extensive military engineering experience on the Eastern Front. He had been promoted up through the ranks to major general and was in charge of building and maintaining roads and bridges in western Russia, Yugoslavia, and Czechoslovakia. His expertise was seen as invaluable for understanding not only the transportation network but also the challenges of maintaining the system in the harsh climate. He wrote several reports while at Fort Hunt and drew extensive maps of the networks that had been under his command. In August 1946, Vierow was extradited to Yugoslavia and charged with war crimes. He was convicted, jailed, and released in 1953.[13]

Another early, and ultimately one of the most important, Germans brought to PO Box 1142 was Brigadier General Reinhard Gehlen. General Gehlen managed the German Eastern Front Intelligence Service from 1942 until nearly the end of the war. He ran a team of henchmen who gathered data any way they could. They were ruthless: torture, threats, murders, and virtually any form of intimidation were their techniques. Because of their intelligence-gathering methods, Gehlen, at the top of the team, knew that if somehow the Russians got their hands on him, the end of his life would come painfully, but probably not quickly. Thus, he had every incentive to join forces with the United States and its allies. He managed to hide the treasure trove of documents he had collected at several secret locations in Europe. Gehlen offered his knowledge and expertise, his team of intelligence experts, and his hidden documents if the United States would give him sanctuary at the end of the war. After weighing who he was and what he and his men had done, with the potential for valuable information on the Soviet Union, the Americans accepted his offer.[14]

When General Gehlen and his men arrived at Fort Hunt, the information-gathering process was different than the interrogation paradigm practiced during the war. Now, in many cases, officers from the Pentagon conducted the interrogations. Rudy Pins and his colleagues, who had become quite adept at gathering information from German POWs, no matter their ranks or levels of expertise, were shunted to the sidelines. Pins recalled that Gehlen and his men were treated as VIP guests. He saw him occasionally, and even escorted the German to a movie shown at Fort Hunt, but other than these occasional encounters, he saw Gehlen only in passing.[15]

General Gehlen and his staff worked under the codename of the Bolero group. In the ten months he and his men were at Fort Hunt, they worked under the supervision of Captain Eric Waldman from the Pentagon, producing numerous reports that focused on Russian military capabilities. Waldman was born in Vienna in 1914, emigrated to the United States in 1938, joined the U.S. Army in 1942, and graduated from Officer Candidate School in the Field Artillery. He transferred to military intelligence in the Pentagon, where he specialized in German military tactics. At the conclusion of the war, he was transferred to PO Box 1142 and was placed in charge of Gehlen and the Bolero group. Studies, such as "Methods of the German Intelligence Service in Russia," "Development of the Russian High Command and its Conception of Strategy During the Eastern Command," and "Development and Establishment of the Russian Political Commissars within the Red Army" gave the United States, the United Kingdom, and their allies a jump start in understanding what potential threats the Soviet Union might pose in the near future.[16]

For the caches of documents, the Gehlen group had hidden away in Europe, the Pentagon folded the collection of these materials into a program to gather thousands and thousands of military, corporate, and public documents, and any other conceivable source of information left behind in the wake of the Third Reich. The program was under the U.S. Army's Document Control Section in Frankfurt, directed by Lieutenant Colonel S. Frederick Gronich. He sent teams to wherever he thought document collection seemed promising, and as materials were gathered, he insisted that his men prepare index cards to provide easy access when the documents reached their final destination.[17]

Edgar Danciger, from Fort Hunt, was ideal for this project. He was fluent in German and Russian, plus he had a good eye for relevant materials. His specialties were the German railway system and the Siegfried line—the German defensive system that stretched for about 390 miles along the western border of the old German Empire. When he returned to Fort Hunt from his document-gathering assignments, he would make every effort to track down the architect or engineer who designed and/or built a structure for which he had plans. If that man was in a POW camp, Danciger would arrange a transfer to Fort Hunt to have the designer explain what was in the plans. Beyond locating documents, with his fluency in Russian, he was a valuable member of the 30 or so men translating captured Russian documents.[18]

Once the Pentagon gathered these reams and reams of materials, they were boxed, cataloged, and shipped to Camp Ritchie, which became the processing center. To deal with the onslaught of documents—an estimated 150 tons of materials were processed after the war—16 men who had been part of the MIRS program at Fort Hunt were transferred to Camp Ritchie. The new name for the program was the German Military Document Section (GMDS). Paul Fairbrook, who was transferred with the program, said the mission for this program was different from MIRS. The documents gathered at Fort Hunt and the new incoming materials were "organized like a library," or more precisely like the Library of Congress for captured German documents. In other words, the new role for Fairbrook and his colleagues was to catalog and create finding aids for these materials, rather than analyze documents to help fight the war. He and his colleagues spent a year at Camp Ritchie with the GMDS project.[19]

To help manage the daunting task of translating and wading through all of the documents from all of the sources, the Pentagon decided to bring over some 200 Germans to help sort and analyze the data. The Germans were vetted both for their potential abilities to work with these documents and for their support of the United States. In this group there were 35 German officers with ranks of captain or higher, including four mid-level generals; 22 lower-level officers; and 120 non-commissioned officers and enlisted men. In its love of codenames, the Pentagon called this program "The Hill," and the nickname for the Germans working on this program was the "hillbillies."[20]

Oddly, the War Department decided to relegate Paul Fairbrook and his MIRS colleagues to cataloging rather than analyzing the new documents. During the war, in addition to analyzing documents, they had prepared three versions of the Red Book and the numerous other enormously valuable reports. It would have seemed only reasonable that they would have played the same role in the GMDS program. They knew the Germans were at Camp Ritchie, and, in fact, Paul Fairbrook said he was annoyed that the American officers spent more time with the Germans than with the Americans. In particular, Paul said he and his colleagues intensely disliked one of the American commanding officers, Colonel George F. Blunda (whom they referred to as "Colonel Blunder") because he, for the most part, ignored his American soldiers and associated with the German officers.

There was some minimal contact between the former MIRS men and some of the Germans. Paul Fairbrook met one German enlisted man who was a skilled artist. He arranged for the German to draw illustrations for his father's stamp catalog. But this connection was an exception to the lack of fraternization between the Americans and Germans.[21]

When the program ended in 1946, the hillbillies had produced over 3,600 pages of valuable information for the United States and its allies. The resulting published reports provided what amounted to "lessons learned" concerning the Third Reich. For example, the report entitled "German Military Transportation" showed how heavily the Germans relied on rail transport, which helped mitigate the fact that oil and rubber were in short supply. British and American military sections had specific questions, such as how the Germans supplied their troops and their procedures for court-martials, and reports were prepared to answer them.[22]

Late in the war, many of the men stationed at PO Box 1142 remained stateside, others were transferred to Europe to help with the monumental task of interrogating German prisoners. Werner Moritz would have preferred to have remained at Fort Hunt, in large measure because his wife would not be able to join him abroad. He was first sent to England and later to France. His nickname of "Lucky" Moritz, or more importantly his good luck, served him well in his new adventure. First, the ship on which he was traveling hit a mine in the Seine River and split in half, but he fortunately was on the half that did not sink. Second, the plane he was traveling on to connect with the Third Army crashed. He walked away, stunned but not severely injured. A nun found him, took him to a French convent to recover, and after several days, he was able to find and join up with his outfit.

Moritz was with Patton's Third Army as it crossed the Rhine River into Germany in late March 1945. He, another interpreter, and several soldiers were allowed to operate independently in the area. The army was moving quickly with little resistance, approaching Nuremberg. He described what happened next: "It was getting dark and we see three guys [German soldiers] marching toward us, one with a white flag raised, two other guys with guns." Werner was not sure what to do, so he called Third Army headquarters and asked what he should do. "The guy from Third Army said to us, 'Well, tell them to drop their guns and march forward' and that's what we did. And they dropped their guns and they came. And they wanted to tell us that they were from a division and the division wanted to surrender. Now I got a division. So now I called Third Army again and I said, 'What am I going to do with these people? It's getting dark.'" The headquarters sent a contingent of engineers who "put wire around that division and called it a prison camp." The German infantry division was likely quite diminished in size from its normal 12,500–15,000 soldiers, but capturing a division was no mean feat!

Moritz continued to operate independently, and on May 23, near Waldering, Bavaria, he recalled, "It was hot as hell, we were all —we had two jeeps. ... We're rolling around and we're passing some houses sitting on the hill and a kid came running down and was hollering, 'Streicher, Streicher!'" Werner asked the boy to tell him more. The boy said Julius Streicher was in the house with a young girl. Werner continued, "We had four MPs and four interrogators. I knocked on the front door. I had my gun ready. [The door] was locked. I walked around the house and looked through the windows. Shades were down. We finally decided we were going to break into the house. ... I asked the MPs to break down the front door. They did. And we heard steps running, feet running. We looked around and went upstairs. We found Streicher in bed with a 15-year-old girl. So I said to him, 'You're Streicher. You're Streicher.'" At first Streicher denied who he was, but eventually said that yes, indeed, he was the notorious Nazi.[23]

"Lucky" Moritz had pulled off one of the greatest feats of anyone associated with PO Box 1142. Julius Streicher was quite possibly the most virulent antisemite in the entire Nazi establishment. After serving in World War I, he joined the Nazi Party in 1921 and became a close friend and one of the earliest supporters of Adolf Hitler. From his headquarters in Nuremberg, he published *Der Stürmer,* a crude, venomous anti-Jewish newspaper that in many ways provided the focus for Hitler's antisemitic policies. Aside from his anti-Jewish newspaper, Streicher was in almost every other way a truly disgusting human being. The fact that he was with a 15-year-old girl when he was captured was typical of his personal degeneracy. He was reviled by nearly everyone else in the Nazi Party, so much so, that party members finally convinced Hitler to strip him of his party positions in 1940. But because of his long-standing connection to Hitler, he was allowed to continue to serve as editor of *Der Stürmer* throughout the war years.

Julius Streicher was captured by a German Jewish-American soldier who had spent time in a concentration camp, and for all he knew at the time, his family had perished in another concentration camp. Further, three of the four MPs with Moritz were African American soldiers. Moritz explained to his African American companions: "We captured a guy here that's of great importance. He hates everything. He hates blacks. He hates Jews, especially Jews, but I want you to know he hates blacks almost as much as he hates Jews." They took Streicher to a hut near the Third Army headquarters and Moritz told one of the black MPs: "Look, I'm going to do things you probably think I'm crazy. And you want to know something? I am crazy. I am crazed. I captured a Nazi of unbelievable mischief. I captured a Nazi who doesn't deserve to live. I would like to shoot him right now, but I know I would be court-martialed and end up in prison. But I'm going to do what I have to do." He had Streicher undress, "I took out my penis and pissed on him. I pissed all over him, his head and everywhere. And he started to move his head and I said, 'Don't move. I have my pistol in my hand. I'll shoot you in the ass.'"[24]

Streicher was transferred to prison and stood trial for war crimes in the International Military Tribunal in Nuremberg. He was found guilty of war crimes on October 1, 1946, and hanged along with nine other Nazis on October 16.

After the war, Werner Moritz remained in Germany to interrogate German prisoners. He recalled that he and his colleagues were allowed to look at the list of potential interrogees, and if someone for whatever reason looked interesting, they could request to interview him. One morning he looked at the list and he recognized a name. "I had him brought down to me. I told him to sit down. I sat down and I said to him, 'Your name, please?' And he said to me, 'Why are you asking me this?' We went to school together. He remembered me. We went to school together and then we had an interesting conversation." The young man (Moritz did not recall his name) had not been part of the Hitler Youth; his father was a socialist, and because of that, his former school friend had had a difficult time finding work, was watched all of the time, and was thoroughly disgusted with the Nazi regime. He said he "was friendly to our side and anything he could tell me, he'd be willing to do. And then we proceeded for an hour. He gave me all kinds of information, not great information, but good information. So that was a piece of luck."[25]

Peter Weiss returned to Europe after the war as a civilian, working for Congress in the Office of Military Government. He interviewed numerous Germans and Austrians. In a follow-up to experiences at Fort Hunt, he came to better recognize former Nazi true believers from what they said, which went something like this: "You know. We had to do this [fight the war] because of the Red Menace from the East. Right? You should understand that." They believed in what they were doing. On the other hand, there were those who tried to make excuses for supporting Hitler. They would say something like: "We were really blind to what was happening. ... It was terrible what we did. We didn't know. We didn't know." From this latter group, Peter spoke to a woman and asked: "'What about all the people who were taken away from their apartments and never came back?' And she said, 'Well. That was only the Jews.' And she looked at me; she didn't know. Well, I hadn't told her I was Jewish. But that was fairly typical."

Later, Peter went to Vienna and Czechoslovakia, where his father came from. By that time (1946), he had learned that his grandfather, uncle, aunt, and cousins on his father's side of the family had all perished in the camps. He was in a civilian uniform, and he went to the apartment where he had lived. "This man came to the door, and I said 'I'm sorry to bother you, but I grew up in this apartment. ... I just wanted to come by and see it again.' He said, 'When did you leave?' I said, 1938 which was the year of the annexation of Austria. And he said, 'Is that right, 1938?' He said, 'Why did you leave?'" Peter observed that the man's reaction was typical of many Austrians. Of course, he left because he and his family really had no other choice. Many said something like "They made us do it. The Germans made us do it." Peter's reaction was "Bullshit. The Germans didn't make them do it. They [the Austrians] voted 98 percent in a plebiscite for annexation."[26]

Two of the Fort Hunt soldiers, Paul Kubala and Rudy Pins, were involved with the interrogation of another notorious German Nazi—Hermann Göring.

Göring believed, with good reason, that he was the heir apparent to Hitler in the Third Reich. Hitler said as much in a 1941 decree. But, as everything was unraveling, the old adage that there is no honor among thieves, or, in this case, no honor among Nazi thugs, took over. As the Red Army was nearly at Berlin's doorstep, Hitler intimated that he would commit suicide rather than surrender and he thought Göring was in the best position to negotiate a peace settlement. This put Göring in a bind. If he did nothing, he could be accused of dereliction of duty; on the other hand, if he started to exert his influence, he could be considered a traitor. Enter another Nazi close to Hitler—Martin Bormann. Bormann and Göring were rivals, and Bormann convinced Hitler that Göring was, indeed, a traitor; the *Führer* then issued an order for Göring's arrest and imprisonment on April 24. Things were moving fast. On April 30, 1945, Hitler committed suicide, and five days later a contingent of the Luftwaffe freed Göring from his confinement. The next day, May 6, Göring surrendered to the Americans in his full uniform, with all of his medals and ribbons.On May 7, Göring appeared with Paul Kubala in still and moving pictures. Kubala acted as his interpreter. Kubala was a major at the time and in charge of the Augsburg interrogation center, or what the Americans jokingly referred to as "Camp Ashcan." He served as the interpreter and liaison between Göring and the military and the media and conducted the earliest interrogations of the German. Shortly after his arrival at Augsburg, the Americans gave Göring an IQ exam and found that his IQ was 138. Then they started a series of interrogations that would last over many months.

After the first couple of weeks, Kubala wrote an assessment of what he and his colleagues had learned to that point. He observed that by no means was Göring "the comical figure he had been depicted as so many times in newspaper reports." He is "neither stupid nor a fool in the Shakespearean sense," but "cool and calculating. He is able to grasp the fundamental issues under discussion immediately. He is certainly not a man to be underrated. Although he tried to soft-pedal many of the most outrageous, crimes committed by Germany, he said enough to show that he is as much responsible for the policies within Germany and for the war itself, as anyone in Germany." Göring took great pride in many of his accomplishments, particularly the development of the Luftwaffe. "On the other hand, he denied having had anything to do with the racial laws and with the concentration camps, with the SS and the atrocities committed both in Germany and outside. Göring is at all times an actor who does not disappoint his audience. His vanity extends into the field of the pathological."

The remainder of the report summarized many of the events in the war, often focusing on his relationship with Hitler. If something went well, he generally took the credit; if something went badly, he would emphasize that he had advised Hitler that what he planned was not a good idea. A case in point was the invasion of Russia. Göring said that "one of his greatest shocks was when Hitler decided to wage war against Russia." He told the *Führer* that "what he was doing was against his own beliefs and contrary to what he had written and promised the people [in] *Mein Kampf*." Hitler retorted that the "Russians were becoming a greater menace every day, and that he would smash the Russian Army before winter." Göring pointed out that even if Germany smashed the Russians, Hitler would still not be able to make peace with the Russians, but Hitler refused to listen. Not long after the setbacks in Russia, Göring said that Hitler became increasingly more ill-tempered.

One line of Göring's questioning pried into where he and his henchmen had hidden the treasures the Nazis had stolen. Göring provided some insights but was mostly cagey as to the hiding places of most of the treasures. Another report, taken from a ledger in Göring's possession, listed his income from 1937 to 1942. This probably was only a fraction of what he had stolen or confiscated during that period, but it still was staggering. He listed 9,201,000 in Reichsmarks, which was equivalent to close to a million American dollars.

Another document can best be described as a moderated discussion between Göring and Hans Heinrich Lammers, who was the Reich Minister and the Chief of Chancellery. In that position, Lammers was the one who managed important documents, such as a paper that could have designated Göring or anyone else as Hitler's successor. At the conclusion of their discussion, Göring said that he wanted "to see to it that there is order and peace, especially until matters regarding the relationship to the Allied forces have been cleared up, to avoid uprisings in connection to communism, which would be very embarrassing to the Americans and English." He continued, arrogantly alleging that "I am the one who can not only help, but who also knows all the episodes of the past." In other words, he was saying he really was not a war criminal but a good guy who could help in Germany's transition from war to peace.[27]

The Allies did not accept Hermann Göring's offer as the best person to assist in Germany's transition from war to peace. Instead, he was transferred to Nuremberg in September 1945 to await trial. Göring was charged with four counts, the most serious of which were crimes against humanity, which included among other atrocities his involvement in the arrest, torture, and murder of 6,000,000 Jews and others in the Holocaust. His portion of the trial took place in March 1946, and he was convicted and sentenced to be hanged on September 30, 1946. He cheated the hangman, however, and committed suicide on October 15, 1946.

Early in 1946, as Göring's trial was wending its way through the legal system, Rudy Pins was offered the chance to travel to Germany to assist in the Nuremberg trials. The United States needed translators and with Pins's experience at Fort Hunt, he was an ideal candidate. He agreed to the assignment with one condition—he wanted to go as a civilian rather than a soldier. He left the army and returned to Cleveland to await his orders and receive his passport. In September 1946, he sailed to Germany and when he arrived in Nuremberg, he was immediately assigned to translating and summarizing transcripts. Many of his colleagues were men he had worked with at PO Box 1142. The trials of some of the most notorious Nazis were drawing to a close, but one of the first interrogations he attended was of Hermann Göring, conducted by the U.S. chief interrogator Dr. Robert Kempner. "Sitting across the table from the man who had recently been one of the most powerful men in the Third Reich aroused mixed emotions in me," Pins recalled. "Here was a man responsible for so much misery—my own as well as that of millions of others—a man who strutted on the world stage bedecked in [medals] on his uniforms." Göring was now dressed in a plain tunic; he had lost a great deal of weight in prison, and "at the moment his main concern was that we share our cigarettes with him. ... He certainly was not browbeaten."[28]

Paul Kubala, who was in the limelight as the first American seen with Göring, who had advanced through the military hierarchy from enlisted man to major and had played such as important role in the American intelligence-gathering program, seems not only to have learned a great deal from Göring; he also benefited materially from his association. He was accused of taking 15 gold watches; two valuable cigarette cases that belonged to Wilhelm Ohnesorge, one of Hitler's close friends; 87,000 Reichsmarks, which was worth $8,750 at the time; plus, other valuables. Exactly if or how he had acquired them was not known. There were also charges of inappropriate treatment of and relationships with female prisoners and for cohabiting with a woman who was not his wife. Later he was accused of taking Göring's ribbons and medals.

Clearly the major was in trouble, and under normal circumstances would have faced a court-martial, but he had made valuable friends in high places. In this case, Kubala's guardian angel, Colonel William "Buffalo Bill" Quinn, wrote a long letter to General Geoffrey Keys, commander of the Seventh Army, admitting that "undoubtedly the charges were true." Then, he continued saying that he "had a warm spot in my heart for Kubala" and that he would appreciate it very much if the general could go easy on him. Keys agreed and offered Kubala discipline under Article of War 104, which provided for wartime discipline for minor infractions of the rules, in lieu of a court-martial. Kubala agreed to accept the 104 discipline and thus was able to continue his military career, rising to the rank of lieutenant colonel.[29]

The men from PO Box 1142 were thus involved in the postwar period. They did their parts in easing the transition of German scientists, as part of Operation *Paperclip*; they continued to collect, translate, and process captured German documents; and some, particularly the German Jewish soldiers, gained some satisfaction with their involvement in the capture, arrest, and interrogation of some of the most notorious Nazis, who had brought so much pain and suffering to them and their families. Most were glad they had served their new country, but they were anxious to get on with their postwar lives.

CHAPTER 10

They Talked, We Listened

"We extracted information in a battle of the wits. I'm proud to say I never compromised my humanity."

GEORGE FRENKEL

On a warm August day in 2006, Fred Michel and George Mandel met for the first time in 60 years, in a picnic area at Fort Hunt. Both men were in their early 80s; their joints were a bit creaky, but they were delighted to reconnect again after so many years. They had become close friends during their time together at PO Box 1142, but when they were both discharged from the army in December 1945, they had lost contact with each other. As it so happened, they only lived a few miles apart for most of their adult lives. Mandel was a chemist who lived in Bethesda, Maryland, and, until recently, Michel had worked as an engineer in the Washington area and lived in Alexandria, Virginia. When he discovered that his old friend had been so close, Fred said, "He [Mandel] was right there, near us all along, teaching at George Washington University."

George Mandel came to the George Washington University in 1949, joined the faculty a year later and continued in numerous capacities until shortly before his death in 2011. One of his colleagues said: "It is difficult to exaggerate all that George Mandel did for our department and our school." He was popular and approachable as a teacher and made significant contributions as a scholar. He created a program called Problem-Based Learning, offered as small-size discussion groups for first- and second-year medical students to help them understand how they would deal with clinical problems in their careers. He established a similar program in his field of pharmacology for senior medical students. One of his students, Julius Axelrod, Ph.D., won the Nobel Prize in Physiology/Medicine in 1970 for his work on a class of neurotransmitters.

Dr. Mandel won numerous teaching and service awards and was an icon at the university.[1]

Fred Michel had distinguished himself in a career in mechanical engineering. After the war, he earned a master's degree in mechanical engineering at Columbia University. He returned to the Washington, DC area and worked for Melpar, Inc. in Alexandria and Arlington for a time, then moved on to the Westinghouse Electric Company as the director at the research laboratory in Churchill, Pennsylvania. He returned to Northern Virginia to work for the U.S. Army, retiring as deputy chief of manufacturing. Among the many awards he received were two medals from the army for Meritorious Civilian Service and a Gold Medal for his contributions in the field of manufacturing. He was also elected as a Fellow of the Society of Manufacturing Engineers. He co-authored two textbooks on manufacturing engineering.[2]

On the day of the reunion, Fort Hunt looked quite different from the thriving military fort in which Fred and George were assigned in the 1940s. Birthday parties, picnickers, and games had replaced the buildings and compounds they remembered. The National Park Service had erected an interpretive marker that briefly described the PO Box 1142 operations as a reminder of where the buildings were located, but the changes and distractions were minor compared to the memories they conjured up from so many years earlier. They remembered that when they went into town and people asked where they were stationed, they were careful to not say anything about Fort Hunt and instead said they were assigned to a post office box, specifically "PO Box 1142." George Mandel recalled that whenever his "family wondered where the hell I was, I told them I was speaking to scientists, or something like that. They didn't know I was interrogating Nazis." His post-military life as a college professor was different from his work at Fort Hunt, but on one occasion the memories came flooding back. He was attending a scientific conference in Paris and made eye contact with another scientist who looked familiar, but he momentarily could not remember why. Then it hit him that the man was a German, whom he had interrogated at Fort Hunt. "He looked at me, and I heard him say to someone in German, 'That was my prison warden.'" The two men chatted and shook hands afterwards, each respectful of the other.

At this 2006 reunion, National Park Service historians had only contacted and interviewed some 15 former soldiers from PO Box 1142. They were already lining up others to interview, and they started planning for another reunion a year later.

On October 5, 2007, the National Park did hold its follow-up reunion. Park staff had interviewed about 30 veterans by that time and had arranged to conduct several more. In addition to the reunion, the park also dedicated a monument and erected a flagpole to the World War II veterans stationed at PO Box 1142. The event was sponsored in part by the George Washington Memorial Parkway and by the Army's Freedom Team Salute. Two dozen veterans came—some in wheelchairs, some using walkers, and others seemingly as spry as they had been 60 years earlier. They were pleased that they finally had the opportunity to share what they had done so many years earlier.

To kick off the event, Wayne Spivey and park historian Brandon Bies raised the flag on the new flagpole. Wayne came to the Fort Hunt event from his home in Georgia. When he left his military career, he had worked as an accountant for the Ford Motor Company until his retirement. He recalled that his "mouth was always dropping open when we heard [the interrogators and German scientists] talking." He continued, "The information they got and the sketches of atoms and molecules and whatnot [was just amazing]." If anyone attending the reunion had asked Wayne about a particular file, he more than likely could have described it in detail. He was quite proud to say that he "was just one of three Southern boys there, walking around hearing German and Russian and Japanese" during his time at Fort Hunt.[3]

George Weidinger and his wife traveled from Cleveland to attend the event. They were thrilled and felt very honored to be included. After the war, George and his wife returned to Cleveland, and he continued his work at the Motch & Merryweather Machinery Company. Before the war, he had worked his way from apprentice to handle some of the more complicated equipment in the plant. When he returned, the factory superintendent asked him to develop the specifications for how various parts were made. The demand for parts, especially during the Korean War, became so great, a major part of his job was to subcontract with other companies around the country to make the parts.

George has remained in Cleveland. In 2011, Nina, his wife of 69 years passed away. They had met and were married six months before he was stationed at Fort Hunt. He recalled that he was frustrated that he could not tell her what he was doing there, but, with a twinkle in his eye, he said, "We had other things to talk about." George was happy that he could begin sharing his experiences from Fort Hunt with Nina and others. Before Nina died, she was admitted to a local area hospice. The care she received there was so outstanding that George wanted to give something back to the center. He started sharing his photograph collection to help raise money for its operation. He and Nina had traveled to 79 countries and his photographs were memories of those trips.[4]

The Freedom Team Salute gave each man an award for his service. Most were delighted for the recognition, especially since what they had done so many years earlier had been kept under wraps. Some were happy to receive their honor but wanted to make it clear that they did not support the way in which prisoners were being treated in the war in Iraq. By then it was widely known that prisoners were subjected to terrible conditions and torture at Abu Ghraib in Iraq and at Guantanamo Bay in Cuba. One veteran voiced his opposition by refusing to receive the award.

Not only were the Fort Hunt veterans opposed to the way Iraqi prisoners were treated; they wanted to make it clear that the way they had treated their prisoners at PO Box 1142 was very different. "We got more information out of a German general with a game of chess or ping pong than they do today with their torture," said Henry Kolm. He knew of whence he spoke. After the war, Kolm was sent to Germany as a translator during the Nuremberg trials. One of his assignments was to play chess with Colonel Rudolf Hess, one of the most notorious of all German war criminals. "He [Hess] loved to play chess, but he hated to lose. He mostly won, but whenever he lost, it was a major calamity. He couldn't wait for the next game to get back at me." Even knowing the horrendous hideous crimes Hess had committed against Jews—he had been the commandant at the Auschwitz and Birkenau death camps—Kolm could still say that "he was a real pleasure to deal with."

After his World War II and postwar experiences, Henry Kolm became a senior scientist and researcher at the Massachusetts Institute of Technology (MIT) in the fields of physics and electromagnetism. He co-founded the MIT Magnet Lab and was involved in the development of world-record electromagnets. He was recognized for his many inventions and contributions to science, such as high-gradient magnetic separation and water filtration, high-speed maglev transportation systems, and development of the electromagnetic aircraft carrier catapult. The maglev train transportation system, which some consider the future of rail transportation, uses two sets of magnets: one set to repel and push the train up off the track, and another set to move the elevated train ahead, taking advantage of the lack of friction. The train travels along a guideway of magnets that control the train's stability and speed. It currently can reach a speed of about 270mph. Discussions are currently underway to build a maglev system to connect Washington with Baltimore. The electromagnetic aircraft carrier catapult on the Gerald R. Ford-class aircraft carriers has replaced the steam-powered systems on earlier ships.

When Henry Kolm retired from MIT, he founded several companies and was named Entrepreneur of the Year in 1981 by *Money* magazine. He was an accomplished pianist with a lifelong passion for classical music, spoke fluent

French and German, and held a first-degree black belt in Korean karate. He received numerous awards for his inventions and contributions to technology.[5]

Another veteran, Arno Mayer, had a slightly different take on the treatment of prisoners in the Middle East. He said he felt "like the military is using us to say, 'We did spooky stuff then, so it's OK to do it now.'" He wanted to make it clear that nothing could be further from the truth. Like Henry Kolm, Arno Mayer had a distinguished career in academia. He had taught for many years in the Department of History at Princeton University. His university biography stated that "he would be the first to say that his teaching and research were decisively influenced by this early wartime experience, which helped shape his perspective of the last century and of European history." It went on to say that Arno "sought to place even the most unthinkable in a wide, comparative historical context, the conflict between reaction and revolutionary change." His publications focused on European historical problems, but he was continuously drawn to his early life, with respect to Nazism and the Holocaust. In his *Why did the Heavens not Darken?* (1988), he postulated that, while the Nazis were always antisemitic, they turned to genocide when the German armies became bogged down in savage military campaigns on the Eastern Front.

Arno Mayer was not merely doing research. He was a wonderful teacher as well. His biography said he was balanced in plumbing "the wellsprings of conservatism as well as his commitment to eminently relevant issues in the trajectory of modern Europe," which made him "a legendary teacher and mentor of students." Finally, "he has earned the respect and affection of undergraduates, graduate students, and colleagues in and outside the [Princeton] Department of History."[6]

John Gunther Dean continued on the same theme as his former colleagues, saying: "We did it [interrogated German prisoners] with a certain amount of respect and justice." If these comments were perhaps a bit more diplomatic than the others, it was for good reason. He had spent his post-World War II career as a diplomat in the American foreign service. He quickly moved up through the ranks and demonstrated his diplomatic skill while stationed in Paris in the late 1960s. He was credited with playing a major role in bringing the United States–North Vietnam peace talks to Paris in 1968. Then, in the early 1970s, while he was stationed in Southeast Asia, he was partly responsible for helping to save thousands of lives after the fall of Saigon in 1975. As the ambassador to Cambodia a little later, he ensured that all American personnel were evacuated just days before the Khmer Rouge entered Phnom Penh and initiated its ruthless reign of terror under Pol Pot.

Later, while Dean was stationed as ambassador to Lebanon, he was helpful in obtaining the release of the first American hostages in Iran. He was also instrumental in orchestrating the withdrawal of Soviet troops from Afghanistan in the 1980s. While he was in Lebanon, however, he drew the ire of the Israeli government and his bosses in the United States when he opened ties with the Palestine Liberation Organization. Because of this and other issues as he tried to balance diplomacy with Arabs and Israelis, he believed he was the target of Israeli assassination attempts.

One of Dean's most pleasant postings was as ambassador to Denmark. The Danes were long-standing friends and allies of the United States, and this assignment was almost completely devoid of controversy. While in Denmark, he endeared himself to the locals, because he became fluent in the Danish language.[7]

The veterans of PO Box 1142 continued to share their views and experiences at the reunion. They believed that torture was not only unnecessary and inhumane; it did not work. George Frenkel elaborated, saying that "during the many interrogations, I never laid hands on anyone. We extracted information in a battle of the wits. I'm proud to say I never compromised my humanity." George's perspective was based on his experience as one of the earliest soldiers stationed at Fort Hunt, then as a trainer for the young men who were being evaluated then trained in interrogation techniques at Camp Ritchie.

When George finished his military service, he went as a civilian to Germany. Like so many, the journey was sobering, when he learned that much of his family had perished in the Holocaust. But while he was there, he met and married Eva, to whom he was married for over 60 years. He worked for a time as a civilian historian in the Office of the Chief of Military History, but, with a growing family, he needed to make a little more money. George found that he could earn more if he rejoined the military doing the same job in the same office. He made the military his career and retired after 20 years. From the military, he moved over to the Voice of America as a writer.[8]

When Peter Weiss received his award, he said: "I am deeply honored to be here, but I want to make it clear that my presence here is not in support of the current war." Of all the speakers at the reunion, Peter Weiss had more credibility to speak about human rights than anyone. He had devoted his legal career to defending human rights around the world. He sought to hold governments accountable, using the principle of "universal jurisdiction," which allows states or international organizations to claim criminal jurisdiction over an accused person regardless of their nationality or of where the alleged crime was committed. In 1977, Peter brought attention to the United States's complicity in the overthrow of the Allende government in Chile with a suit concerning the detention and death of American journalist Charles Horman. He also showed his tenacity, keeping the heat on the government, which led to indictments against officials from both countries in 2011 and convictions for two Chilean officials in 2015.

Peter loved to find and use obscure federal laws to seek justice in human rights cases. In 1979, he used the Alien Tort Statute to hold a Paraguayan official accountable inside the United States for the torture and murder of the 17-year-old son of a Paraguayan dissident.[9] The case was *Filártiga v. Peña-Irala*, and it established a basis, since limited, for holding individuals and corporations accountable for human rights abuses.[10]

As the president of the Hague Appeal for Peace and the Lawyers Committee on Nuclear Policy, and as one of the founders of the International Association of Lawyers Against Nuclear Arms, he was a leader in the efforts to achieve the statement by the International Court of Justice in 1996 that the use of nuclear weapons would violate international law.[11]

Collectively, as a group, these veterans had more reason than most to torture the German prisoners they had interrogated. The Nazi regime had driven them and their families out of Europe, and most had family or loved ones who were victims of the Holocaust. Nevertheless, they made the powerful message that torture is not only inhumane but also does not bring the desired result of extracting important intelligence from captives.[12]

When the 2007 event ended, the George Washington Memorial Parkway chief ranger, Vincent Santucci, park historian Brandon Bies, and their park colleagues continued their quest to contact and interview as many men stationed at PO Box 1142 as possible. Time was their enemy, because by October 2007, World War II veterans were dying at a rate of about 30 every hour. They interviewed several veterans only days or weeks before they died. They learned that Daniel Pritchard, a veteran of the escape and evasion program, who lived in the Cleveland area, was not well but was interested in speaking with them. A team made arrangements to meet with him in July 2008, but just as they were ready to leave, Pritchard's family called to say that he had fallen into a coma. Several days later, Daniel came out of the coma and asked where the National Park Service rangers were. They jumped on a plane to interview Pritchard. His son was present and was able to fill in a few details his father had shared with him. Daniel passed away a short time later.[13]

At the conclusion of the 2007 reunion, David Vela, who at the time was the superintendent at the George Washington Memorial Parkway and later was the acting director of the National Park Service, concluded the ceremony by saying: "The National Park Service is committed to telling your story, and now it belongs to the nation."

Today, few remnants of PO Box 1142 remain at Fort Hunt Park. A small original building stands near the entrance. The early 1900-gun emplacements, where a few German prisoners were blindfolded and held for several hours, are still there. The rest of the park is a popular picnic and recreation area. On most warm weekends, families gather to eat their picnic lunches, play baseball, and have fun. In the middle of the park, the monument to PO Box 1142 stands, reminding visitors of what happened there. It is difficult to imagine that a bustling POW camp, a center for analyzing thousands of captured German documents, and buildings that housed programs for escape and evasion for American soldiers were once there.

CHAPTER 11

Go into Something Because You Really Like It

"Go into something because you really like it, and then do it with a drive and enthusiasm so that it isn't work."

JOHN KLUGE

Like the men who attended the reunions at Fort Hunt, the veterans of PO Box 1142 went on to successful careers after the war. Some continued in intelligence work. Most were glad for their experiences at Fort Hunt but chose career fields that were quite different from their work there. Many were leaders in their fields. Several were successful in business. Others had distinguished academic careers. Some had military careers, while others left the army but moved over to careers in government. Still others returned to the jobs they left before their military service. And one man, John Kluge, became one of the richest men in the country.[1]

John Kluge was already an entrepreneur while he was a student at Columbia University. He had a lucrative job as the tutor to Lin Jing (known in English as K. M. James Lin), the adopted son of Lin Sen, the President of China. When he graduated, he went to work for Otten Brothers (Paper) Company under an unusual arrangement that would characterize his business deals later in life. He asked the company to pay his expenses but without a salary. In return, if he doubled sales, the company promised to give him a one-third interest in the company. He met his goal. Yet, even with his success in paper sales and his share in the company, when he was discharged from the army, he sold his interest in the company, took the profit, and, with a partner, purchased radio station WGAY in Silver Spring, Maryland for $15,000. He had read an article in the *Wall Street Journal* that said the start-up costs for radio stations were substantially less than the new television industry. This, plus the consumer expense of purchasing a television (the cheapest television in 1946 was $100, equivalent to $1,336 today) and the reliance of Americans on their trusty radios during the Great Depression and World War II made a great deal of sense to Kluge. His partner agreed to operate the station while Kluge sold advertising spots. Within a short time, the station was a financial success.

John Kluge understood that putting all of one's eggs in one basket was not a good business model, so as he was setting up, then running his radio station, he acquired the franchise to sell Fritos snacks in the northeast. He could see that large supermarkets would quickly replace the mom-and-pop grocery stores and concentrated his sales efforts on this growing side of the grocery business. Diversity was one part of the Kluge business model, another was articulated by his business partner, Stuart Subotnick, who said that he and Kluge had "never gone where the herd goes. By the time the herd shows up, it's too expensive."

John Kluge put this part of his philosophy into practice in 1959 when he acquired principal interest in the struggling Metropolitan Broadcasting Company with its independent television and radio stations. The company was suffering because it could not compete with the powerful broadcasting networks—CBS, NBC, and ABC. Kluge saw a niche for independent stations and started buying them, when available, at reasonable prices. In the process, he changed the name of the company to Metromedia and continued to diversify. He purchased a large outside billboard company, the Ice Capades, and the Harlem Globetrotters. He was careful to keep expenses low, but he continuously looked for opportunities. He thought the game show *Jeopardy* would attract an audience and acquired the early version of the program, as well as programs featuring Jacques Cousteau. He also took advantage of the opportunity to purchase syndicated re-runs of popular shows.

By the mid-1980s, John Kluge decided to sell the various parts of his Metromedia empire for an estimated $4.5 billion, which was one of the most lucrative sales of a business up to that point. In 1987, *Forbes* Magazine reported that John Kluge was the richest man in the United States. Kluge continued with several business interests, but his focus shifted to philanthropy, giving $110 million to his alma mater, Columbia University, and $60 million to the Library of Congress, among his most generous gifts. His gift to Columbia grew by $400 million upon his death. The money he gave to Columbia was designated for student aid, paying back many times over the assistance he had received when he attended college. He also donated his large estate near Charlottesville, Virginia, valued at $45 million, to the University of Virginia.[2]

Whereas John Kluge made his mark in business, Silvio Bedini made his as a historian at the Smithsonian Institution in Washington, DC. When Silvio was discharged from the army, however, the Smithsonian was not in his thoughts.

He had returned to Ridgefield, Connecticut, to work with his brothers in the family contracting business. His particular skill was landscaping, and it seemed that would be his life's work. But he was also interested in history, and more specifically, the history of technology. He had bought an antique wooden clock with brass movements for $20, which became the catalyst for his interests. Then, in 1958, he accepted an invitation to write a brochure to commemorate the 250th anniversary of his town. The brochure grew into a 411-page book entitled *Ridgefield in Review*, which he wrote in partnership with his wife. This hastened his transition from landscaper to historian. It also did not hurt that Allen Nevins—one of the most well-known historians of the day—wrote a glowing introduction to the book.

Silvio's interest in antique clocks expanded into broader areas of technology and science, and he became fascinated with the works of Galileo during the Renaissance. As he followed his interests, he shared his findings in published papers. His work and his passion for historical technology came to the attention of Robert P. Multhauf, who was recruiting historians for the new Smithsonian Museum of History and Technology, then under construction on the National Mall in Washington, DC. At the age of 44, Silvio was offered a position with the new museum. He quickly became a fixture for some of his interesting discoveries, for his ability to share his finds with a wide audience, and for his administrative abilities. He stumbled onto an equatorial sundial from the Ming dynasty in a junk heap behind an auto repair shop in California. He sleuthed his way into the archives holding Christopher Columbus's correspondence. The local press in Washington could not wait to hear about what he had found. The *Washington Post* even published what it called "The Great Bedini's Rare Gifts." For much of his tenure, he served as the deputy director and for a time as the acting director of the museum.

His enduring legacy, however, was his enormous contribution to knowledge. He published 50 books and articles. Twenty of his books are currently listed on Amazon.com. He was fascinated with Benjamin Banneker, for whom a high school in Washington, DC is named. Silvio chronicled the life of this remarkable free African American man, who was a leading figure in early American science and mathematics and who surveyed the plat of the new nation's capital. In his book, *The Pope's Elephant*, he shared the story that grew out of a discovery he had made while visiting the underground tunnels in Rome. While there he found the tomb of Hanno—the white elephant that was the pet of Pope Leo X. In the early 1500s, Leo lived a life of excesses of the flesh that drew the ire of Martin Luther and others, but, for the people of Rome, his elephant brought great pleasure. *The Literary Review* said that

Bedini's *The Pope's Elephant* was "A work of extraordinary scholarship. ... Crisply written and amply illustrated, it shines a bright light on two short lives, that of Leo and Hanno, and that of the age they embodied."[3]

John Kluge excelled in business; Silvio Bedini was a superb historian; Dieter Kober made an indelible mark in music. When Dieter left his military service, he picked up right where he had left off with his passion for music. He went to Chicago and planned to pursue a career as a music critic, but his life's direction changed and instead he received a master's degree in musicology and a doctorate of fine arts from the Chicago Musical College. In the process he felt a pull toward conducting classical music, and with that in mind, he went to Salzburg, Austria, where he studied under the guidance of Igor Markevitch at the Mozarteum.

In 1952, the trajectory of his musical career, and, for that matter, the trajectory of classical music in Chicago, changed forever. He recognized that there was a dearth of chamber music in the city. He decided to change that and brought together a group of 11 musicians to perform numbers by Bach and Handel at the University of Chicago. The Chicago Chamber Orchestra was born, and Deiter Kober would be its conductor for 61 years. Not only did he bring together the orchestra, but he was determined to make classical chamber music accessible to everyone. They performed primarily at the Art Institute of Chicago, all around the Chicago area, and on tours around the country. Concerts generally were free, with one big fundraising performance each year to help cover the expenses. To help pay the bills, Dieter taught at the City Colleges of Chicago from 1950 to 1989. Members of the orchestra worked for low wages or for free to ensure that the concerts would be accessible to a wide audience.

In 1987, on the occasion of the chamber orchestra's 35th anniversary, the City of Chicago declared October 17 as Chicago Chamber Orchestra Day, and on that evening the ensemble performed its annual fundraising concert. The day before, Dieter Kober sat down for an interview with Pulitzer Prize-winning historian and journalist Studs Terkel on the latter's weekly Chicago radio program. Dieter talked about his orchestra and why it was so important to Chicago culture. He believed it was important to mix the classics with contemporary music to attract a wide audience. For the contemporary music, a benefactor might commission a work by a local composer to be premiered by the orchestra. To further enhance the audience's experience, he would explain something about each piece so they would better understand what they were hearing. For example, his orchestra would perform Beethoven symphonies with 35–36 artists. Concertgoers were surprised at the size of the group, since most had seen groups like the Chicago Symphony perform Beethoven with 80–100 artists. Dieter explained that the first performance of the *Fourth Symphony* was in Prince Lobkowitz's palace, which could accommodate no more than 35 artists—thus the Chicago Chamber Orchestra's performance was identical in size to its debut.

In addition to free performances in Chicago, the orchestra had an arrangement through a grant to perform for Chicago public school children, primarily from low-income areas. The orchestra would send recordings to the schools for the teachers to share with the children. Then they would be bused to a central location where they would listen to and interact one-on-one with Dieter Kober and his orchestra. Dieter said that this was likely the first-time inner-city children were exposed to Beethoven and Handel. He said they were enthralled with this new experience.[4]

Dieter conducted a concert of a local chamber group in East Germany one year before the fall of the Berlin Wall in 1989, then returned with his Chicago group in 1994 to perform in unified Germany. Dieter Kober passed away in 2015, but his orchestra lives on. It also lives on with recordings of performances he conducted, such as the highly regarded performance of the complete Handel's *Water Music*.[5]

In the MIRS section of PO Box 1142, Dieter Kober was one of the younger members of the group. One of his contemporaries who became a very good friend was Paul Fairbrook. When Paul returned home from the army, he decided to take advantage of the GI Bill to further his education. He applied to the hotel management program at Cornell University but was turned down for admission. It seemed that almost everyone wanted to enroll in that program. He next applied to Brown University, in part because a colleague in the army was a professor there. He was denied admission there as well, but the same day he received his denial letter, he called the admissions officer at the college and asked if he could come to meet with him—that day. He said he could get there by 4:00 in the afternoon. On the train ride from New York to Providence, Rhode Island, where Brown is located, he chatted with another passenger who helped him prep for his interview. He convinced the admissions person that he would be a great student and was admitted to the school.

Brown University was perfect for Paul. He found that his writing experience for the MIRS program under the tutelage of Professor Tucker was already paying dividends. Rather than having to take the lowest level English—affectionally referred to as "Bonehead English"—he was allowed to take an advanced literature class, which encouraged him to major in comparative literature. Paul graduated and after a series of jobs, finally settled on his life's work in food management. In the interim period, he was married, received a master's degree from Michigan State University in food management, then accepted a job at Northern Illinois University in De Kalb, Illinois. The college grew, his job changed, and he started looking for another opportunity. The opportunity came when he applied for, was offered, and accepted the position of Dean of the Culinary Institute of America (often referred to as the other CIA).

At the time, the school was located in New Haven, Connecticut, but it was quickly gaining the reputation as the premier chef's school in the country. The school eventually moved to Hyde Park, New York, and over its seven decades has trained over 50,000 students—many as chefs in the finest restaurants in America. Paul was the dean, and his boss was Ms. Frances Roth, a well-established attorney in Connecticut. She had founded the school and hired Paul Fairbrook to manage the curriculum and help raise money. He quickly realized that funding for the school was in a precarious state. The income was based almost solely on tuition. Paul tried to stabilize the funding by admitting more students, but he also established the requirement that all students needed to be high school graduates. Most of the instructors were European, which was another problem. Their way of dealing with students was to berate them constantly, which drove some of the more sensitive ones away. Of the curriculum offerings, Paul recognized the need for creating and teaching a new course in restaurant management. He understood that no matter how talented a chef might be, if he/she opened a restaurant and was clueless as to the business side of the operation, it was doomed to failure.

The CIA was a wonderful opportunity, but Paul became restless after a couple of years for two reasons. He admitted that he needed positive feedback from his director—Ms. Roth—which he never received. He also came to the realization that talking about food management was one thing, but what he craved was the actual hands-on management of food services. He resigned from his post at the school and went on his own as a consultant, assisting in opening restaurants, and landed the plum job of helping with advanced food planning for the World's Fair in Montreal—"Expo 67."

He returned to university food management in 1965, when he received a call from the University of the Pacific in Stockton, California. He accepted the job, packed his family—his wife, four children, and a dog—into a station wagon and moved to California. Paul and his family loved Stockton. His job was perfect. He managed the food services at the university—everything from dormitory dining rooms to hot dogs and peanuts at college football games. Stockton had excellent schools for his children. When they finished with public schools, they could attend the university free of charge. The city was near San

Francisco, Yosemite National Park, Lake Tahoe, and many other attractions. Moreover, Paul could continue with his consulting business. Paul remained in Stockton and ran the university food services program for 20 years. Since then, he has continued his consulting work, has written numerous books and articles on food management, and has received several prestigious awards for his work.[6]

"Lucky" Werner Moritz's luck continued after the war when he settled in Charlotte, North Carolina in 1963. He had an eye for finding business opportunities and concluded that the printing business, more precisely printing on fabrics, had enormous potential in the southern textile industry. He became a pioneer in the field and in 1969, he and his partners obtained a patent for fabric printing on pile fabrics, like towels. He started small, but grew and eventually acquired several companies which he consolidated into Hydro Prints, Inc. His company continued to grow and eventually became Automated Prints, Inc., which was listed on the American Stock Exchange.[7]

Much like Werner Moritz, Edgar Danciger became an entrepreneur, developing and perfecting a product that was in demand in postwar America. He moved to New York and worked during the day manufacturing wire cable rope and attended classes at night, eventually receiving a degree in engineering. From his day job of making wire cable, Edgar recognized a need for a product called pre-stressed concrete strand (concrete that required internal reinforcement with taut steel cable for stability). Edgar moved his family to Jacksonville, Florida, and created the Florida Wire and Cable Company. Not only did he create the company; he designed and built all of the manufacturing equipment. The company started with four employees and when he sold it 30 years later, there were 500. He saw the booming economy in Florida as a place that would need the product he produced. His gamble paid off, in that many of the new bridges and high-rise buildings required his pre-stressed concrete cable.

From his early life on the sea, he never lost his love for sailing. Edgar belonged to at least four yacht clubs and participated in competitive ocean sailing. His wife said that whenever they would sail past the Statue of Liberty, Edgar would start to cry. She added that he had such an intense love affair with his adopted country—the United States—he was delighted to pay his taxes. He actively supported local institutions in Jacksonville, such as the symphony and the Salvation Army, and he endowed a scholarship at the University of North Florida for mechanical engineering students.[8]

Leslie Willson completed his military service, then returned to the University of Texas to complete his college degree in journalism and a master's degree in German. He met his wife in the graduate program. He and his new wife moved to New Haven, Connecticut, where Leslie completed his Ph.D. in German literature at Yale. Following the completion of his doctorate, Leslie taught at Wesleyan College, Northwestern University, Duke and Penn State, and then returned to his beloved alma mater, the University of Texas, as a professor in 1966. He remained there until his retirement in 1992. He lived in the same house until his death in 2007.

Leslie was a popular teacher and he served as chairman of the German Department. His academic specialty was translating important German works into English, such as novels by Michael Krüger, Ulla Berkéwicz, and Gerhard Köpf. Leslie was the cofounder and first president of the American Literary Translators Association and was editor and publisher of a groundbreaking German literary magazine, *Dimension,* featuring contemporary German-language authors. He was recognized for his scholarly work with awards from the Goethe Institute and German government.[9]

Rudy Pins offered a great deal about his early life in Germany and in the United States. Further, his descriptions of his work at PO Box 1142 were the most illuminating. His older brother, Jacob Pins, a well-known artist in Israel, collaborated with Rudy to produce Rudy's autobiography from his early childhood until he completed his work after the war at Nuremberg. But from that time until his death in 2016, much of Rudy's life story is a mystery. In 2014, he was interviewed in a lengthy article in the *Honolulu Star Advertiser.* He had moved to Honolulu in retirement, and he shared his experiences as a child in Germany, his life as a teenager in Cleveland, and his experiences at Fort Hunt and Nuremberg. Regarding later life, he only mentioned that he had worked for a trade publishing business in New York. He did not say which company, how long he worked there, or what he published.[10]

In his interview with the National Park Service historians, they asked him about his work after his military service. More specifically, they asked if the government tried to recruit him into any of the federal intelligence services. He responded that he "did work for the government for a while." They probed a little deeper asking, "when you worked for the government, was it anything to do with intelligence or anything?" He said it was. They then asked "Oh, really? Okay, and what was that?" He said: "Well, I don't intend to go into that," and that ended that part of the conversation.[11]

Trying to piece together Rudy's life between the end of the war and the early 2000s is, and likely will remain, an unsolved puzzle.[12] He never married and did not have any children. His brother married but did not have children. His parents were killed in the Nazi death camps. Thus, without any Pins descendants, family members are not a possible source of information. Rudy's obituary simply said: "April 23, 2016, Rudolph L. Pins, 95, of Honolulu, an army veteran, died in Honolulu. He was born in Höxter, Germany. No survivors. Private services."[13]

While we know very little about Rudy's later life, he continued to share his recollections and helped us understand more and more about Fort Hunt while he was stationed there. On a September Sunday morning in 2014, the CBS *Sunday Morning* program featured Rudy and Fort Hunt, along with park historian Brandon Bies. The reporter, Seth Doane, asked Rudy, "How was it to live with a secret like that?"

"Well, you get used to it. Your fellow soldiers had the same secret." Rudy said before describing the camp. "It was a secret installation for the interrogation of POWs—Japanese, Italian, and German, but mainly German."

"What did the Nazis, what did Hitler, do to your family?" Doane asked.

"Destroyed it. Humiliated it." Rudy went on to say his parents were killed in Hitler's death camps during the Holocaust.

The reporter asked Rudy what he did at Fort Hunt. "I used to sit across from enemy soldiers who in combat would've killed me, and I probably would've killed them," he said. "My job was to get as much useful information as possible. You were face-to-face with the forces that destroyed your family." He continued, "They were the enemy. They were treated as the enemy. But you can't let your emotions get away from you. You also have a job to do."

Doane showed Rudy notes from one of his interrogations and said, "In one of those interrogation notes you wrote, 'So-and-so is a very stupid Nazi.'" What did Rudy think of that?

"He probably was!"

Pins concluded saying, "You don't get people to talk by beating 'em or waterboarding or anything of that nature." The interrogations were "never physical," but "psychological? Yes." If there was one postwar theme expressed by the soldiers stationed at Fort Hunt, it was this: No matter how much the Americans hated their German enemies and no matter how much potential information they might possess and not reveal, they never resorted to physical abuse to squeeze information from them.[14]

We likely will never know if, indeed, Rudy Pins ever worked for the CIA or some other United States intelligence agency. In contrast, there is absolutely no question that Angus Thuermer worked for the agency. In fact, he often referred to himself as the CIA's "spooksman," who, whenever a reporter asked him a question, would always reply, "No comment."

After his service in the navy and his assignment at PO Box 1142, Angus joined the CIA for a 26-year career that included postings as station chief in New Delhi and Berlin during the Cold War. After he died in 2010, his family joked that he described his job as helping sources get out of tight spaces, or occasionally into them. They said in one instance, Thuermer "smuggled a source out of India by putting him and a bottle of oxygen in a box, which was boarded onto the cargo bay of a Pan Am flight out of New Delhi. For another mission, he arranged to have Chinese dissidents carried over the mountains of Nepal into India on the back of an elephant. Then, there was Soviet leader Josef Stalin's daughter, Svetlana, whom he helped spirit out of New Delhi to the United States, in part by hiding her in a luggage cart at an airport."

Just before he retired in 1978, Angus was the CIA station chief in Berlin for two years. This was at the height of the Cold War, and because he likely knew as much as any outsider about the comings and goings of the East German Stasi spy agency, he was absolutely certain that the other side's spook agency did everything in its power to know what he was doing as often as possible. For fun, after the Cold War and as the East German spy records became available, he put in a request for the surveillance reports on his activities. He was upset to find that they were mostly mundane and included things like that he had driven his Volkswagen bus the wrong direction on a one-way street.[15]

It is not surprising that the men who made such enormous contributions to America's success in winning World War II would achieve so much success after the war. The Jewish refugees from Europe often expressed their gratitude that the United States not only accepted them on its shores but allowed them to contribute to the defeat of Adolf Hitler. Most said their experiences at Fort Hunt helped them as they navigated their careers later in life. Most also kept the secrets of their duties at PO Box 1142 to themselves but were delighted when they could finally share their stories, years later. Also, when given the opportunity, several veterans wanted to make it clear that when they interrogated German prisoners, they did not resort to corporal punishment but generally achieved success in gaining important information. This gave them credibility to criticize the treatment of prisoners in the Middle East conflicts.

In summary, we owe a great debt of gratitude to these men.

Epilogue

In 2007, shortly after I was appointed chief historian of the National Park Service, I was invited to be the keynote speaker at the anniversary of the attack on Pearl Harbor on December 7 that year. Early that morning, I squeezed into my National Park Service dress uniform, and my wife and I headed to Pearl Harbor. At 7:55a.m., the exact time the Japanese attack commenced, there was a moment of silence and a navy ship passed by with the sailors and marines standing at attention, "guarding the rail." Hawaii Air National Guard F-15s flew over in the "missing man" formation. At the conclusion of the ceremony, I watched as a family went to the USS *Arizona*, to witness a diver carefully insert the ashes of their husband/father into the ship. He had survived the December 7 attack and wanted to join his fellow crewmates who had fallen that day and were permanently entombed in the wreckage. I gave my talk but felt like it was insignificant, given the enormity of the day's events.

Later that day, I witnessed the dedication of a new monument to the 429 sailors and marines killed on the USS *Oklahoma*. The battleship was hit by multiple torpedoes and capsized within minutes on that fateful day. This was a special day for the ship's survivors. Many came for the dedication ceremony, and I had the opportunity to spend time with them. I spoke at length with Paul Goodyear, who was one of the leaders in the effort to erect the memorial. He introduced me to his fellow shipmates. Two of the men described their experience of being trapped in the bottom of the ship when the *Oklahoma* flipped over. In what they thought was their tomb, believing they only had minutes more to live, rescuers were able to drill through the hull and save them. Probably for my benefit, one gentleman said to the other: "I let you get out first. I have never, ever let anyone go in front of me." Another sailor said he was just getting ready to take a shower when the ship was hit, and he said, "I had to make a quick decision. Should I get dressed or not?" He said, "I jumped overboard as naked as a jay bird!" They had fun with me, but it did not take long for them to shift to talking about their comrades who died that day.

I also met Ed Vezey, an officer on the ship, who gave the keynote address at the dedication of the USS *Oklahoma* monument. Ed recalled that early on the morning of December 7, he and his roommate Frank Flaherty had to make a big decision: "We had to decide if we were going to the beach, swim, talk, and eat hot dogs or if we were going to go to breakfast first and then go to the beach, swim, talk, and eat hot dogs. In those days there were no girls in the navy, so we looked forward to going to the beach." As they contemplated their days' activities, a frantic message came over the loudspeaker that the ship was under attack; minutes later the *Oklahoma* was hit by numerous torpedoes and rolled over. Ed continued, "we don't know for sure what happened to Frank, but we do know he held a light for the men to escape from the below deck when the electricity went out. When the metal doors closed, Frank was trapped." A day that began so innocently ended with his friend Frank as one of 429 men killed that day. Frank Flaherty and his fallen shipmates are memorialized on the marble shafts that make up the memorial.[1]

The Japanese attack on Pearl Harbor was a complete surprise, which exposed America's unpreparedness for war. But, almost overnight, the American people sprung into action, determined to win the war as quickly as possible. On December 8, men lined up at military recruiting offices nationwide to join various branches of the service. Among them, Bob Feller, who was emerging as the star pitcher for the Cleveland Indians, joined the U.S. Navy, giving up three years at the prime of his baseball career. He was the first of some 500 former, present, and future Major League Baseball players who joined or were drafted into the military during the war.[2]

Men and women went to work, building the ships, airplanes, tanks, and the other tools of war at breakneck speed. Earlier that year, the SS *Patrick Henry*, the first of 2,710 Liberty ships, was launched in September 1941. Construction took 150 days from start to finish. A year later, with the urgency of getting these vessels in the water, the SS *Robert E. Peary* took four days, 15 hours, and 29 minutes to complete from start to launch. Fifteen companies, in 13 states, built the "Ugly Duckling" Liberty ships in 18 shipyards.[3] Airplane factories produced some 300,000 military aircraft during the war. Of that number, 12,731 B-17 Flying Fortress bombers were produced at the astonishing rate of one every four days at the height of production. More than 50,000 Sherman tanks were constructed—one every three hours or 45–50 per day. At the end of the war, this adage was often stated that the machine shops were as important as machine guns in winning the war.[4]

One glaring deficiency, which in part contributed to America's lack of vigilance before the surprise attack on Pearl Harbor, was the pre-war weakness in intelligence gathering. In recognizing this fact, the United States War Department quickly moved on multiple fronts to rectify the deficiencies. It borrowed heavily from its British Allies, who had already tried and tested many ideas and strategies, but it also tailored its program to its own needs and requirements. As an example, the training programs at Camp Ritchie were important for providing many of the tools needed to gather intelligence in and near the battlefields and at PO Box 1142. Recruiting German Jews to interrogate German soldiers and sailors, listen in on prisoner conversations, and translate, analyze, and prepare the "Order of Battle" and other reports from captured German documents gave leaders the tools to understand their enemy's strengths, weaknesses, and abilities. And the escape and evasion program gave flyers the equipment to evade capture if possible and the tools to help prisoners escape. Even if they remained incarcerated, they at least were able to keep in touch with their home base.

John Gunther Dean observed that "PO Box 1142 made a major contribution in many ways of showing the importance of intelligence before we [the United States] had an intelligence operation." And the operations at "1142 obeyed the laws. Listening and using your brain to get somebody's knowledge … was perfectly all right. Nobody ever interrogated with force." He continued saying that as far as he could tell, "we obeyed the international conventions on prisoners." [5]

We owe a huge debt of gratitude to the men—like John Gunther Dean— who were willing to share their experiences at PO Box 1142. Their stories are yet another pillar added to the edifice of our understanding of America's involvement in World War II. Information gleaned from interrogations, eavesdropping, and captured documents were crucial in intelligence-gathering operations. One historian said that by D-day, General Dwight Eisenhower probably knew more about German military strength than Hitler because of the extraordinary Allied intelligence apparatus.[6]

Intelligence gathering was multifaced, with groups of experts breaking enemy codes, others in the underground observing and passing along their findings, air reconnaissance spying on enemy activities, and still others feeding false, but convincing, information to the enemy. Intelligence gathering was such a crucial piece in the Allied victory. David Kahn, a leading expert in cryptology, wrote that it is "impossible to quantify the impact of intelligence on [World War II, but] some historians claim it hastened the end of the conflict by two years."[7]

General Dwight D. Eisenhower went even further, and shortly after the Allied victory in Europe wrote that "the intelligence … [gathered] before and during this campaign has been of priceless value to me. It has simplified my task as a commander enormously. It has saved thousands of British and American lives and in no small way, contributed to the speed with which the enemy was routed and eventually forced to surrender."[8]

Of the men who shared their experiences at PO Box 1142, most had no interest in military service before the war; nearly all went into non-military professions after the war. But, like the millions of Americans who fought on the battlefield, worked in the factories, served in various non-combat roles, or sacrificed at home so that the troops would have everything they needed, they devoted their energies to winning the war. No one questioned what they were doing or why. After the war, they returned to their pre-war jobs, found new jobs, opened small businesses, attended or returned to school, taught in schools, got married, and produced the "baby boomer" generation.

So how do we assess the importance of the work at PO Box 1142? Or more importantly, how did the men assigned there view their own importance or what they gained from their experience there? Everyone thought the work they did was valuable and were happy they could finally talk about what they did. This has been a constant theme throughout this work. Some shared the value of their experience later in life. Henry Kolm, among others, recognized that the collaborative nature of their work prepared them for their careers. He said that before coming to Fort Hunt, he was not very people oriented, but the time there "taught me a lot about people, about running a team, and about organizing things." Others said the discipline was valuable. If they were late for anything, they were punished, so it did not take long for them to be punctual. Recognizing and respecting authority was important as well.

Still others provided their assessments of the overall value of the work at Fort Hunt. John Gunther Dean mused that the significance of PO Box 1142 might best be understood as a history lesson. The respectful way in which they dealt with prisoners paid dividends in the information they gathered. Present and future programs would do well to learn from what they did. Thus, "history," he said, "looks at a problem with a little bit of hindsight, but only if people learn from history will it have an impact on the future."[9]

When Rudy Pins was asked if he thought PO Box 1142 helped turn the tide of the war, or, more precisely, if he thought it made a difference, he answered: "I would hope so. But, you know, it's like a jigsaw puzzle. You need all the pieces to get the picture, and we got some of the pieces" but not all.[10]

Finally, Paul Fairbrook expressed the feelings of many of his World War II colleagues when asked why his service at Fort Hunt was so important to him. "First, I was able to revenge in whatever way I could my loss of my uncle, my aunt, and my cousins—my family—to the Holocaust. I had the chance to really do something about that. Second and equally important, I had the chance to thank the United States for letting me and my family in. Because of that, I, my children, and my grandchildren are all doing well in this wonderful country."[11]

Bibliography

Articles

"300,000 Airplanes." *Air & Space Magazine*, May 2007. https://www.airspacemag.com/history-of-flight/300000-airplanes-17122703/.

Ambrose, Stephen E. "Eisenhower and the Intelligence Community in World War II." *Journal of Contemporary History,* 16 (1981): 153–166.

Azmy, Baher. "International Human Rights Pioneer Peter Weiss Celebrates 90." Center for Constitutional Rights, December 8, 2015. https://ccrjustice.org/home/blog/2015/12/08/international-human-rights-pioneer-peter-weiss-celebrates-90.

"Belgium Refugee Eager to Fight for Uncle Sam." *Pittsburgh Post Gazette*, March 3, 1943.

Bland, John Paul. "Secret War at Home: The Pine Grove Furnace Prisoner of War Interrogation Camp." Cumberland County (Pennsylvania) Historical Society, 2006.

Brown, David. "Kindertransport Exhibit Highlights Family Separation in 1930s." Leo Baeck Institute, September 27, 2018. https://www.lbi.org/news/kindertransport-exhibition-highlight-family-separation-1930s/.

"Captured Nazi Ship Taken to Puerto." http://iagenweb.org/wwii/FeatureWWIIOdenwald.html#:~:text=November%201941&text=Washington%20(AP)%E2%80%94The%20Navy,at%20San%20Juan%2C%20Puerto%20Rico.&text=She%20was%20enroute%20to%20Germany%20from%20Japan%20when%20she%20was%20seized.

ClevelandSeniors.com. "George Weidinger: Shortening the War through PO Box 1142." http://www.clevelandseniors.com/people/george-weidinger.htm.

Cress, Joseph. "Pine Grove POWs: Pine Grove Furnace was once a Prisoner of War Interrogation Camp used during WWII." *The Sentinel,* October 6, 2014.

Dickson, Paul and Thomas B. Allen "Marching on History: When a 'Bonus Army' of World War I veterans converged on Washington, MacArthur, Eisenhower and Patton were there to meet them" *Smthsonian Magazine.* February 2003 https://www.smithsonianmag.com/history/marching-on-history-75797769./.

Dvorak, Petula. "A Covert Chapter Opens For Fort Hunt Veterans As Files on Nazi POWs Are Declassified, Their Interrogators Break Their Silence." *Washington Post,* August 20, 2006. https://www.washingtonpost.com/archive/politics/2006/08/20/a-covert-chapter-opens-for-fort-hunt-veterans-span-classbankheadas-files-on-nazi-pows-are-declassified-their-interrogators-break-their-silence-span/5ae16af8-9c6d-414b-9d5e-c64e10f0241a/.

Dvorak, Petula. "Fort Hunt's Quiet Men Break Silence on WWII." *Washington Post*, October 6, 2007. https://www.washingtonpost.com/wpdyn/content/article/2007/10/05/AR2007100502492.html.

Egner, Kate. "Ann Pamela Cunningham." *Digital Encyclopedia of George Washington.* https://www.mountvernon.org/library/digitalhistory/digital-encyclopedia/article/ann-pamela-cunningham.

Ellison, Matt. "The German Strategic Mastermind Behind America's Post-War Order." *Palladium*, 2019. https://palladiummag.com/2019/04/12/the-german-strategic-mastermind-behind-the-post-world-war-ii-liberal-order/.

Findagrave.com. "Paul Kubala." https://www.findagrave.com/memorial/49242434/paul-kubala.

Forum Jacob Pins. "Rudy Pins: Erinnerungen 1920-1948 (dt)." Autobiography in German published by his brother Jacob Pins (translated into English). http://www.jacob-pins.de/?article_id=286&clang=0.

Graham, Dave. "New book reveals horror of Nazi camp brothels." *Reuters*, August 17, 2009. https://www.reuters.com/article/us-germany-nazis-brothels/new-book-reveals-horror-of-nazi-camp-brothels-idUSTRE57G45X20090817.

GW School of Medical and Heath Sciences. "H. George Mandel Ph.D." https://smhs.gwu.edu/news/h-george-mandel-phd.

Holl, Richard E. "Swastikas in the Bluegrass State: Axis Prisoners of War in Kentucky, 942–46." *The Register of the Kentucky Historical Society*, 100 (Spring 1992): 139–165.

"Helmut Ruge, German POW #1." World War II Pacific: The early years. http://www.ww2pacific.com/ruge.html.

"Isle Resident Part of Secrets of POW Camp." *Honolulu Star Advertiser*, November 12, 2014.

"Israel honors GI who told the Nazis, 'We are all Jews'." *The Times of Israel*, November 27, 2016.

Kahn, David. "The Rise of Intelligence." *Foreign Affairs*, 85 (September–October 2006): 125-134.

Legacy.com. "Edgar Danciger." https://www.legacy.com/obituaries/staugustine/obituary.aspx?n=edgardanciger&pid=157083223&fhid=12961.

Legacy.com. "Frederick Michel." https://www.legacy.com/obituaries/washingtonpost/obituary.aspx?n=frederickmi-chel&pid=128958113.

Legacy.com. "Henry H. Kolm." https://www.legacy.com/obituaries/wickedlocal-sudbury/obituary.aspx?n=henry-h-kolm&pid=144598916.

Legacy.com. "Walter Thomas Cini." https://www.legacy.com/obituaries/name/walter-cini-obituary?pid=19816363.

Lemyre, Rick. "Secret World of Camp Tracy Revealed." *The Press: Brentwood, Discovery Bay, Oakley, and Antioch* (California), January 28, 2010, updated Nov 22, 2013.

Matthews, Sam. "The Tale of Camp Tracy." *Tracy (California) Press*, November 22, 2008.

Miller, Michael E. "How the Nazi telegram that helped drive Hitler to suicide was nearly forgotten in a S.C. safe." *Washington Post*, July 10, 2015. https://www.washingtonpost.com/news/morning-mix/wp/2015/07/10/how-the-nazi-telegram-that-helped-drive-hitler-to-suicide-was-nearly-forgotten-in-a-s-c-safe/.

"Nazi Captives Not Subjected to Harsh Measures." *The (Lakeland, Florida) Ledger*, October 7, 2007.

North Carolina State University Extension Service, "Tobacco Grower's Information," https://tobacco.ces.ncsu.edu/tobacco-fertility-nutrients/

Obituary for Edgar Danciger: https://www.jacksonville.com/article/20120417/BUSINESS/801254725.

Post, Robert C. "Silvio A. Bedini, 1917–2007." *Technology and Culture*, 49, (April 2008): 522-529.

Povich, Shirley. "At Redskins-Eagles Game, Crowd Was Kept Unaware That War Had Begun." *Washington Post*, December 7, 1991. https://www.washingtonpost.com/wp-srv/sports/longterm/general/povich/launch/war.htm.

Princeton University. "Arno J. Mayer." https://dof.princeton.edu/about/clerk-faculty/emeritus/arno-j-mayer.

The University of Texas at Austin. "A. Leslie Willson." https://liberalarts.utexas.edu/germanic/_files/pdf/depnotables/willson.pdf.

United States Holocaust Memorial Musuem. "The Immigration of Refugee Children to the Unites States." *Holocaust Encyclopedia.* https://encyclopedia.ushmm.org/content/en/article/the-immigration-of-refugee-children-to-the-united-states

USMM.org. "Liberty Ship SS Robert E. Peary built in 4 days, 15 hours, 29 minutes." http://www.usmm.org/peary.html.

Shapiro, T. Ross. "Obituary: Angus Thuermer, Swashbuckling former CIA Official." *Pittsburgh Post-Gazette,* May 11, 2010.

"Story of Marcus McDilda – Kempeitei Torture – WW2 FEPOW." (Story written by a Mr. White). *Forces War Records,* August 11, 2015. https://www.forces-war-records.co.uk/blog/2015/08/11/lieutenant-marcus-mcdilda-captured-tortured-interrogated.

Williams, Mike. "P.O. Box 1142: The Secrets of Fort Hunt." https://www.lastingtributesfuneralcare.com/obituaries/Spencer-Gulick/#!/Obituary.

Worldcat.org. "Schlicke, Heinz M." https://www.worldcat.org/identities/lccn-n82029005/.

Yoon-Hendricks, Alexandra. "You Asked, We Answered: Abandoned Delta Hotel Once Served as WWII Interrogation Center." *Sacramento Bee,* May 20, 2019, updated June 5, 2019.

Zimmerman, Dwight Jon. "Churchill's Deal With the Devil: The Anglo-Soviet Agreement of 1941." DefenseMediaNetwork, July 12, 2011. https://www.defensemedianetwork.com/stories/churchills-deal-with-the-devil/

Books

Alford, Kenneth D., *Nazi Plunder: Great Treasure Stories of World War II.* New York: De Capo, 2003.

Angress, Werner. *Witness to the Storm: A Jewish Journey from Nazi Berlin to the 82nd Airborne, 1920–1945.* Scotts Valley, California: CreateSpace Independent Publishing Platform, 2012.

Bedini, Silvio A. *The Life of Benjamin Banneke.* New York: Macmillan, 1972.

Bedini, Silvio A. *The Pope's Elephant.* New York: Penguin, 2000.

Brikill, Paul. *The Great Escape.* New York: W. W. Norton, 2004.

Chernow, Ron. *Washington: A Life.* New York: Penguin Press, 2010.

Childs, David. *Wings and Tracks.* Caldwell, Idaho: Caxton Printers, 2009.

Cini, Carol E. *The Spy and His CIA Brat.* CreateSpace Independent Publishing Platform, 2017.

Corbin. Alexander. *The History of Camp Tracy: Japanese WWII POWs and the Future of Strategic Interrogation.* Fort Belvoir, Virginia: Ziedon Press, 2009.

Dickson, Paul and Thomas B. Allen. *The Bonus Army: An American Epic.* London: Walker Books, 2004.

Eddy, Beverley Driver, *Ritchie Boy Secrets: How a Force of Immigrants and Refugees Helped Win World War II.* Guilford, Connecticut: Stackpole Books 2021.

Fairbrook, Paul. "Autobiography of Paul Fairbrook, 1923–2017," edited by Carolyn Chandler, 2018 (not published).

Happel, Jörn. *Der Ost-Experte: Gustav Hilger - Diplomat im Zeitalter der Extreme* (in English *The East Expert—Gustav Hilger: Diplomat in the Age of Extremes*). Berlin: Ferdinand Schöningh GmbH, 2017.

Henderson, Bruce. *Sons and Soldiers: The Untold Story of the Jews Who Escaped the Nazis and Returned with the US Army to Fight Hitler.* New York: Harper Collins, 2017.

Jacobsen, Annie. *Operation Paperclip: The Secret Intelligence Program that Brought Nazi Scientists to America.* Boston: Little Brown and Company, 2014.

Kluge, John, Jr., *John Kluge Stories.* New York: Columbia University Press, 2009.

Lewis, Emanuel Raymond. *Seacoast Fortifications of the United States: An Introductory History.* Annapolis: Naval Institute Press, revised edition, 1993.

Maher Neil M. *Nature's New Deal: The Civilian Conservation Corps and the Roots of the American Environmental Movement.* New York: Oxford University Press, 2009.

Mallett, Derek R. *Hitler's Generals in America: Nazi POWs and Allied Military Intelligence.* Lexington: University Press of Kentucky, 2013.

Mayer, Arno J. *Why Did the Heavens Not Darken?: The Final Solution in History.* New York: Pantheon, 1988.

Mulligan, Timothy P. *Lone Wolf: The Life and Death of U-Boat Ace Werner Henke.* Norman, Oklahoma: University of Oklahoma Press, 1995.

Neitzel, Sönke and Harald Welzer. *Soldiers: German POWs on Fighting, Killing and Dying* Toronto: Penguin Random House of Canada, 2012.

Neufeld, Michael J. *Von Braun: Dreamer of Space, Engineer of War.* New York: Alfred A. Knopf, 2007.

Nicholas, Lynn H. *The Rape Of Europa: The Fate of Europe's Treasures in the Third Reich and the Second World War.* New York: Vintage Books, 1994.

Ross, Steven J. and Wolf Gruner (editors). *New Perspectives on Kristallnacht: After 80 Years, the Nazi Pogrom in Global Comparison (The Jewish Role in American Life: An Annual Review)* 17th edition. East Lafayette, Indiana: Purdue University Press, 2019.

Scalia, Joseph Mark. *Germany's Last Mission to Japan: The Failed Voyage of U-234.* Annapolis: Naval Institute Press, 2000

Sheskin, Ira M. and Arnold Dashefsky. "United States Jewish Population, 2020," in *American Jewish Yearbook, 2020.* Cham SUI: Springer, 2021.

Shoemaker, Lloyd R. *The Escape Factory: The Story of MIS-X.* New York: St. Martin's Press, 1992.

Stern, Guy. *Invisible Ink: A Memoir.* Detroit: Wayne University Press, 2020.

Thompson, Gilbert (editor). *Pioneers of Medicine Without a Nobel Prize.* London: Imperial College Press, 2014.

Tobias, Henry J. *A History of the Jews of New Mexico.* Albuquerque: University of New Mexico Press, 1990.

Tuccille, Jerome. *The War Against the Vets: The World War I Bonus Army during the Great Depression.* Potomac, Maryland: Potomac Press, 2018.

Ward, Bob. *Dr. Space: The Life of Wernher von Braun.* Annapolis: Naval Institute Press, 2009.

Williams, Eric. *The Wooden Horse: The Classic World War II Story of Escape.* New York: Skyhorse, 2014.

Government Publications

Coyne, George Kermit. "History of P.O. Box 1142: Naval Prisoner of War Interrogations Conducted by the Military Intelligence Staffs of MIS-Y & Op-16-Z," May 17, 2010. George Washington Memorial Parkway, National Park Service, Arlington Virginia.

Davis, Timothy. *Highways in Harmony: George Washington Memorial Parkway, Virginia, Maryland, Washington, D.C.* (Washington, DC: National Park Service, 1994).

EDAW, Inc. "Cultural Landscape Report," Mount Vernon Memorial Highway, vol. 1. Alexandria, Virginia, 1989.

Fairbrook, Paul (although not listed as author in the publication). "Political Indoctrination and Morale Building in the German Army" (Washington, DC: Washington MIRS, Military Branch, Military Intelligence Service, War Department, December 21, 1944).

Fairbrook, Paul (although not listed as author in the publication). "Organization of the High Command of the German Army," Fall 1944. Copy made available by Paul Fairbrook. No publication data.

"History and Operation of MIRS, London and Washington Branches," May 1, 1943, to 14 July 14, 1945.

Laird, Matthew R. Ph.D. "By the River Potomac: An Historic Resource Study of Fort Hunt Park,' George Washington Memorial Parkway, prepared for the National Park Service, National Capital Region, August 2, 2000." Washington, DC.

"Order of Battle of the German Army," February 1944 (Washington, DC: Military Intelligence Division, Department of War).

"Order of Battle of the German Army," March 1945. (Washington, DC: Military Intelligence Division, Department of War).

Government Documents

Assistant Chief of Staff, G-2, Intelligence Division, Captured Personnel and Materials Branch, Enemy POW Interrogation File (MIS-Y), 1943–45, Reports, U-Boats, Ships, and other Naval Material, Box 730, National Archives and Records Administration (NARA) 165.

CIA.gov. Freedom of Information Act Release of information on Gustav Hilger from the CIA: HILGER, GUSTAV_0038.pdf (cia.gov).

Clinton, William J. "Executive Order 12937." https://fas.org/sgp/clinton/eo12937.html.

Coastal Defense Study Group. "The Endicott and Taft Reports." https://cdsg.org/product/the-endicott-and-taft-reports./.

Cornell University Library. Kubala, Paul Interrogations in the General William Donovan Nuremberg Collection. http://lawcollections.library.cornell.edu/nuremberg?f%5Bwitness_tesim%5D%5B%5D=Hermann+Goering.

Griffith, Sanford, Discussion I-IV, Series of Talks by Sanford Griffith, prepared for the Third Army School, San Antonio, TX, April 20, 1942. Record Group 165, Records of the War Department General and Special Staffs; Office of the Director of Intelligence (G-2), Subordinate Office and Branches, Captured Personnel and Material Branch, NARA.

Gross, Dan. "Paul Kubala (1907–1967)."

Herbert Hoover Presidential Library and Museum. "The Great Depression." https://hoover.archives.gov/exhibits/great-depression.

Jewish Virtual Library. "Eric Waldman on the US Army's Trusteeship of the Gehlen Organizations During the Years 1945–1949." https://www.jewishvirtuallibrary.org/cia-relationship-with-nazi-general-reinhard-gehlen-during-world-war-ii.

Library of Congress. "United States Statutes at Large." https://www.loc.gov/law/help/statutes-at-large/71st-congress/session-2/c71s2ch354.pdf.

Library of Congress. "Washington's Diaries" (Available Online), at: https://www.loc.gov/loc/lcib/0010/gwdiary.html.

National Register of Historic Places. U.S. Department of the Interior. National Park Service.

Report No. 116, Source ETO-536-MI, February 26, 1943, Record Group 165, Records of the War Department General and Special Staffs; Office of the Director of Intelligence (G-2), Subordinate Office and Branches, Captured Personnel and Material Branch. NARA.

Transcripts of "Man on the Street" interviews following the attack on Pearl Harbor. https://tile.loc.gov/storage-services/service/afc/afc1941004/afc1941004_sr01b/afc1941004_sr01b.xml.

U.S. Senate. "Report of the Senate Select Committee on Intelligence Committee Study of the Central Intelligence Agency's Detention and Interrogation Program together with Foreword by Chairman Feinstein and Additional Minority Views." December 9, 2014. https://www. intelligence.senate.gov/sites/default/files/publications/CRPT-113srpt288.pdf.

Viero, Walter biography,http://www.lexikon-der-wehrmacht.de/Personenregister/V/VierowWalter-R. htm.https://vault.fbi.gov/Arthur%20Rudolph%20/Arthur%20Rudolph%20Part%201% 20of%201/view.

Website for the USS *Oklahoma* Memorial: https://www.nps.gov/perl/learn/historyculture/ uss-oklahoma.htm.

Films, Audio and Visual Media

Ades, Lisa, (director). *GI Jews: Jewish Americans in World War II*. New York: Turquoise Films, Channel Thirteen, 2017.

Bauer, Christian. *The Ritchie Boys*. New York: Docurama Films, 2004.

CBS News. "Memories of a POW Camp outside Washington, DC." *Sunday Morning*, September 21, 2014. https://www.cbsnews.com/news/memories-of-a-pow-camp-outside-washington-d-c/.

Fesler, Pam. "Former GIs Spill Secrets Of WWII POW Camp." *All Things Considered*, National Public Radio, August 18, 2008. https://www.npr.org/templates/story/story.php?storyId=93649575.

Teitel, Amy Shira. "Wernher von Braun: History's most controversial figure? Pivotal to the history of spaceflight, von Braun's Nazi past makes him incredibly difficult to talk about." *Al Jazeera*, 2013. https://www.aljazeera.com/opinions/2013/5/3/wernher-von-braun-historys-most-controversial-figure/.

Terkel, Studs. "Interviewing Dieter Kober on the occasion of the Chicago Chamber Orchestra's 40th Anniversary." Studs Terkel Radio Archive, Oct 16, 1987. https://studsterkel.wfmt.com/ programs/interviewing-dieter-kober-occasion-chicago-chamber-orchestras-40th-anniversary.

Tsuyoshi, Masuda. "Unearthed Tapes Explain a Piece of World War Two History." *NHK*, December 22, 2020. https://www3.nhk.or.jp/nhkworld/en/news/backstories/1423/.

Wertheim, Jon. "Stories from members of the Ritchie Boys, a secret U.S. WWII intelligence unit bolstered by German-born Jews." *60-Minutes*, CBS, May 9, 2021.

Thesis

Kleinman, Steven M. "The History Of MIS-Y: US Strategic Interrogation During World War II.". Thesis submitted to the Faculty of the Joint Military Intelligence College in partial fulfillment of the requirements for the degree of Master of Science of Strategic Intelligence, August 2002.

Oral History Interviews

Ahrens, James, interview by Vincent Santucci, September 29, 2010, George Washington Memorial Parkway, National Park Service, Arlington, Virginia.

Bedini, Silvio, interview by Brandon Bies and Matthew Virta, October 15, 2007, George Washington Memorial Parkway, National Park Service, Arlington, Virginia.

Bies, Brandon, multiple interviews with Robert K. Sutton between 2007–2021.

Braun, Wernher von, oral history interview: https://www.nasa.gov/sites/default/files/atoms/files/von_braun_interviews.pdf.

Buck, Daniel, interview (by phone) by Vincent Santucci and David Lassman, October 25, 2010, George Washington Memorial Parkway, National Park Service, Arlington, Virginia.

Danciger, Edgar, interview by David Lassman (by phone), November 8, (year not stated), George Washington Memorial Parkway, National Park Service, Arlington, Virginia.

Dean, John Gunther, interview by Brandon Bies, Vincent Santucci, Sam Swersky, Eric Oberg, October 2, 2007, George Washington Memorial Parkway, National Park Service, Arlington, Virginia.

Dennis, Lawrence interview by David Lassman, June 7, 2009, George Washington Memorial Parkway, National Park Service, Arlington, Virginia.

Dierkes, Dana, interview by Robert K. Sutton, January 11, 2021.

Fairbrook, Paul interview by Brandon Bies and Vincent Santucci, February 15, 2008, George Washington Memorial Parkway, National Park Service, Arlington, Virginia.

Fairbrook, Paul interviews by Robert K. Sutton, March 18, 2018, and December 19, 2020.

Feller, Bob interview by Robert K. Sutton, November 11, 2008.

Fichtner, Hans interview by Brandon Bies and Vincent Santucci, April 22, 2010, George Washington Memorial Parkway, National Park Service, Arlington, Virginia.

Frenkel, George, interviews by Brandon Bies, Sam Swersky, and Doug Heimlich, December 5, 2006, and January 18, 2007, George Washington Memorial Parkway, National Park Service, Arlington, Virginia.

Gajdosch, Franz, interviews by Brandon Bies May 6 and October 25, 2010, George Washington Memorial Parkway, National Park Service, Arlington, Virginia.

Graber, Norman, interview by Brandon Bies, May 14–15, 2007, George Washington Memorial Parkway, National Park Service, Arlington, Virginia.

Grau, Dieter, interview by Brandon Bies, Vincent Santucci, and Jackie Dannenberg (widow of an Operation *Paperclip* engineer), April 21, 2010, George Washington Memorial Parkway, National Park Service, Arlington, Virginia.

Hacker, Victor, interview by Brandon Bies and Vincent Santucci, January 16, 2008, George Washington Memorial Parkway National Park Service, Arlington, Virginia.

Hess, Bill, interviews by Brandon Bies, Matthew Virta, and Samuel Swersky, November 21, 2006 (Colonel Steve Kleinman joined in on March 9, 2007), George Washington Memorial Parkway, National Park Service, Arlington, Virginia.

Holderer, Oscar, interview by Brandon Bies and Vincent Santucci, April 23, 2010, George Washington Memorial Parkway, National Park Service, Arlington, Virginia.

Jones, David and Thomas Griffin, interview by Brandon Bies, Vincent Santucci, and Matthew Virta, Nov 6, 2008, George Washington Memorial Parkway, National Park Service, Arlington, Virginia.

Kloss, Robert, interview by Vincent Santucci and David Lassman, May 6, 2010, George Washington Memorial Parkway, National Park Service, Arlington, Virginia.

Kluge, John interview by Brandon Bies, Matthew Virta and Vincent Santucci, May 16, 2008, George Washington Memorial Parkway, National Park Service, Arlington, Virginia.

Kober, Dieter, interview by Brandon Bies, January 17–18, 2008, George Washington Memorial Parkway, National Park Service, Arlington, Virginia.

Kolm, Henry, interview by Brandon Bies and Sam Swersky, May 7–8, 2007, George Washington Memorial Parkway, National Park Service, Arlington, Virginia.

Leonhard, Anton, interview by Brandon Bies, Vincent Santucci, and David Lassen, April 2, 2010, George Washington Memorial Parkway, National Park Service, Arlington, Virginia.

Mandel, George, interview 1 by Brandon Bies and Sam Johnson, July 13, 2006; interview 2 by Brandon Bies, Sam Swarovski, Vincent Santucci, and Matthew Virta from NPS, plus John Bardal from the *National Geographic* (second interview conducted at the National Geographic.), January 29, 2007. Both interviews housed at the George Washington Memorial Parkway, National Park Service, Arlington, Virginia.

Mayer, Arno, interview by Brandon Bies and Vincent Santucci, September 16, 2008, George Washington Memorial Parkway, National Park Service, Arlington, Virginia.

Mayer, Arno, interview by Robert K. Sutton, December 13, 2020.

Michel, Fred and Lucille, interview by Brandon Bies, May 30–31, 2006, George Washington Memorial Parkway, National Park Service, Arlington, Virginia.

Moritz, Werner, interview by Brandon Bies, July 23–24, 2007, George Washington Memorial Parkway, National Park Service, Arlington, Virginia.

Nipkow, Louis Al, interview by Brandon Bies, Vincent Santucci, and Colonel Steven Kleinman, February 17, 2008, George Washington Memorial Parkway, National Park Service, Arlington, Virginia.

Nottingham, Howard, interview by Brandon Bies and Matthew Virta, April 19, 2007, George Washington Memorial Parkway, National Park Service, Arlington, Virginia.

Patton, Ralph, interview by Brandon Bies, Vincent Santucci, and David Lassman, February 10, 2009, George Washington Memorial Parkway, National Park Service, Arlington, Virginia.

Pins, Rudy, interview by Brandon Bies and Sam Swersky, September 14-15, 2006, George Washington Memorial Parkway, National Park Service, Arlington, Virginia.

Rosenthal, Roberta and Stephen Rosenthal, interview by Robert K. Sutton, August 23, 2020.

Salomon, Ernest, interview 1 and 2 by Brandon Bies and Vincent Santucci, late November 2008 (specific day not specified) and December 3, 2008; interview 3 by Brandon Bies, Vincent Santucci and Dan Grose, March 12, 2009 (by telephone from Tokyo). All three interviews housed at the George Washington National Parkway, National Park Service, Arlington, Virginia.

Santucci, Vincent, multiple interviews by Robert K. Sutton between 2007–2021.

Schueman, Walter, interview by Brandon Bies (joined briefly by Vincent Santucci), September 17, 2010, George Washington Memorial Parkway, National Park Service, Arlington, Virginia.

Spivey, Wayne, interview by Brandon Bies, August 20–31, 2006, George Washington Memorial Parkway, National Park Service, Arlington, Virginia.

Stern, Guy, interview by Robert K. Sutton, May 18, 2021.

Syphax, Burke, interview by Brandon Bies, March 6, 2007, George Washington Memorial Parkway, National Park Service, Arlington, Virginia.

Thuermer, Angus MacLean, interview by Brandon Bies, Sam Swersky, and Vincent Santucci, October 25, 2006, George Washington Memorial Parkway, National Park Service, Arlington, Virginia.

Weidinger, George, interview by Brandon Bies and Vincent Santucci, November 29, 2007, George Washington Memorial Parkway, National Park Service, Arlington, Virginia.

Weidinger, George, interview by Robert K. Sutton, March 12, 2021.

Weiss, Peter, interview by Brandon Bies, September 13, 2006, George Washington Memorial Parkway, National Park Service, Arlington, Virginia.

Weiss, Peter interview by Robert K. Sutton, April 26, 2021.

Willson, A. Leslie, interview by Brandon Bies, December 14, 2007, George Washington Memorial Parkway, National Park Service, Arlington, Virginia.

Winick, Charles, interview by Brandon Bies, September 16, 2010, George Washington Memorial Parkway, National Park Service, Arlington, Virginia.

Endnotes

Introduction

1 This poem, "The New Colossus," at the base of the Statue of Liberty was written by Emma Lazarus (1849–87), considered by many as the first major American Jewish poet.

2 https://www.haaretz.com/jewish/.premium--1.5408033. Determining precise numbers for Jewish populations in the United States is not an exact science. Some names that appear to be Jewish, such as Cohen or Levy, probably are Jewish, but possibly not. Other names like Smith, Davidson, or the Portuguese names listed above, do not necessarily sound Jewish but may be. Thus, it is difficult to determine from the census who is Jewish and who is not; Ira M. Sheskin and Arnold Dashefsky, "United States Jewish Population, 2020," *American Jewish Yearbook, 2020* (Cham SUI: Springer, 2021).

3 Ibid.

4 Luis Gold was my wife's great-great-grandfather. The precise date he arrived in New Mexico is not known, but the best estimate is that he arrived in 1857–58, https://www.findagrave.com/memorial/48249527/luis-gold; Henry J. Tobias, *A History of the Jews of New Mexico* (Albuquerque: University of New Mexico Press, 1990), 42; George A. McMath, "National Register of Historic Places Inventory, Nomination Form: Meier & Frank Building," National Park Service, December 30, 1981; Arthur A. Hart 'National Register of Historic Places Inventory, Nomination Form: Alexander House', National Park Service, February 24, 1972.

5 United States Jewish Population: Lisa Ades (director), "GI Jews: Jewish Americans in World War II" (New York: Turquoise Films, Channel Thirteen, 2017).

6 Here and in the remainder of this study, I will spell antisemitism this way, because the Anti-Defamation League (ADL) uses this spelling. In its website, the ADL says it "has adopted the spelling of 'antisemitism' instead of 'anti-Semitism'. After reviewing the history and consulting with other leading experts, we've determined that this is the best way to refer to hatred toward Jews. The word 'Semitic' was first used by a German historian in 1781 to bind together languages of Middle Eastern origin that have some linguistic similarities. The speakers of those languages, however, do not otherwise have shared heritage or history. There is no such thing as a Semitic peoplehood. Additionally, one could speak a Semitic language and still have anti-Semitic views." https://www.adl.org/spelling.

7 When Roddie Edmonds arrived home in Tennessee after the war, he did not tell anyone in his family or anyone else about his experience in the prison camp. He literally took the story with him to the grave when he died in 1985. He had, however, kept diaries of his wartime experiences and included this story in one of his diary entries. His son, the Reverend Chris Edmonds, learned about the incident in the prison camp and was able to track down several men who had been present at the time. They provided witness statements to *Yad Vashem*, the Holocaust center in Israel, and in 2015, *Yad Vashem* recognized Edmonds as "Righteous Among the Nations," Israel's highest honor for non-Jews who risked their lives to save Jews

during the Holocaust. "Israel honors GI who told the Nazis, 'We are all Jews',", *The Times of Israel*, November 27, 2016.

8 Ades, "GI Jews."

9 In 1995, President William J. Clinton issued Executive Order 12937, which declassified virtually every previously classified record from World War II, https://fas.org/sgp/clinton/eo12937.html. In addition, the Nazi War Crimes Disclosure Act (15 U.S.C. § 552) of 1998 further opened the documents to the American public.

10 Lloyd R. Shoemaker, *The Escape Factory: The Story of MIS-X* (paperback edition, New York: St. Martins Press, 1992). The reference to the suppression of the book came from interviews with Vincent Santucci, Chief Ranger at George Washington Memorial Parkway 2007–08.

11 Matthew R. Laird, Ph.D., "By the River Potomac," An Historic Resource Study of Fort Hunt Park, George Washington Memorial Parkway, prepared for the National Park Service, National Capital Region, Washington, DC, August 2, 2000.

12 Multiple conversations with Brandon Bies and Vincent Santucci between 2007 and 2021. I became involved in the program when I was chief historian of the National Park Service in 2007. I was able to help cover the cost of travel to several interviews; I was also the biggest promoter of the program in the National Park Service.

Chapter 1

1 Ron Chernow, *Washington: A Life* (New York: Penguin Press, 2010), 87–108.

2 Excerpts from George Washington's Diaries, online version from the Library of Congress, https://www.loc.gov/loc/lcib/0010/gwdiary.html.

3 Laird, "By the River Potomac," 12–15.

4 https://tobacco.ces.ncsu.edu/tobacco-fertility-nutrients/.

5 Chernow, *Washington*, 109–110; Laird, "By the River Potomac," 12–21.

6 Ibid, Appendix E, 141–146 (plan for River Farm).

7 Chernow, *Washington*, 805–817.

8 https://www.mountvernon.org/library/digitalhistory/digital-encyclopedia/article/ann-pamela-cunningham.

9 There was one 16-inch gun manufactured and placed on the Pacific side of the Panama Canal entrance. The Endicott and later Taft Reports on Coastal Defenses have been reprinted by the Coastal Defense Study Group, https://cdsg.org/product/the-endicott-and-taft-reports/; Emanuel Raymond Lewis, *Seacoast Fortifications of the United States: An Introductory History* (Annapolis: Naval Institute Press, revised edition, 1993).

10 Laird, "By the River Potomac," 27–66.

11 Dr. Burke Syphax, a well-known surgeon who taught at Howard University for many years, recalled his time at Fort Hunt in an interview in 2007. His son Stephen was the resource manager for National Capital Parks-East, National Park Service and managed the cultural and natural resources for Fort Washington and Piscataway Park on the Maryland side of the Potomac River: Burke Syphax interview by Brandon Bies, March 6, 2007, George Washington Memorial Parkway, National Park Service, Arlington, Virginia.

12 Laird, "By the River Potomac," 27–66.

13 https://www.loc.gov/law/help/statutes-at-large/71st-congress/session-2/c71s2ch354.pdf; Timothy Davis, *Highways in Harmony: George Washington Memorial Parkway, Virginia, Maryland, Washington, D.C.* (Washington, DC: National Park Service, 1994); EDAW, Inc.,

"Cultural Landscape Report," Mount Vernon Memorial Highway, vol. 1, Alexandria, Virginia, 1989.

14 A good summary of Hoover's program can be found at https://hoover.archives.gov/exhibits/great-depression.

15 Of the numerous books on the Bonus Army, Jerome Tuccille, *The War Against the Vets: The World War I Bonus Army during the Great Depression* (Potomac, Maryland: Potomac Press, 2018) is the most recent. However, many historians consider Paul Dickson and Thomas B. Allen, *The Bonus Army: An American Epic* (London: Walker Books, 2006) as the classic treatment of the Bonus Army.

16 https://www.smithsonianmag.com/history/marching-on-history-75797769/.

17 Laird, "By the River Potomac," 71–75.

18 Neil M. Maher, *Nature's New Deal: The Civilian Conservation Corps and the Roots of the American Environmental Movement* (New York: Oxford University Press, 2009).

19 Laird, "By the River Potomac," 75–87.

20 Ibid, 88–117.

21 Ibid, 118–123.

22 Dana Dierkes, interview by Robert K. Sutton, January 11, 2021.

23 Brandon Bies, interview by Robert K. Sutton, February 4, 2021.

Chapter 2

1 George Weidinger, interview by Brandon Bies and Vincent Santucci, November 29, 2007, George Washington Memorial Parkway, National Park Service, Arlington, Virginia.

2 Ibid. A more detailed piece on George Weidinger can be found at http://www.clevelandseniors.com/people/george-weidinger.htm.

3 Rudy Pins, interview by Brandon Bies and Sam Swersky, September 14-15, 2006, George Washington Memorial Parkway, National Park Service, Arlington, Virginia; http://www.jacob-pins.de/?article_id=286&clang=0.

4 https://encyclopedia.ushmm.org/content/en/article/the-immigration-of-refugee-children-to-the-united-states. There was a similar program in the United Kingdom. It is described at https://www.lbi.org/news/kindertransport-exhibition-highlight-family-separation-1930s/.

5 Pins, interview.

6 Guy Stern was not stationed at Fort Hunt, but his early life in Germany, his time at Camp Ritchie, his memoir, and his interview provided insights that have been invaluable for this study. Guy Stern interview with Robert K. Sutton, May 18, 2021; Guy Stern, *Invisible Ink: A Memoir* (Detroit: Wayne University Press, 2020), 1–52.

7 Arno Mayer, interview by Brandon Bies and Vincent Santucci, September 16, 2008, Gerorge Washington Memorial Parkway, National Park Service, Arlington, Virginia; Arno Mayer interview with Robert K. Sutton, December 13, 2020.

8 John Gunther Dean, interview by Brandon Bies, Vincent Santucci, Sam Swersky, and Eric Oberg, October 2, 2007, George Washington Memorial Parkway, National Park Service, Arlington, Virginia.

9 Steven J. Ross and Wolf Gruner (editors), *New Perspectives on Kristallnacht: After 80 Years, the Nazi Pogrom in Global Comparison (The Jewish Role in American Life: An Annual Review)*, 17th edition (East Lafayette, Indiana: Purdue University Press, 2019). This collection of essays is the most recent analysis of *Kristallnacht*. The summary was taken mostly from Chapter 2: "'Worse than Vandals': The Mass Destruction of Jewish Homes and Jewish Responses During the 1938 Pogrom" by Wolf Gruner.

10 Dean, interview.

11 Werner Moritz, interview by Brandon Bies, July 23–24, 2007, George Washington Memorial Parkway, National Park Service, Arlington, Virginia.

12 At the time of Norman's birth, Jaslo was within the Austro-Hungarian Empire.

13 Norman Graber, interview by Brandon Bies, May 14–15, 2007, George Washington Memorial Parkway, National Park Service, Arlington, Virginia.

14 Walter Schueman, interview by Brandon Bies (joined briefly by Vincent Santucci), September 17, 2010, George Washington Memorial Parkway, National Park Service, Arlington, Virginia.

15 Dieter Kober, interview by Brandon Bies, January 17–18, 2008, George Washington Memorial Parkway, National Park Service, Arlington, Virginia.

16 Paul Fairbrook, interview by Brandon Bies and Vincent Santucci, February 15, 2008, George Washington Memorial Parkway, National Park Service, Arlington, Virginia; Paul Fairbrook, interviews by Robert K. Sutton, March 18, 2018, and December 19, 2020.

17 Fred and Lucille Michel, interview by Brandon Bies, May 30–31, 2006. George Washington Memorial Parkway, National Park Service, lington, Virginia.

18 https://www.biography.com/political-figure/henry-kissinger.

19 George Mandel, interview by Brandon Bies and Sam Johnson, July 13, 2006; interview 2 by Brandon Bies, Sam Swarovski, Vincent Santucci, and Matthew Virta from NPS, plus John Bardal from the *National Geographic* (second interview conducted at the *National Geographic*), January 29, 2007. Both interviews housed at the George Washington Memorial Parkway, National Park Service, Arlington, Virginia.

20 Henry Kolm, interview by Brandon Bies and Sam Swersky, May 7–8, 2007, George Washington Memorial Parkway, National Park Service, Arlington Virginia.

21 Peter Weiss, interview by Brandon Bies, September 13, 2006. George Washington Memorial Parkway, National Park Service, Arlington, Virginia. Peter was admitted to Harvard, but attended St. John's College in Annapolis instead. His parents could afford St. John's along with the scholarship he received but could not afford to send him to Harvard; Peter Weiss interview with Robert K. Sutton, April 26, 2021.

22 Edgar Danciger, interview by David Lassman (by telephone), November 8, year unstated. George Washington Memorial Parkway, National Park Service, Arlington, Virginia.

23 Ernest Salomon, interview 1 and 2 by Brandon Bies and Vincent Santucci, late November 2008 (specific day not specified) and December 3, 2008. Interview 3 by Brandon Bies, Vincent Santucci, and Dan Gross, March 12, 2009 (by telephone from Tokyo). All three interviews housed at the George Washington Memorial Parkway, National Park Service, Arlington, Virginia.

24 "Belgium Refugee Eager to Fight for Uncle Sam," *Pittsburgh Post Gazette* , March 3, 1943.

Chapter 3

1 https://bleacherreport.com/articles/90449-the-most-forgotten-game-ever-played-dec-7-1941; A longtime iconic sports writer in Washington, DC recalled the game on its 50th anniversary; Shirley Povich, "At Redskins-Eagles Game, Crowd Was Kept Unaware That War Had Begun," *Washington Post,* December 7, 1991, https://www.washingtonpost.com/wp-srv/sports/longterm/general/povich/launch/war.htm.

2 https://www.loc.gov/collections/interviews-following-the-attack-on-pearl-harbor/about-this-collection/; https://tile.loc.gov/storage-services/service/afc/afc1941004/afc1941004_sr01b/afc1941004_sr01b.xml.

3   Stern, interview.

4   Mayer, interview; Fairbrook, interview; Moritz, interview; Pins, interview.

5   Ibid.

6   Steven M. Kleinman, "The History Of MIS-Y: US Strategic Interrogation During World War II," thesis submitted to the Faculty of the Joint Military Intelligence College in partial fulfillment of the requirements for the degree of Master of Science of Strategic Intelligence, 25–37.

7   Rick Lemyre, "Secret World of Camp Tracy Revealed," *The Press: Brentwood, Discovery Bay, Oakley, and Antioch* (California), Jan 28, 2010, updated Nov 22, 2013; Lieutenant Colonel Corbin's comprehensive study of Camp Tracy is in Alexander Corbin, *The History of Camp Tracy: Japanese WWII POWs and the Future of Strategic Interrogation* (Fort Belvoir, Virginia: Ziedon Press, 2009).

8   Louis Al Nipkow, interview by Brandon Bies, Vincent Santucci, and Colonel Steven Kleinman February 17, 2008, George Washington Memorial Parkway, National Park Service, Arlington, Virginia.

9   Sam Matthews, "The Tale of Camp Tracy," *Tracy (California) Press*, November 22, 2008.

10 Alexandra Yoon-Hendricks, "You Asked, We Answered: Abandoned Delta Hotel Once Served as WWII Interrogation Center," *Sacramento Bee*, May 20, 2019, updated June 5, 2019, https://www.sacbee.com/news/local/beyond-sacramento/article230125464.html.

11 For sports fans, Marwood is the current home of Ted Leonsis, who owns the Washington Capitals hockey team and the Washington Wizards basketball team.

12 Kleinman, "History of MIS-Y," 38.

13 Laird, "By the River Potomac," 90–91.

14 Ibid; Howard Nottingham, interview by Brandon Bies and Matthew Virta, April 19, 2007, George Washington Memorial Parkway, National Park Service, Arlington, Virginia. Nottingham attended the December 7 Redskins game at Griffith Stadium.

15 Laird, "By the River Potomac," 92–95.

16 Victor Hacker, interview by Brandon Bies and Vincent Santucci, January 16, 2008, George Washington Memorial Parkway, National Park Service, Arlington, Virginia.

17 Following the revelations of torture of prisoners at Abu Ghraib in Iraq, a congressional report titled "Lawfulness of Interrogation Techniques under the Geneva Conventions" outlined what was appropriate under the Geneva Conventions, https://www.everycrsreport.com/reports/RL32567.html.

18 George Kermit Coyne, "History of P.O. Box 1142: Naval Prisoner of War Interrogations Conducted by the Military Intelligence Staffs of MIS-Y & Op-16-Z," May 17, 2010, George Washington Memorial Parkway, National Park Service, Arlington, Virginia.

19 The history of Pine Grove Furnace during World War II is told by local resident John Paul Bland, *Secret War at Home: The Pine Grove Furnace Prisoner of War Interrogation Camp* (Cumberland County (Pennsylvania) Historical Society, 2006). Also, a summary of the history is in Joseph Cress, "Pine Grove POWs: Pine Grove Furnace was once a Prisoner of War Interrogation Camp used during WWII," *The Sentinel*, Oct 6, 2014, https://cumberlink.com/news/local/history/pine-grove-pows-pine-grove-furnace-was-once-a-prisoner-of-war-interrogation-camp-used/article_780cf746-4d0a-11e4-bddd-d763f93fb84b.html.

Chapter 4

1   Stern, interview.

2   The quote and information about Sanford Griffith can be found in Kleinman, "History of
    MIS-Y," 50. The citation for the material in the National Archives is "Discussion I-IV," Series
    of Talks by Sanford Griffith, prepared for the Third Army School, San Antonio, TX, April 20,
    1942, Record Group 165, Records of the War Department General and Special Staffs; Office
    of the Director of Intelligence (G-2), Subordinate Office and Branches, Captured Personnel
    and Material Branch, National Archives and Records Administration NARA.
3   Kleinman, "History of MIS-Y," 49–69.
4   Paul Kubala (1907–1967), datasheet prepared by Dan Gross.
5   George Frenkel, interviews by Brandon Bies, Sam Swersky, and Doug Heimlich, December 5,
    2006, and January 18, 2007, George Washington Memorial Parkway, National Park Service,
    Arlington, Virginia.
6   Kober, interview.
7   Bruce Henderson, *Sons and Soldiers: The Untold Story of the Jews Who Escaped the Nazis and
    Returned with the US Army to Fight Hitler* (New York: Harper Collins, 2017), 131–148; *The
    Ritchie Boys*, directed by Christian Bauer (New York: Docurama Films, 2007).
8   Fairbrook, interview.
9   Walter Schueman, interview by Brandon Bies, September 17, 2010, George Washington
    Memorial Parkway, National Park Service, Arlington, Virginia.
10 Mandel, interview.
11 Henderson, *Sons and Soldiers*, 279–281; *The Ritchie Boys*.
12 Mayer, interview.
13 Weiss, interview.
14 Leslie Willson, interview by Brandon Bies, December 14, 2007, George Washington Memorial
    Parkway, National Park Service, Arlington, Virginia; Peter Weiss, interview with Robert K.
    Sutton, April 26, 2021.
15 Roberta Rosenthal and Stephen Rosenthal, interview by Robert K. Sutton, August 23, 2020.
16 *The Ritchie Boys*.
17 Ibid; Bruce Henderson, *Sons and Soldiers*, 291–296.
18 Ibid, 167–171, 176–178, 277–286; *Ritchie Boys*. Bruce Henderson does an outstanding job of
    describing Werner Angress's exploits before, during, and after the war. After the war, Angress
    finished college, received a Ph.D. from the University of California at Berkley, and taught at
    several colleges, ending up at SUNY Stony Brook. Werner published numerous books and
    articles, including his memoir, *Witness to the Storm: A Jewish Journey from Nazi Berlin to the
    82nd Airborne, 1920–1945* (Scotts Valley, California, CreateSpace Independent Publishing
    Platform, 2012).
19 Stern, interview.

Chapter 5

1   Laird, "By the River Potomac," 91.
2   Ibid, 100; Helmut Ruge, a German navy (*Kriegsmarine*) radio operator who pretended to be
    a civilian crewman aboard the *Odenwald*, a German merchant ship functioning as a military
    ship. He arrived in the United States on December 13, 1941, and became the first German
    POW of World War II. He probably was not at Fort Hunt, http://www.ww2pacific.com/ruge.
    html, and http://iagenweb.org/wwii/FeatureWWIIOdenwald.html. Other German sailors from
    the *U-210*, the *U-701*, and the *U-354* arrived at Fort Hunt and were interrogated between
    August 6 and September 8, 1942.

3   The Mycke transcript is reproduced in Laird, "By the River Potomac," 101–109. The original document is in Assistant Chief of Staff, G-2, Intelligence Division, Captured Personnel and Materials Branch, Enemy POW Interrogation File (MIS-Y), 1943–45, Reports, U-Boats, Ships, and other Naval Material, Box 730, NARA 165.

4   HILGER, GUSTAV_0038.pdf (cia.gov).

5   Ibid.

6   Cited in Matt Ellison, "The German Strategic Mastermind Behind America's Post-War Order," *Palladium,* 2019, https://palladiummag.com/2019/04/12/the-german-strategic-mastermind-behind-the-post-world-war-ii-liberal-order/.

7   Ibid.

8   Pins, interview; a recent biography of Gustav Hilger, in German is Jörn Happel, in his *Der Ost-Experte: Gustav Hilger - Diplomat im Zeitalter der Extreme* (Berlin: Schoeningh Ferdinand GmbH, 2017) (in English: *The East Expert—Gustav Hilger: Diplomat in the Age of Extremes*).

9   Angus MacLean Thuermer, interview by Brandon Bies, Sam Swersky, and Vincent Santucci, October 25, 2006, George Washington Memorial Parkway, National Park Service, Arlington, Virginia.

10   Ibid.

11   Henke's life and death are chronicled in Timothy P. Mulligan, *Lone Wolf: The Life and Death of U-Boat Ace Werner Henke* (Norman, Oklahoma: University of Oklahoma Press, 1995).

12   Pins, interview.

13   Richard E. Holl, "Swastikas in the Bluegrass State: Axis Prisoners of War in Kentucky, 1942—46," *The Register of the Kentucky Historical Society,* 100 (Spring 1992),139–165.

14   Cited in Kleinman, "History of MIS-Y," 139–142. The name Gustav Sader and the names of the interrogators were verified by Dan Gross. Sader's rank was not specified.

15   Paul Kubala was one of the more important officers assigned to Fort Hunt, but information about him and much of his career is sketchy. He served in the army in World War II, then transferred to the air force after the war. He rose to the rank of Lieutenant Colonel and, when he died in 1967, he was buried in Arlington National Cemetery. His two daughters have written biographical sketches of their father, which are reproduced in an article prepared by Dan Gross: "Paul Kubala (1907-1967)"; Dan Gross datasheet: Findagrave.com citation for Paul Kubala at https://www.findagrave.com/memorial/49242434/paul-kubala.

16   Quoted in https://www.defensemedianetwork.com/stories/churchills-deal-with-the-devil/.

17   Abbreviated copy of the English translation of transcript from Kleinman, "History of MIS-Y," 130–137; Taken from Report No. 116, Source ETO-536-MI, February 26, 1943, Record Group 165, Records of the War Department General and Special Staffs; Office of the Director of Intelligence (G-2), Subordinate Office and Branches, Captured Personnel and Material Branch, NARA.

18   Sönke Neitzel and Harald Welzer, *Soldiers: German POWs on Fighting, Killing and Dying* (Toronto: Penguin Random House of Canada, 2012), 205.

19   The last group—the post-World War II Germans—will be discussed in far more detail in Chapter 9;.Laird, "By the River Potomac," 100–112.

20   Pins, interview.

21   The V-1 was technically a missile or buzz bomb.

22   Mandel, interview.

23   Kolm, interview.

24   Salomon, interview.

25 There are numerous articles by and about Hellmuth Hertz. One succinct piece is in Chapter 9 of Gilbert Thompson (editor), *Pioneers of Medicine Without a Nobel Prize* (London: Imperial College Press, 2014); Fred and Lucille Michel, interview.

26 Joseph Mark Scalia, *Germany's Last Mission to Japan: The Failed Voyage of U-234* (Annapolis: Naval Institute Press, 2000).

27 A partial list of Heinz Schlicke's publications can be found at https://www.worldcat.org/identities/lccn-n82029005/.

28 Kolm, interview.

29 Ibid; Pins, interview.

Chapter 6

1 Henderson, *Sons and Soldiers*, 131–32.

2 Willson, interview; Kleinman, "The History of MIS-Y," 100–105.

3 Coyne, "History of P.O. Box 1142."

4 Weidinger, interview; Moritz, interview.

5 Willson, interview.

6 Cited in Kleinman, "The History of MIS-Y," 101.

7 Franz Gajdosch, interview by Brandon Bies, October 25, 2010, George Washington Memorial Parkway, National Park Service, Arlington, Virginia.

8 Pins, interview.

9 Neitzel and Welzer, *Soldiers*, 347.

10 Wayne Spivey, interview by Brandon Bies, August 20–31, 2006, George Washington Memorial Parkway, National Park Service, Arlington, Virginia.

11 https://www.washingtonpost.com/wp-dyn/content/article/2007/10/05/AR2007100502492.html; https://www.washingtonpost.com/archive/politics/2006/08/20/a-covert-chapter-opens-for-fort-hunt-veterans-span-classbankheadas-files-on-nazi-pows-are-declassified-their-interrogators-break-their-silence-span/5ae16af8-9c6d-414b-9d5e-c64e10f0241a/; https://www.npr.org/templates/story/story.php?storyId=93649575.

12 Anton Leonhard, interview by Brandon Bies, Vincent Santucci, and David Lassen, April 2, 2010. George Washington Memorial Parkway, National Park Service, Arlington, Virginia.

13 Gajdosch, interview.

14 Salomon, interview.

15 Leonhard, interview.

16 Stern, interview.

17 Kolm, interview; Bill Hess, interview by Brandon Bies, Matthew Virta, and Samuel Swersky, November 21, 2006. Colonel Steve Kleinman joined in on March 9, 2007.

18 John Kluge, interview by Brandon Bies, Matthew Virta, and Vincent Santucci, May 16, 2008, George Washington Memorial Parkway, National Park Service, Arlington, Virginia.

19 Dean, interview.

20 In his oral history interview, Arno Mayer said Wernher von Braun made this comment. He referred to the famous German rocket scientist several times in the context of Fort Hunt. The problem is that there is no indication that Braun ever was at Fort Hunt. He came through Fort Strong in Boston instead. There is a strong likelihood that Mayer may well have met Braun there, since he shuttled between the two places. Mayer also includes Braun in the shopping expedition in Washington, DC.

21 Ibid.

22 Ibid; Willson, interview. Both men agreed to share the letter and envelope. Willson kept the letter—since he had written to Mrs. Eisenhower—and Mayer kept the envelope. The envelope and the letter are both filed in the George Washington Memorial Parkway headquarters.

23 Peter Weiss, interview with Robert K. Sutton, April 26, 2021.

24 https://www.forces-war-records.co.uk/blog/2015/08/11/lieutenant-marcus-mcdilda-captured-tortured-interrogated.

25 https://www.intelligence.senate.gov/sites/default/files/publications/CRPT-113srpt288.pdf.

26 Pins, interview.

Chapter 7

1 "History and Operation of MIRS, London and Washington Branches," (May 1, 1943–July 14, 1945), 12.

2 Ibid, 13.

3 Ibid, 5.

4 Fairbrook, interview.

5 Kober interview.

6 Kluge, interview.

7 Charles Winick interview by Brandon Bies and Vincent Santucci, September 16, 2010, George Washington Memorial Parkway, National Park Service, Arlington, Virginia.

8 Kluge, interview.

9 Winick, interview.

10 Kober, interview.

11 Ibid; Fairbrook, interview.

12 Thuermer, interview; An article in Reuters discussed a new book by Robert Sommer, *Das KZ Bordell* (The Concentration Camp Brothel) that chronicles brothels established in concentration camps, https://www.reuters.com/article/us-germany-nazis-brothels/new-book-reveals-horror-of-nazi-camp-brothels-idUSTRE57G45X20090817.

13 Kober, interview; Fairbrook, interview.

14 Kober, interview.

15 Winick, interview.

16 Kluge, interview.

17 Kober, interview.

18 *The Ritchie Boys.*

19 "Order of Battle of the German Army," February 1944 (Washington, DC: Military Intelligence Division, Department of War), iii, iv.

20 "History and Operation of MIRS," 14, 94–95.

21 Schueman, interview.

22 "History and Operation of MIRS," 89.

23 Kluge, interview.

24 Ibid.

25 Ibid.

26 "Political Indoctrination and Morale Building in the German Army (December 1944)" Copy provided by Paul Fairbrook.

27 "Organization of the High Command of the German Army (Fall 1944)." Copy made available by Paul Fairbrook.

28 Kober, interview.

29 Kluge, interview.
30 Fairbrook, interview.
31 Kober, interview.
32 Kluge, interview.
33 "History and Operation of MIRS," 5.

Chapter 8

1 Augustus W. Soule, Jr., interview with Brandon Bies and Sam Swersky, May 9, 2007, Goerge Washington Memorial Parkway, National Park Service, Arlington, Virginia.

2 Silvio Bedini interview by Brandon Bies and Matthew Virta, October 15, 2007, George Washington Memorial Parkway, National Park Service, Arlington, Virginia. National Park Service staff interviewed Silvio Bedini on October 15, 2007, while he was bedridden. His son and daughter were present. A month later, he passed away; Daniel Buck interviewed (by phone) by Vincent Santucci and David Lassman, October 25, 2010, George Washington Memorial Parkway, National Park Service, Arlington, Virginia; Shoemaker, *The Escape Factory*, 52–53.

3 These numbers are taken from Ibid, 202; confirmed in Silvio Bedini interview.

4 Lawrence Dennis, interview by David Lassman, June 7, 2009, George Washington Memorial Parkway, National Park Service, Arlington, Virginia.

5 Much of the information about Spencer Gulick was drawn from his obituary page at https://www.lastingtributesfuneralcare.com/obituaries/Spencer-Gulick/#!/Obituary. Additional information is from a summary of his oral history interview prepared by John Ellif of the Friends of Fort Hunt Park.

6 David Jones and Thomas Griffin, interview by Brandon Bies, Vincent Santucci, and Matthew Virta, Nov 6, 2008, George Washington Memorial Parkway, National Park Service, Arlington, Virginia. David Jones rose to the rank of major general in the United States Air Force. His lifelong buddy Thomas Griffin rose to the rank of major in the air force. I had the great privilege of meeting both men, along with two of their Doolittle Raider colleagues at the World War Memorial in Washington, DC on Veterans Day, November 11, 2008.

7 There are literally dozens of books written on German prison camps (especially on *Stalag Luft III*), and many on the Great Escape alone, along with film treatments of the event. Two sources that are particularly good and these, written by men who were actually prisoners in the camp: Eric Williams, *The Wooden Horse: The Classic World War II Story of Escape* (New York: Skyhorse, 2014); Paul Brikill, *The Great Escape* (New York: W. W. Norton, 2004).

8 Robert Kloss, interview by Vincent Santucci and David Lassman, May 6, 2010, George Washington Memorial Parkway, National Park Service, Arlington, Virginia.

9 James Ahrens, interview by Vincent Santucci, September 29, 2010, George Washington Memorial Parkway, National Park Service, Arlington, Virginia.

10 Ralph Patton, interview by Brandon Bies, Vincent Santucci, and David Lassman, February 10, 2009, George Washington Memorial Parkway, National Park Service, Arlington, Virginia.

11 David Childs, *Wings and Tracks* (Caldwell, Idaho: Caxton Printers, 2009), 2, 7, 59. Even with his severe injuries, David Childs lived to the age of 96 and passed away just days short of his 97th birthday. Additional biographical information is in his obituary can be found at https://www.columbiagorgenews.com/obituaries/david-childs/article_4a555222-d020-5d28-a805-a99f9e64676e.html. He was my first cousin, once removed—my mother's first cousin. He outlived everyone in his generation. He wrote this book about his World War II adventures and his life on the family farm in Gilliam County, Oregon, cited above.

12 https://www.legacy.com/obituaries/name/walter-cini-obituary?pid=19816363; Carol E. Cini, *The Spy and His CIA Brat* (CreateSpace Independent Publishing Platform, 2017).

13 Shoemaker, *The Escape Factory*, 55–57. When Shoemaker first published his book in 1990, neither the American military nor the National Archives had released and information about PO Box 1142. Like everyone else at Fort Hunt, Shoemaker had been sworn to secrecy, but he published his book anyway. The Department of Defense purchased as many copies as it could get its hands on in an attempt to keep it out of circulation. It is still very difficult to purchase, with prices on the secondary market often reaching into several hundred dollars.

14 https://www.pearsonfuneralhome.com/obituaries/William-Cory/#!/Obituary.

15 An oral history interview with Kenneth Kurtenbach can be found at https://collections.ushmm.org/search/catalog/irn80133; Shoemaker, *The Escape Factory*, 71–72, 160–168.

Chapter 9

1 Dean, interview; Michel, interview.

2 https://www.legacy.com/obituaries/tampabaytimes/obituary.aspx?n=heinz-schlicke&pid=17492772.

3 Weiss, interview.

4 Dan Gross has compiled a comprehensive list of *Paperclip* scientists from files at the National Archives. He has put the list in an Excel file, which is summarized here.

5 NASA conducted several interviews with Wehrner von Braun, excerpts which are included in: https://www.nasa.gov/sites/default/files/atoms/files/von_braun_interviews.pdf. There are many biographies of Wehrner von Braun: Amy Shira Teitel, "Wernher von Braun: History's most controversial figure? Pivotal to the history of spaceflight, von Braun's Nazi past makes him incredibly difficult to talk about," *Al Jezeera*, 2013, found at https://www.aljazeera.com/opinions/2013/5/3/wernher-von-braun-historys-most-controversial-figure/; Michael J. Neufeld, *Von Braun: Dreamer of Space, Engineer of War* (New York: Alfred A. Knopf, 2007); Bob Ward, *Dr. Space: The Life of Wernher von Braun* (Annapolis: Naval Institute Press, 2009 edition).

6 Mayer, interview; Mayer, interview by Robert K. Sutton.

7 Dieter Grau interview by Brandon Bies, Vincent Santucci, and Jackie Dannenberg (widow of an Operation *Paperclip* engineer), April 21, 2010, George Washington Memorial Parkway, National Park Service, Arlington, Virginia.

8 Hans Fichtner, interview by Brandon Bies and Vincent Santucci, April 22, 2010, George Washington Memorial Parkway, National Park Service, Arlington, Virginia; Oscar Holderer, interview by Brandon Bies and Vincent Santucci, April 23, 2010, George Washington Memorial Parkway, National Park Service, Arlington, Virginia.

9 Dan Gross database on *Paperclip* scientists and engineers.

10 The heavily redacted FBI file on Arthur Louis Hugo Rudolph is available at https://vault.fbi.gov/Arthur%20Rudolph/Arthur%20Rudolph%20Part%201%20of%201/view.

11 Annie Jacobsen, *Operation Paperclip: The Secret Intelligence Program that Brought Nazi Scientists to America* (Boston: Little Brown and Company, 2014).

12 Pins, interview; Weiss, interview. This story is one of the instances in which there is a discrepancy in stories. According to Rudy Pins, Oshima was fluent in German but not English, and he liked brandy and drank a bottle a day. Peter Weiss could not remember the name of the Japanese diplomat, but said it was the military attaché to Berlin, which Oshima was at one time, and that it was possibly Oshima. He said the man loved bourbon. A recent article in

the Japanese media publication NHK uncovered and published an article describing an oral history interview with Oshima shortly before he died in 1975. The story by Masuda Tsuyoshi is entitled "Unearthed Tapes Explain a Piece of World War Two History," *NHK* (December 22, 2020), https://www3.nhk.or.jp/nhkworld/en/news/backstories/1423/.

13 Walter Vierow's military career in documented in http://www.lexikon-der-wehrmacht.de/ Personenregister/V/VierowWalter-R.htm; His work at Fort Hunt is in Derek R. Mallett, *Hitler's Generals in America: Nazi POWs and Allied Military Intelligence* (Lexington: University Press of Kentucky, 2013), 122–24, 137.

14 Ibid, 162–67.

15 Pins, interview.

16 Mallett, *Hitler's Generals*, 139–40; Eric Waldman described his experience with Gehlen and his group in detail, debriefing with the CIA in 1969, titled "Debriefing of Eric Waldman on the US Army's Trusteeship of the Gehlen Organizations During the Years 1945–1949." Reproduced in https://www.jewishvirtuallibrary.org/cia-relationship-with-nazi-general-reinhard-gehlen-during-world-war-ii.

17 Mallett, *Hitler's Generals*, 140–41.

18 Edgar Danciger, interview by David Lassman (by telephone), November 8, (year not stated), George Washington Memorial Parkway, National Park Service, Arlington, Virginia.

19 Paul Fairbrook, interview by Robert K. Sutton, November 11, 2020.

20 Mallett, *Hitler's Generals*, 153–60.

21 Fairbrook, interview by Robert K. Sutton, November 11, 2020; Derek Mallett confirmed that Paul Fairbrook's assessment of the situation that the former MIRS staff were likely relegated to translating and cataloging German documents.

22 Mallett, *Hitler's Generals*, 153–60.

23 Moritz, interview.

24 Ibid.

25 Ibid.

26 Weiss, interview; Weiss, interview by Robert K. Sutton.

27 The declassified interrogation reports for Hermann Göring and others are conveniently collected in this website: http://lawcollections.library.cornell.edu/nuremberg?f%5Bauthor_ tesim%5D%5B%5D=Paul+Kubala%2C+Major%2C+MI%2C+Commanding.

28 Pins, interview.

29 The case against Paul Kubala is detailed in Kenneth D. Alford, *Nazi Plunder: Great Treasure Stories Of World War II* (New York: De Capo, 2003), 53–60; Dan Gross found a long piece by Kubala's daughter, Lady Josette Kubala Walton, describing her father's activities in World War II. Obviously, she was defending her father. She stated that Kubala's son from his first marriage was selling German medals that he claimed were from Göring. There was no evidence that Kubala either did or did not take Georing's medals. Dan Gross "Paul Kubala (1907–1967)" datasheet.

Chapter 10

1 https://smhs.gwu.edu/news/h-george-mandel-phd.

2 https://www.legacy.com/obituaries/washingtonpost/obituary.aspx?n=frederick-michel&pid=128958113.

3 Brandon Bies interview by Robert K. Sutton, February 4, 2021; Petula Dvorak, "A Covert Chapter Opens For Fort Hunt Veterans As Files on Nazi POWs Are Declassified, Their

Interrogators Break Their Silence," *Washington Post*, August 20, 2006, https://www.washing-tonpost.com/archive/politics/2006/08/20/acovert-chapter-opens-for-fort-hunt-veterans-span-classbankheadas-files-on-nazi-pows-are-declassified-their-interrogators-break-their-silence-span/5ae16af8-9c6d-414b-9d5e-c64e10f0241a/.

4   As of this writing, George Weidinger is still living. He is hard of hearing but still as sharp as ever. He has continued to provide information for this book. George Weidinger interview; George Weidinger correspondence with Robert K. Sutton, January 19, 2021; An article about George's work for the hospice can be found at https://www.hospicewr.org/Western-Reserve-CareLink/February-2014/The-Man-Behind-the-Lens.

5   Henry Kolm, "Nazi Captives Not Subjected to Harsh Measures," *The (Lakeland, Florida) Ledger* (October 7, 2007); https://www.legacy.com/obituaries/wickedlocal-sudbury/obituary.aspx?n=henry-h-kolm&pid=144598916.

6   As of this writing, Arno Mayer is still living. He has continued to share his memories and insights from his experiences at Fort Hunt. Mayer, interview with Robert K. Sutton; https://dof.princeton.edu/about/clerk-faculty/emeritus/arno-j-mayer; Arno J. Mayer, *Why Did the Heavens Not Darken?: The Final Solution in History* (New York: Pantheon, 1988).

7   https://www.legacy.com/obituaries/nytimes/obituary.aspx?n=john-dean&pid=193100190.

8   Frenkel, interview.

9   Alien Tort Statute (28 U.S.C. § 1350; ATS), also called the Alien Tort Claims Act (ATCA),

10   In the case of *Kiobel v. Royal Dutch Petroleum* (2013), the U.S. Supreme Court reasoned that nothing within the Alien Tort Statute indicated that it was intended to apply extraterritorially. A case would need to touch and concern the territory of the United States with "sufficient force."

11   Much of the information about Peter's postwar activities are drawn from a tribute to him on the occasion of his 90th birthday, to honor his achievements in the field of human rights, https://ccrjustice.org/home/blog/2015/12/08/international-human-rights-pioneer-peter-weiss-celebrates-90.

12   Petula Dvorak, "Fort Hunt's Quiet Men Break Silence on WWII," *Washington Post*, October 6, 2007, https://www.washingtonpost.com/wp-dyn/content/article/2007/10/05/AR2007100502492.html.

13   Vincent Santucci interview with Robert K. Sutton, March 31, 2008; Bies, interview, February 4, 2021. After the reunion, the park's budget for continuing the oral history project was drying up. As chief historian of the National Park Service, I was able to transfer some of my budget to the park to continue the program.

Chapter 11

1   The following brief biographies are for the veterans in this story. Unfortunately, most are now gone, so I am not able to follow up with them. For some, I have information on them after they left their service at Fort Hunt; for others, I do not. If you happen to read this chapter and have a loved one or relative who is not included here, it does not reflect deliberate omission, but rather that I do not have information on them after they left their military service.

2   https://www.immigrantentrepreneurship.org/entries/john-werner-kluge/#Business_Beginnings; There are multiple articles, testimonials, and other sources about John Kluge. One of the most interesting and intimate sources was written by his son, who compiled stories and advice given to him as a child by his father in John Kluge, Jr., *John Kluge Stories* (New York: Columbia University Press, 2009).

3   Robert C. Post, "Silvio A. Bedini, 1917–2007", *Technology and Culture*, 49 (Apr, 2008), 522–529; Silvio A. Bedini, *The Pope's Elephant* (New York: Penguin, 2000); Silvio A. Bedina, *The Life of Benjamin Banneker* (New York: Macmillan, 1972).

4   The full interview by Studs Terkel of Dieter Kober is available at https://studsterkel.wfmt.com/programs/interviewing-dieter-kober-occasion-chicago-chamber-orchestras-40th-anniversary. Included in this recording are several musical performances of the Chicago Chamber Orchestra.

5   Dieter Kober interview; Dieter Kober's obituary can be found at https://www.chicagotribune.com/entertainment/ct-dieter-kober-obit-ent-1008-20151007-column.html.

6   As of this writing (January 2021), Paul Fairbrook still lives in Stockton, California. He is as sharp as ever and has provided tremendous help for this project. I have spoken with him on numerous occasions. We have had some fun with comparing notes on Stockton. I lived there from 1957–67, just blocks away from where he currently lives. He mentioned the president of the University of the Pacific, Robert Burns. I went to school with Ron Burns, his son. I told him I sold peanuts and soft drinks at the football games just a couple of years before he went there. In addition to the National Park Service interview and my discussion with Paul, he compiled an autobiography, which has been enormously helpful: Paul Fairbrook, "Autobiography of Paul Fairbrook, 1923 – 2017," edited by Carolyn Chandler, 2018 (not published).

7   Moritz, interview; Werner Moritz obituary, found at https://www.legacy.com/obituaries/charlotte/obituary.aspx?n=werner-moritz&pid=145869474; the documentation for his patent can be found at https://patents.google.com/patent/US3468694.

8   Edgar Danciger's post-World War II biography was drawn from his obituaries at https://www.jacksonville.com/article/20120417/BUSINESS/801254725 https://www.legacy.com/obituaries/staugustine/obituary.aspx?n=edgardanciger&pid=157083223&fhid=12961.

9   When Leslie Willson passed away, the Germanic Studies program posted an obituary in his honor at https://liberalarts.utexas.edu/germanic/_files/pdf/depnotables/willson.pdf.

10   "Isle Resident Part of Secrets of POW Camp," *Honolulu Star Advertiser*, November 12, 2014.

11   Pins, interview.

12   Brandon Bies interview with Robert K. Sutton February 4, 2021. I asked Brandon Bies if he found out, either on or off the record, where Rudy worked after the war. Brandon thinks he might very well have worked for the CIA. I contacted the CIA through its website and through its chief historian's office. I was directed to CIA.gov, then to the Freedom of Information Act Reading Room. That source was a dead end.

13   Honolulu, Hawaii, https://obits.staradvertiser.com/2016/05/07/rudolph-l-pins/.

14   CBS News, "Memories of a POW camp outside Washington, D.C.," September 21, 2014, https://www.cbsnews.com/news/memories-of-a-pow-camp-outside-washington-d-c/.

15   Much of this information and the lengthy quote were taken from the excellent obituary in the T. Ross Shapiro, "Obituary: Angus Thuermer / Swashbuckling former CIA official," *Pittsburgh Post-Gazette*, May 11, 2010, https://www.post-gazette.com/news/obituaries/2010/05/11/Obituary-Angus-Thuermer-Swashbuckling-former-CIA-official/stories/201005110245.

Epilogue

1   https://www.nps.gov/perl/learn/historyculture/uss-oklahoma.htm.

2   Bob Feller interview with Robert K. Sutton, November 11, 2008 (he had just turned 90, days earlier).

3   http://www.usmm.org/peary.html.

4   https://www.airspacemag.com/history-of-flight/300000-airplanes-17122703/.

5   Dean, interview.

6   Stephen E. Ambrose, "Eisenhower and the Intelligence Community in World War II," *Journal of Contemporary History* 16 (1981), 156.

7   David Kahn, "The Rise of Intelligence," *Foreign Affairs,* 85 (September–October 2006) 132.

8   Eisenhower to (British) General Stewart Menzies (May 1945) quoted in Ambrose, "Eisenhower and the Intelligence Community in World War II," 65–66.

9   Kolm, interview; Dean, interview.

10   CBS News, "Memories of a POW camp outside Washington, D.C.," September 21, 2014).

11   Paul Fairbrook appeared with two other Camp Ritchie veterans on the CBS *60-Minutes* program (May 9, 2021). In a follow-up interview with Rabbi Jason Guasdoff of Temple Israel in Stockton, California (June 10, 2021), Paul discussed his experience on *60-Minutes* and his service in World War II at Camp Ritchie and Fort Hunt. He concluded with this quote, www.youtube.com/watch?v=jG9mUuKkIOo.

Index